Masterworks of Literature Series

William S. Osborne, Editor
Southern Connecticut State College

The Power of Sympathy
and
The Coquette

The Power of Sympathy

by WILLIAM HILL BROWN

and

The Coquette

by MRS. HANNAH W. FOSTER

Edited for the Modern Reader by
William S. Osborne
Southern Connecticut State College

New College and University Press, Inc.
Albany, NY 12203

Library of Congress Card Number 70-130902

New Material, Introduction and Notes
by WILLIAM S. OSBORNE

23456789012 CCCC 8765432109

Contents

Editor's Note

It seems appropriate, particularly for the student of American literature, to publish *The Power of Sympathy* and *The Coquette* in a single volume. The novels are representative pieces of early native fiction, exhibiting the weaknesses and the strengths of the many tales of seduction and intrigue so popular with women readers in the last decades of the eighteenth century. By having the two novels in a single volume, the student can easily compare the works; and, if he wishes, by referring to *Charlotte Temple* (edited by Clara M. and Rudolph Kirk, already published in the Masterworks of Literature Series), he can judge objectively the relative merit of each of the three authors.

Introduction

"With respect to novels," Noah Webster wrote, "... it may be said with truth, that some are useful, many of them pernicious, and most of them trifling. A hundred volumes of modern novels may be read, without acquiring a new idea." Too often they corrupted the morals of young readers who ought "not [to] see the vicious part of mankind" exposed—even made notorious, Webster declared—in the pages of popular fiction.[1] In his attack on "pernicious" fiction, in great demand by young women in the last decades of the eighteenth century, Webster spoke the conservative New England mind and repeated in large part what the critics of the novel in England had already said. Since novels were indeed fiction, they recited for innocent readers a series of adventures which had never happened, which were frankly lies; they gave young people false notions about life, making attractive pictures of vice and questionable conduct. "It is as incumbent a duty to attend to the books a young lady reads," enjoined the editor of the *Weekly Magazine*, "as to the company she keeps; for if it is allowed, that the frequent hearing of loose conversation naturally prepares the mind for the admittance of vicious ideas, it cannot be denied that books, in which love is the only theme, and intrigues the sole business of the actors, are more dangerous than even bad company."[2] In spite of the elab-

[1] Noah Webster, "On the Education of Youth in America," *A Collection of Essays and Fugitiv[e] Writings on Moral, Historical, Political and Literary Subjects* ([Boston], 1790), p. 29.

[2] "Novels not only pollute the imaginations of young women," the editor continued, "but likewise give them false ideas of life, which too often make them act improperly; owing to the romantic turn of thinking they imbibe from their favorite studies. They read of characters which never existed, and never can exist; and when all the wit and invention of a luxuriant fancy are stretched to paint a young man all perfection in body and mind, it is hardly possible for a girl to avoid falling in love with the phantom, and being out of humour with the piece of plain mortality which she afterwards marries, and finds, to her great disappointment and mortification, he does not act like the image her fondness had dressed up to her view."
Quoted in G. Harrison Orians, "Censure of Fiction in American Romances and Magazines: 1789-1810," *PMLA*, LII (March, 1937), 198-99.

9

orate arguments against fiction by teachers and editors of women's magazines and clergymen, young women continued to read novels which authors were very willing to supply.

These authors, in the first decades when American novels were published in the country, were well aware of the public interest in their work; therefore, like their English predecessors, notably Samuel Richardson, they wrote a rudimentary novel— more often than not, a tale of seduction and intrigue. Acknowledging their readers' tastes, they fashioned what they believed to be lively tales of amorous adventures, sometimes based on fact. "[D]idactic essays," William Hill Brown observed in *The Power of Sympathy*, "are not always capable of engaging the attention of young ladies. We fly from the labored precepts of the essayist to the sprightly narrative of the novelist." Mindful, however, of the critics' censure of fiction, Brown and his fellow authors wrote their tales with an eye on the ethics of the times, just as their English predecessors, notably Samuel Richardson, had also done. The stories were heavily moral, since the function of the novel as its earliest practitioners in America saw it was largely utilitarian. "[L]et the American fair ... reject with disdain every insinuation derogatory to their true dignity and honor," Mrs. Hannah Foster proclaimed in *The Coquette*. "Let them despise and forever banish [those persons] who can glory in ... the ruin of [their] reputation." Fiction-writers in America—like teachers and editors and clergymen—prided themselves too on being guardians of their readers' morals.

They prided themselves also on being Americans. Royall Tyler deplored, in the preface to *The Algerine Captive* (1797), the fact that so much English fiction was printed in the country, that so few novels read in America were "of our own manufacture." Because novels are often "picture[s] of the times," Tyler argued, the young reader "is insensibly taught to admire the levity, and often the vices[,] of the parent country. ... the English Novel ... impresses on the young mind an erroneous idea of the world, in which she is to live. It paints the manners, customs, and habits of a strange country; excites a fondness for false splendour; and renders the homespun habits of her country disgusting." He urged his countrymen to write "our own books of amusement and ... exhibit our own manners."[3] Sharing with

[3] Royall Tyler, *The Algerine Captive; or, the Life and Adventure of Doctor Updike Underhill* (Walpole, New Hampshire, 1797), pp. ix-xi *passim*.

Tyler this nationalistic sentiment, many of the early novelists fleshed out their tales of seduction with what passed as American scenes and American characters who preached the virtues of American democracy.

Brown's young hero in *The Power of Sympathy* expounds an American ideal when he writes a correspondent: "I wish people would . . . not dispute for any precedence or superiority but [cultivate] good nature and sociability. . . . Inequality among mankind is a foe to our happiness. . . . Upon what grounds its right is founded I could never yet be satisfied." A short while later he speaks again the author's mind: "All men [in America] are declared free and equal; and their tempers are open, generous and communicative. It is the same," he concludes, "in all those countries where the people enjoy independence and equal liberty." One of the characters in Mrs. Foster's novel pleads a decorous militantism for women in America:

> We think ourselves interested in the welfare and prosperity of our country; and consequently, we claim the right of inquiring into those affairs which may conduce to or interfere with the common weal. We shall not be called to the Senate or the field to assert its privileges and defend its rights, but we shall feel for the honor and safety of our friends . . . who are thus employed. . . . Why, then, should the love of our country be a masculine passion only? Why should government which involves the peace and order of the society of which we are a part be wholly excluded from our observation?

The proper conduct of life in America, the early novelists indicated, included a respect for the ideals upon which the country was founded.

The virtues of American democracy, however, were only a minor appeal in the early fiction. A far more significant one was the story itself. To remove the onus that fiction was indeed *fiction,* authors announced that their tales were in the main true—assuming hopefully that the gulf between censure and acceptance might be bridged if fiction was largely fact. Tyler in *The Algerine Captive* assured the critics that his narrative would have its ultimate interest to the readers as fact, not as fiction. Brown informed the readers that *The Power of Sympathy* was "founded in truth"; Mrs. Foster declared that *The Coquette* too was "founded in fact." So many English novels of seduction and intrigue were largely fancy, figments of an author's fertile imagi-

nation; but many American tales purported to be verbatim accounts which authors and often readers were aware of.

Still another appeal in the early fiction was the utilizing of the very popular doctrine of sensibility, so fashionable in many English novels. Brown wrote,

> Hail *Sensibility!* Sweetener of the joys of life! Heaven has implanted thee in the breasts of his children to soothe the sorrows of the afflicted, to mitigate the wounds of the stranger who falleth in our way. *Thou* regardest with an eye of pity those whom *wealth* and *ambition* treat in terms of reproach. Away, ye seekers of power—ye boasters of wealth. Ye are the Levite and the Pharisee who restrain the hand of charity from the indigent and turn with indignation from the way-worn son of misery. But *Sensibility* is the good Samâritan who taketh him by the hand and consoleth him and poureth wine and oil into his wounds. Thou art a pleasant companion. . . .

Sensibility in the American novel was largely sugary sentiment, and writers encouraged their women readers to indulge their hearts. "[I]t is the heart that gives [life] a relish," one of Brown's characters declaimed. Well might readers share the sentiment of another of Brown's characters who was "worked into a fit of melancholy" and "impressed with feelings of sympathetic sorrow" after she had heard a particularly sad tale. And well might readers endorse the sentiment of a friend of the erring heroine in *The Coquette:* "Have you sorrows? I will soothe and alleviate them. Have you cares? I will dispel them. Have you pleasures? I will heighten them. Come, then, let me fold you to my expecting heart. My happiness will be partly suspended until your society renders it complete."

Readers should identify with the characters: watching their conduct closely, associating themselves with the experiences related in the novels (vicariously, it was assumed), they could read the writers' admonitions with profit—or at least with awareness of possible consequences. It was a sign of heart, Brown advised his readers, if the pages of novels were damp with "large drops of sorrow" and "dews of sympathy." Although soberer critics of the novel, and some readers as well, frowned on the doctrine of sensibility—this extravagance of heart, it was a characteristic of American writing for a half century to come, in the prose of Irving and Cooper and Simms and in the poems of Bryant and Poe and the household poets of New England.

With so much attention paid to the embellishments in the fiction, there was little time for conscious artistry in the early novel. Like their English predecessors, the American novelists wrote their stories as a series of letters. Letters provided the simplest literary style, supposedly, and lent conviction to what was recorded. Fiction-writers developed no real plot, simply told their tales matter-of-factly. The writing was turgid, self-conscious, melodramatic. Characters were rarely individualized, conventional types often repeated several times in the same story. Novel readers in the beginning were not critical on the whole, as long as the tales were sentimental appeals to the heart.

Such a tale was the first American novel, *The Power of Sympathy* (1789) by William Hill Brown, a minor Boston poet, essayist and dramatist now turned fiction-writer.[4] To forestall criticism of the novel, Brown made painfully evident the moral purpose of the book by prefixing it with a solemn warning "to the young ladies of United Columbia" which the printer, as it has been pointed out, set in eleven different kinds and sizes of print.[5] The thin narrative was merely a convenient vehicle for the author's accounts of several amorous adventures.

The novel, in letter form, begins with young Harrington's announcement to his friend Worthy of his "benevolent scheme" to seduce a young woman whose parents are unknown. "I will . . . take this beautiful sprig," he tells his friend, "and transplant it to a more favorable soil where it shall flourish and blossom under my own auspices. In a word, I mean to remove this fine girl into an elegant apartment. . . ." A tearful protest from Harriot, however, melts the young man's resolve. Lust turns to love. And Worthy, sensibly, lauds young Harrington's "extremely praiseworthy and honorable" action. Harrington's change of heart from gay libertine to honorable lover is somewhat unusual, for would-be seducers are not often so easily dissuaded in the pages of fiction—as the author illustrates by telling the stories of Ophelia and Fidelia and Maria. "Surely there is no human vice of so black a die," Brown apostrophizes through one of his

[4] The fact that William Hill Brown was indeed the author of *The Power of Sympathy* was only established relatively recently. See Milton Ellis, "The Author of the First American Novel," *American Literature*, IV (January, 1933), 359-68.

[5] Lillie Deming Loshe, *The Early American Novel* (New York, 1907), pp. 7-8.

characters, "so fatal in its consequences—or which causes a more
general calamity, than that of *seducing* a female from the path
of honor."

An "unknown friend" sends young Harrington a letter: "I
disclose an affair, which materially concerns you. Harriot must
not be[come] your wife. . . . She is your *sister*." Harriot's
mother, it is discovered, was his father's mistress. When Harriot
learns the identity of her parents, she suffers great anguish; and
her sudden "decaying health" will not long sustain her life.
Writing a long letter to young Harrington, she analyzes in great
detail for the readers her "warring passions" of love for brother
and love for husband. And then she dies. Harrington sees the
world as a "dreary desert" without Harriot. "I prepare to leave
it," he writes his friend: "the fatal pistol is charged." His family
finds his body in his room, a copy of Goethe's *The Sorrows of
Werther* lying on a bedside table.

In stressing the fatal consequences of seduction upon the un-
fortunate lovers, Brown repeats a theme already familiar to
many eighteenth-century novel readers—a theme Richardson, the
master workman in tales of seduction and intrigue, had em-
ployed. The sins of the father, a reformed rake, are visited on
his children. The elder Harrington's adulterous affair with Maria
is nearly countered with his son's illicit affair with Maria's
daughter. Father, son, daughter suffer for the father's indis-
cretion; and death and suicide are the only means to avoid an
incestuous union.

The seduction narratives in *The Power of Sympathy* are sup-
plemented with beneficial discussions on female education, liter-
ature, manners, the delights of rural living, patriotism—all
obviously aimed at improving the minds of the young readers.
Among the author's "hints" on female education is the sur-
prising comment that fiction so popular with young women is
read just "to kill time—to attract the attention . . . for an hour,
but leave[s] not one idea on the mind." To court the critics'
favor, Brown is willing to concede a point. Nor are fiction-
writers always concerned with inculcating principles of "strict
morality" for their young readers. Indeed, the real danger of
desultory or low fiction is emphatically borne out by a young
woman from Connecticut, who imbibed wrong notions of hu-
man nature from her reading and discovered too late that some
of her friends were deceitful and that men, treacherous and

insincere, "consult[ed] interest oftener than honesty." The young woman played the coquette and ended her life in a public tavern where she gave birth to a dead child and died herself a few days later. The tragedy of Elizabeth Whitman, which Brown summarizes in a footnote in *The Power of Sympathy*, gave Mrs. Foster the story for *The Coquette*, published eight years later. Novels not concerned with "the chaste principles of true friendship, rational love, and connubial duty," Brown continues, ". . . [are] totally unfit to form the minds of women, of friends, or of wives." The few novels which contain "excellent sentiments" —among them, *The Power of Sympathy*, the author implies— should be widely read and appreciated, for they speak "the language of the heart."

Brown urged his readers to show proper respect and "veneration . . . to the characters of the clergy":

> The ministers of no nation are more remarkable for learning and piety than those of this country. The fool may pretend to scorn, and the irreligious to contemn, but every person of sense and reflection must admire that sacred order, whose business is to inform the understanding and regulate the passions of mankind. Surely, therefore, that class of men will continue to merit our esteem and affection, while virtue remains upon earth.

Winning perhaps the ministers' reluctant approval of *The Power of Sympathy*, he made equally politic gestures to other formidable critics of the novel—among them, Noah Webster. Brown recommended Webster's *Grammatical Institute of the English Language* (1785) to his readers "as the best work in our language to facilitate the knowledge of grammar." "I cannot but think Mr. Webster intended his valuable book for the benefit of his countrywomen," Brown declared; "while he delivers his *rules* in a pure, precise, and elegant style, he *explains* his meaning by *examples* which are calculated to inspire the female mind with a thirst for emulation and a desire of virtue." He also recommended Timothy Dwight's *The Conquest of Canaan* (1785)[6] and

[6]Timothy Dwight, minister, poet, later president of Yale College, was a hostile critic of the novel; from the pulpit he often railed against the "worthless frivolit[ies]" young people engaged in. "Both parents are bound to teach their children," he once said; "and their children . . . are bound to learn, to be industrious, and to be economical; to fill up their time with useful employments; to methodize it, that it may be thus filled up; and to feel, that the loss of time [and] the neglect of talents . . . are

Joel Barlow's *The Vision of Columbus* (1787) and lamented the fact that *"American* literature boast[ed] so few productions from the pens of the ladies." The praise of the critics of the novel and the comments about American books and American writers were intentional as Brown warmed enthusiastically to a defense of American literature: poetry and that sub-literary form, the novel.[7]

As a moralist, Brown suggests the proper conduct of a young woman: "though her heart may be pure, her conduct is a tacit invitation to the seducer." He lists the vanities to which a young woman is susceptible: pride, fashion, material pleasures, irreverence, envy. The best guide to proper conduct is that which *"will bear the test of reflection"* and which will support the *"consciousness of acting right."* The middle ground in conduct and example is the well-favored ground; and if a young woman can walk this ground, she keeps her self-respect and wins the approval of society.

> She mixes with the world seemingly indiscriminantly; and because she would secure to herself that satisfaction which arises from a consciousness of acting right, she views her conduct with an eye of scrutiny. Though her temper is free and unrestrained, her heart is previously secured by the precepts of prudence. For prudence is but another name for virtue. Her manners are unruffled; and her disposition is calm, temperate, and dispassionate, however she may be surrounded by the temptations of the world.

It was Brown's intent that *The Power of Sympathy* would promote "lessons of instruction" which would be helpful to "the young ladies of United Columbia": it might well be a "mirror by which [they] may regulate [their] conduct and amend

all serious violations of their duty to God. The parents are bound to inspire, and the children to imbibe, a contempt, an abhorrence, for [any] worthless frivolity ... [to avoid] that sinful waste of the golden hours of life; that sickly devotion to amusement; that shameful, pitiable dependence on trifling[s].... Few persons are more to be pitied ... than those, who find their enjoyment only in diversions; and cling to a ride, a dance, a visit, a play, or a novel, to keep them from sinking into gloom and despondence...." Timothy Dwight, *Theology Explained and Defended in a Series of Sermons* (New York, 1854), III, 445.

[7]Mrs. Susanna Rowson acknowledged the prejudice against fiction when she wrote in the preface to *Charlotte Temple* (1791) that a mere novel "stands but a poor chance for fame in the annals of literature"; nevertheless, she believed that her story would earn greater applause than that given to "the most elegant, finished piece of literature whose tendency might deprave the heart or mislead the understanding."

[their] lives." As an author writing in America, he made observations and drew conclusions—always with appeals to sensibility —"in such a manner as may directly improve the mind and promote the economy of human life." The heavy moralizing, the sensationalism, the sentiment, and the epistolary form marked Brown's close imitation of similar elements in eighteenth-century English fiction. The first American novel had the ingredients of the popular fiction of the day.

As a tract for young women, *The Power of Sympathy* was perhaps eminently successful; as a novel, it fell short of being a satisfactory piece of fiction. The author's noble purposes did not conceal the book's glaring weaknesses. The handling of plot, character, dialogue, and style reveal Brown's ineptness in managing the demands of the novel form.

The plot is tenuous. The Harriot-Harrington narrative is lost in the other narratives of seduction and intrigue and in the digressions on manners and morals. A sense of proportion is missing; and the modern reader does not know which story, if any, commands his closer attention, his greater power of sympathy. The characters are types long familiar to the modern reader: the young libertine Harrington, reminiscent of Richardson's Lovelace; the reformed rake, the elder Harrington; the injured heroine Harriot; the warm-hearted friends and advisors to the young people, Mrs. Holmes and Worthy. All are equally responsive to the tugs of sentiment. All simply play out the role the author has assigned them in the melodrama.

Although some of the characters were drawn from life, as well as the incidents in which they figured, Brown sacrificed potentially dramatic material to the demands of the popular fiction of the day. There were probably models for Harriot and Fidelia. and the history of Ophelia re-created a notorious Boston scandal involving the two Apthorp sisters and the husband of one of them.[8] Brown, who apparently knew the family, showed extremely bad taste in giving such prominence to the scandal. The family tried to suppress *The Power of Sympathy,* and the success of its efforts makes the first American novel an exceedingly

[8]See Tremaine McDowell, "Last Words of a Sentimental Heroine," *American Literature*, IV (May, 1932), 174-77; also, Tremaine McDowell, "The First American Novel," *American Review*, II (November, 1933), 73-81. In the first article McDowell reproduced letters which Frances Apthorp wrote to members of the family and to her seducer in the days immediately preceding her suicide.

rare book today. Yet, the basis in fact did nothing to improve the reality of the novel.

Nor is the dialogue distinguished: it is artful and contrived. The characters speak for the most part a starchy prose. One letter reads like the next; nothing is familiar or intimate, simply refined phrasing and exquisite epithet. When a particular sentiment cannot apparently be adequately freighted in prose, it is offered in richly ornamental verse.[9] The reality that Richardson sometimes achieved in the letters in his novels, when they express the commonplaces of life, is utterly lacking in Brown's story.

The Power of Sympathy is the product of a man who had knowledge about the demands of the novel, but who had not the ability to manipulate that knowledge into an effective tale—a practitioner in the new form, but not a master of it. With so much to criticize and so little to praise, the modern reader is tempted to dismiss the pioneer work in American fiction; however, the novel can be read with profit by the social historian and the student of American literature. No matter how absurd it may be, Brown's work is remarkable because it largely sets the pattern for American fiction. Melodramatic, pietistic, didactic, sentimental, The Power of Sympathy exemplifies the taste of readers and writers of native fiction for fifty years.

Of all the tales of seduction and intrigue by writers in America, The Coquette (1797) by Mrs. Hannah Foster appeals still to the modern reader whose taste in the novel is more sophisticated.[10] Mrs. Foster's story avoids the excessive sentimentality of The Power of Sympathy and the extravagant sensationalism of Charlotte Temple, perhaps the most popular novel of its kind.[11] The narrative focuses on the career of Eliza

[9]One of the more elaborate passages in prose is a Dantesque vision of the lower world shown to the elder Harrington, now remorseful over his guilty conduct.

[10]For information about Mrs. Foster, see Robert L. Shurter, "Mrs. Hannah Webster Foster and the Early American Novel," American Literature, IV (November, 1932), 306-8.

[11]According to R. W. G. Vail (in Susanna Haswell Rowson, the Author of Charlotte Temple: a Bibliographical Study [Worcester, Massachusetts, 1933]), Charlotte Temple has appeared in over 200 editions. The most recent one is edited by Clara M. and Rudolph Kirk, published in the Masterworks of Literature Series, College and University Press, New Haven, 1964.

Wharton, the coquette; the character of Eliza and her seducer is convincing; the style is not nearly so sententious as that in many novels of the period.

Although Mrs. Foster, the wife of a clergyman, had her own reservations about time spent in novel reading,[12] she discovered a particular interest in the story of Elizabeth Whitman of Hartford, Connecticut. The young woman was apparently a cousin of Mrs. Foster's husband, and her seduction was common gossip in the Connecticut Valley. The story "founded in fact" could hardly be objected to by critics of the novel; readers could sympathize with it; the moralist could respond to it.

The influence of Richardson, whose novels Mrs. Foster believed could be read with profit,[13] is apparent in *The Coquette*. Clarissa and Lovelace and their friends reappear in Eliza and Sanford and their friends. The digressions on problems of conduct and conscience, the didactic strain in the novel, the analysis of sentiment—the "moral lectures," Mrs. Foster called them—show the English author's influence as well; but they are far more skillfully managed here than in much American fiction. In spite of the thick prose, the letters have naturalness and variety as the correspondents reveal Eliza's impetuousness and Sanford's scheming and provide drama and suspense (as much as the epistolary form allowed at least) and give unity to the narrative.

For the modern reader the depiction of character is the reward for examining *The Coquette*. Eliza Wharton is one of the few women in early American fiction who emerge as a real person. A strong-willed young woman, recently freed from a restricting family circle, she had only "lately entered society," anxious—she informs Sanford—"to enjoy my freedom in . . .

[12]"Novels are the favourite, and the most dangerous, kind of reading, now adopted by the generality of young ladies . . . ," she wrote in *The Boarding School*, a series of essays on female education. "They often pervert the judgment, mislead the affections, and blind the understanding." However, Mrs. Foster added a few pages later: ". . . I would not be understood to condemn all novels indiscriminately; though great prudence is necessary to make a useful selection. Some of them are fraught with sentiment; convey lessons for moral improvement, and exhibit striking pictures of virtue rewarded; and vice, folly, and indiscretion punished; which may prove encouragements to imitate, or warnings to avoid similar practices. . . . Those, which are sanctioned by the general voice of delicacy and refinement, may be allowed a reading; yet none should . . . be suffered to monopolize too large a portion of [one's] time." Hannah Foster, *The Boarding School* (Boston, 1798), pp. 18-24 *passim*.

[13]*The Boarding School*, pp. 160-61.

pleasures suited to my age and sex." Self-assured, independent, she is not ready to assume "the tedious round of domestic duties" and "the pedantic conversation of scholars" until she has engaged in "unmeaning pleasantr[ies]" with men who delight her fancy. She will settle down, she announces to her friends, "when I have sowed my wild oats."

To her friend Lucy Freeman she is frankly mischievous in her remark that she puts on a *"madamish"* face before she reads a letter from Mr. Boyer, the young minister who is courting her. "So sweet a repast ...," she tells Lucy, "was rather sickening to my taste." At times she shows a disarming naivete in the ways of the world as she listens to the blandishments of Sanford, "whose profession it is to blast [women's] reputation"—so her friends inform her. She knows that her temperament is perhaps "too volatile" and admits to "that unrestrained levity of disposition, that fondness for ... coquetry," which Sanford encourages. She is restless and cannot yet turn to marriage as her friends have done. Marriage, she confides to Lucy, "is the tomb of friendship. It appears to me a very selfish state." She has "no notion of becoming a recluse" and recoils at "forming [any] connection which must confine me to the duties of domestic life and make me dependent for happiness, perhaps, too, for subsistence, upon ... people who will ... scrutiniz[e] every part of my conduct. ..." She finds Sanford exciting and gallant and deceiving—as she was warned he would be.

When Sanford marries for money, Eliza still is attracted to him for the glamor he sheds, for the apparent freedom he has as a man to do as he pleases and to come and go as he wishes. He is "productive of agreeable sensations"—a man who treats her yet, she tells her friends defensively, with "affections and tenderness of a brother" and with whom she feels "little restraint." However, she does feel forsaken; her will weakens and she becomes a "victim of her own indiscretion." At the time of her death, alone and friendless in a tavern, she honestly appraises her conduct. She is self-perceptive when she arrives at wisdom, too late.

What is real about Eliza Wharton is that she is a rebel against the tired proprieties of her age, as Herbert Ross Brown has pointed out.[14] Nervous, impulsive, fun-loving, she speaks frankly

[14]Hannah Foster, *The Coquette*, ed. Herbert Ross Brown (New York, 1939), p. xviii.

about the kind of life she wants to lead, to the chagrin of her friends. Her tragedy is that in her rebellion she exceeded the one convention of her age which she herself believed in.[15] Unlike the young women in *The Power of Sympathy*, whose similar conduct lost them self-pride, Eliza is a person whose plight is convincing. The reader witnesses her tragedy through the letters; in *The Power of Sympathy* he notes only casually the agony of self-recrimination.

Sanford is equally believable as a character. In the beginning he, like young Harrington, is the self-confident cavalier, intent on winning his goal: "I fancy the young woman is a coquette; and if so, I shall avenge my sex by retaliating the mischiefs she meditates against us," he writes his friend Deighton. "Not that I have any ill design, but only to play off her own artillery by using a little unmeaning gallantry. And let her beware of the consequences." He is captivating to many of Eliza's friends, with manners that make him welcome at dances and dinners, although they properly identify him as "a rake," "a Chesterfieldian," "a second Lovelace." To him, seducing a woman is a kind of game with the stakes not particularly high; "If she will play with a lion, let her beware the paw, I say." And he is confident of his powers: "the gaiety of our dispositions, the insinuating graces of our manners, and the irresistible charms of our persons and address. The qualifications are very alluring. . . ."

But Sanford's pride is roused when he sees Eliza's attraction to Mr. Boyer: "I felt a glow of jealousy, which I never experienced before, and vowed revenge for the pain it gave me. . . ." Eliza's apparent aloofness, he protests to his friend, "mortifies me extremely, as it is the first time I ever failed." And pride is injured too when he realizes that so many of Eliza's friends speak against him: "I must own myself," he admits to Deighton, "a little revengeful, too, in this affair. I wish to punish her friends . . . for their malice towards me, for their cold and negligent treatment of me. . . ." The conquest might have been differ-

[15] Elizabeth Whitman, whose seducer has been inconclusively identified as Pierrepont Edwards, Johathan Edwards' son, has had two sympathetic defenders: Mrs. Caroline W. H. Dall, *The Romance of the Association; or One Last Glimpse of Charlotte Temple and Eliza Wharton* (Cambridge, 1875); and Charles K. Bolton, *The Elizabeth Whitman Mystery* (Peabody, Massachusetts, 1912). It is Bolton's conclusion that Elizabeth Whitman's character has been fashioned for all time, however, in the character of Mrs. Foster's heroine, Eliza Wharton.

ent, Eliza might have kept the day had not circumstances put Sanford in control.

When he wins Eliza, he is almost of two minds. The game is won—"the girl is my own." Yet he is not anxious to claim the reward—"I shall take my own time. . . ." A desire to satisfy his passion is tempered momentarily by real affection for Eliza, "a fine girl." Nevertheless, it is the prize ultimately which he seeks: "my reformation," he rationalizes, "like most others of the kind, will prove unstable." Having made the decision, he rejoices at his success: "If a lady will consent to enter the lists against an antagonist of her honor, she may be sure of losing the prize."

Sanford, like Eliza, is a real person: vain, sensitive, honest, even likeable. His hurt pride, his moments of indecision, his concern for Eliza make him human and not the black villain of so many conventional romances.

In the end, appropriate novel-justice is dealt Eliza and Sanford in a way to assuage the consciences of the outraged readers of the day. But Mrs. Foster has the good sense to let Eliza and her friends and Sanford tell the tale. Eliza's agonizing review of her own conduct at the end of the novel—although it may well be Mrs. Foster's—is Eliza's, growing naturally out of her misfortunes. The "confessions" which Brown wrote for the women in *The Power of Sympathy* are set pieces; even Mrs. Rowson admitted in the narrative of *Charlotte Temple* that she would be "a niggard" if she omitted "an opportunity of pointing out the way to others."[16] Such confessions are required by the convention of the novel, but Eliza's rise naturally out of personal distress which the reader has shared. Mrs. Foster has given early American fiction an interest it did not have before: a candid discussion of a social problem and a sensible depiction of character. The weaknesses of *The Coquette* are the weaknesses of other novels in the tradition: the sentimentality, the digressions, the epistolary form, the proprieties of the age which largely dictated the subject matter for the popular novel. Yet the honest treatment of Eliza's story gives a dignity to a theme so often overwhelmed in fiction of the period.

The Power of Sympathy and *The Coquette* are, nevertheless, period pieces: plot is incidental, many of the characters are

[16]Susanna Rowson, *Charlotte Temple*, ed. Clara M. and Rudolph Kirk (New Haven, 1964), p. 67.

poorly conceived, dialogue is ponderous, style is often pedantic. Yet Mrs. Foster in *The Coquette* sometimes achieves a clarity of expression in her narrative that one does not read again until he examines Mark Twain. The modern reader can view them as representative novels of seduction and intrigue and can observe in them a number of the significant elements to appear in American fiction in the first half of the nineteenth century.

Selected Bibliography

Brown, Herbert Ross. *The Sentimental Novel in America 1789-1860*. New York: Pageant Books, Inc., 1959.

Brown, William Hill. *The Power of Sympathy*. Ed. Herbert Ross Brown. Boston: New Frontiers Press, 1961.

Cowie, Alexander. *The Rise of the American Novel*. New York: American Book Company, 1948.

Foster, Hannah. *The Coquette*. Ed. Herbert Ross Brown. New York: Columbia University Press, 1939.

Loshe, Lillie Deming. *The Early American Novel*. New York: Columbia University Press, 1907.

Orians, G. Harrison. "Censure of Fiction in American Romances and Magazines: 1789-1810," *PMLA*, LII (March, 1937), 195-214.

Quinn, Arthur Hobson. *American Fiction*. New York: Appleton-Century, Inc., 1936.

Van Doren, Carl. *The American Novel: 1789-1939*. Rev. Ed. New York: The Macmillan Company, 1940.

A Note on the Texts

The Power of Sympathy was published in two volumes in 1789 by Isaiah Thomas and Company in Boston. The number of reprints of the novel has been small, the most recent, with an introduction by Herbert Ross Brown, appearing in 1961. The present edition follows the text of the first edition of Brown's novel. Brown wrote a nervous style; only changes in punctuation and minor revisions in the text have been made, however, to conform with modern English practice.

The Coquette was printed in one volume in 1797 by Samuel Etheridge for E. Larkin in Boston. According to Lyle H. Wright, in *American Fiction 1774-1850*, there were thirty editions of the novel by 1840. The most recent edition, with an introduction by Herbert Ross Brown, appeared in 1939. The present edition follows the text of the first edition of Mrs. Foster's novel. Only changes in punctuation and minor revisions in the text have been made to conform with modern English practice.

W.S.O.

THE

POWER of SYMPATHY

OR, THE

TRIUMPH of NATURE

FOUNDED in TRUTH

FAIN would he strew life's thorny way with flowers,
And open to your view Elysian bowers;
Catch the warm passions of the tender youth
And win the mind to sentiment and truth.

PREFACE

Novels have ever met with a ready reception into the libraries of the ladies, but this species of writing hath not been received with universal approbation: futility is not the only charge brought against it. Any attempt, therefore, to make these studies more advantageous has at least a claim upon the patience and candor of the public.

In novels which *expose* no particular vice, and which *recommend* no particular virtue, the fair reader, though she may find amusement, must finish them without being impressed with any particular idea: so that if they are harmless, they are not beneficial.

Of the Letters before us, it is necessary to remark that this error on each side has been avoided: the dangerous consequences of seduction are exposed, and the advantages of female education set forth and recommended.

Letter I

HARRINGTON to WORTHY

Boston

You may now felicitate me—I have had an interview with the charmer I informed you of. Alas! where were the thoughtfulness and circumspection of my friend Worthy? I did not possess them and am graceless enough to acknowledge it. He would have considered the consequences before he had resolved upon the project. But you call me, with some degree of truth, a strange medley of contradiction: the moralist and the amoroso—the sentiment and the sensibility—are interwoven in my constitution, so that nature and grace are at continual fisticuffs. To the point:

I pursued my determination of discovering the dwelling of my charmer and have at length obtained access. You may behold my Rosebud; but should you presume to place it in your bosom, expect the force of my wrath to be the infallible consequence.

I declared the sincerity of my passion—the warmth of my affection—to the beautiful Harriot. Believe me, Jack, she did not seem inattentive. Her mien is elegant—her disposition inclining to the melancholy; yet her temper is affable, and her manners easy. And as I poured my tender vows into the heart of my beloved, a crimson drop stole across her cheek; and thus I construe it in my own favor as the sweet messenger of hope:—

"Do not wholly despair, my new friend; excuse the declaration of a poor artless female. You see I am not perfectly contented in my situation. [Observe, Jack, I have not the vanity to think this distress *altogether* upon my account.] Time therefore may disclose wonders, and perhaps more to your advantage than you imagine. Do not despair then."

Such vulgar, uncongenial souls, as that which animates thy clay cold carcass, would have thought this crimson drop nothing more than an ordinary blush! Be far removed from my heart,

31

such sordid, earthborn ideas: But come, thou spirit of celestial language that canst communicate by one affectionate look—one tender glance—more divine information to the soul of sensibility than can be contained in myriads of volumes!

Hail, gentle God of Love! While thou rivetest the chains of thy *slaves,* how dost thou make them leap for joy as with delicious *triumph.* Happy enthusiasm! that while it carries us away into captivity can make the heart to dance as in the bosom of content. Hail, gentle God of Love! Encircled as thou art with darts, torments, and ensigns of cruelty, still do we hail thee. How dost thou smooth over the roughness and asperities of present pain with what thou seest in reversion! Thou banishest the Stygian glooms of disquiet and suspense by the hope of approaching Elysium. Blessed infatuation!

I desire you will not hesitate to pronounce an *amen* to my hymn to love as an unequivocal evidence of your wish for my success.

Letter II

WORTHY to HARRINGTON

New York

Wish you success! In what? Who is this lady of whom you have been talking at such an inconsistent rate? But before you have leisure to reply to these inquiries, you may have forgotten there is such a person as she whom you call Harriot. I have seen many juvenile heroes, during my pilgrimage of two and twenty years, easily inflamed with new objects—agitated and hurried away by the impetuosity of new desires; and at the same time they were by no means famous for solidity of judgment, or remarkable for the permanency of their resolutions. There is such a tumult, such an ebullition of the brain in these paroxysms of passion, that this new object is very superficially examined. These, added to partiality and preposession, never fail

to blind the eyes of the lover. Instead of weighing matters maturely, and stating the evidence fairly on both sides in order to form a right judgment, every circumstance not perfectly coincident with your particular bias comes not under consideration, because it does not flatter your vanity. "Ponder and pause" just here; tell me seriously whether you are in love, and whether you have sufficiently examined your heart to give a just answer.

Do you mean to insinuate that your declaration of love hath attracted the affection of the pensive Harriot? If this should be the case, I wish you would tell me what you design to do with her.

Letter III

HARRINGTON to WORTHY

Boston

I cannot but laugh at your dull sermons, and yet I find something in them not altogether displeasing; for this reason I permit you to prate on. "Weigh matters maturely!" Ha! ha! why art thou not arrayed in canonicals! "What do I design to do with her?" Upon my word, my sententious friend, you ask mighty odd questions. I see you aim a stroke at the foundation upon which the pillar of my new system is reared. And will you strive to batter down that pillar? If you entertain any idea of executing such a task, I foresee it will never succeed and advise you timely to desist. What! dost thou think to topple down my scheme of pleasure? Thou mightest as well topple down the pike of Teneriffe.

I suppose you will be ready to ask, why, if I love Harriot, I do not marry her. Your monitorial correspondence has so accustomed me to reproof that I easily anticipate this piece of impertinence. But *whom* shall I marry? That is the question. Harriot has no father—no mother—neither is there aunt, cousin, or kindred of any degree who claim any kind of relationship to her. She is companion to Mrs. Francis and, as I understand,

totally dependent on that lady. Now, Mr. Worthy, I must take the liberty to acquaint you that I am not so much of a republican as formally to wed any person of this class. How laughable would my conduct appear were I to trace over the same ground marked out by the immaculate footsteps, to be heard openly acknowledging for my bosom companion any daughter of the democratic empire of virtue!

To suppose a smart, beautiful girl would continue as a companion to the best lady in Christendom, when she could raise herself to a more eligible situation, is to suppose a solecism. She might as well be immured in a nunnery. Now, Jack, I will show you my benevolent scheme; it is to take this beautiful sprig and transplant it to a more favorable soil where it shall flourish and blossom under my own auspices. In a word, I mean to remove this fine girl into an elegant apartment, of which she herself is to be the sole mistress. Is not this a proof of my humanity and goodness of heart? But I know the purport of your answer; so pray thee keep thy comments to thyself and be sparing of your compliments on this part of my conduct, for I do not love flattery. A month has elapsed since my arrival in town. What will the revolution of another moon bring forth?

Letter IV

Miss HARRIOT FAWCET to Miss MYRA HARRINGTON

Boston

I have somehow bewitched a new lover, my dear Myra—a smart, clever fellow, too—and the youth expresses such fondness and passion that I begin to feel afraid even to pity him; for love will certainly follow. I own to you I *esteem* him very much, but must I go any farther? He is extremely generous—polite—gay. I believe if you were to see him your partiality in his favor would exceed mine.

I never saw my poor swain so seemingly disconcerted and abashed as he was a few days ago. He appeared to have something very particular to communicate, but his tongue faltered. Ought not one to help out a modest youth in such cases?

Letter V

Miss MYRA HARRINGTON to Mrs. HOLMES

Boston

Are the rural pleasures of Belleview, my dear friend, so engaging as to debar us of the pleasure of your company forever? Do your dear groves, and your books, still employ your meditating mind? Serious sentimentalist as you are, let me ask whether a ball, a concert or serenade would not afford you the satisfaction of a contemplative walk in your garden, listening to the love tales of the melodious inhabitants of the air?

Raillery apart—when shall I take upon myself the honor to wait upon you here? I want to advise with you on certain points of female conduct, and about my new dress. I have heard you say lessons to a volatile mind should be fresh and fresh applied, because it either pretends to despise them or has a tendency to degeneracy. Now you must know I am actually degenerating for want of some of your mentor-like lessons of instruction. I have scarcely any opinion of my own; these fashions, changing about so often, are enough to vitiate the best taste in the world.

I forgot to tell you my brother has been at home this month; but, from certain indubitable symptoms, I suspect the young man to be in love.

Heigh Ho! what is become of Worthy? The time of my liberty steals away, for you know I was to have three or four months of liberty before I gave myself up to his authority and relinquished all my right and title to the name of Myra Harrington.

Letter VI

HARRINGTON to WORTHY

Boston

Abashed—confounded—defeated, I waited upon my beloved with my head well furnished with ready made arguments, to prevail on her to acquiesce in my benevolent scheme. She never appeared so amiable—grace accompanied every word she uttered and every action she performed. "Think, my love," said I, in a tone something between sighing and tears, and took her hand in a very cordial manner, "Think, my love, on your present, unhappy, menial situation in the family of Mrs. Francis." I enlarged on the violence of my passion—expatiated most methaphysically on our future happiness and concluded by largely answering objections. "Shall we not," continued I, "obey the dictates of nature, rather than confine ourselves to the forced, unnatural rules of—and—and shall the halcyon days of youth slip through our fingers unenjoyed?"

Do you think, Worthy, I said this to Harriot? Not a syllable of it. It was impossible; my heart had the courage to dictate, but my rebellious tongue refused to utter a word. It faltered—stammered—hesitated.

There is a language of the eyes, and we conversed in that language; and though I said not a word with my tongue, she seemed perfectly to understand my meaning—for she *looked* (and I comprehended it as well as if she had *said*), "Is the crime of dependence to be expiated by the sacrifice of virtue? And because I am a poor, unfortunate girl, must the little I have be taken from me?" "No, my love," answered I, passionately, "it shall not."

Of all those undescribable things which influence the mind, and which are most apt to persuade, none is so powerful an

orator—so feelingly eloquent as beauty. I bow to the all-conquer-
ing force of Harriot's eloquence—and what is the consequence? I
am now determined to continue my addresses on a principle the
most just, and the most honorable.

How amiable is that beauty which has its foundation in good-
ness! Reason cannot contemplate its power with indifference.
Wisdom cannot refrain from enthusiasm, and the sneering exer-
tions of wit cannot render it ridiculous. There is a *dignity* in
conscious virtue that all my impudence cannot bring me to de-
spise; and if it be beauty that subdues my heart, it is *this* that
completes the triumph. It is here my pompous parade, and all
my flimsy subterfuges, appear to me in their proper light. In
fine, I have *weighed matters maturely*; and the alternative is
Harriot must be mine, or I miserable without her. I have so well
weighed the matter that even this idea is a *flash* of joy to my
heart. But, my friend, *after lightning comes the thunder*: my
father is mortally averse to making any matrimonial engagement
at so early a period. This is a bar in my way, but I must leap
over it.

Letter VII

Mrs. HOLMES to Miss HARRINGTON

Belleview

Although my attachment to Belleview is not so romantic as
your airy pen has described it, I think its quiet and amusements
infinitely preferable to the bustle and parade with which you are
surrounded.

The improvements made here by my late husband (who in-
herited the virtues of his parents, who still protect me and
endeavor to console the anguish of his loss by the most tender
affection) have rendered the charms of Belleview superior in my
estimation to every gilded scene of the gay world.

It is almost vanity to pretend to give you a description of the
beauty of the prospect, the grandeur of the river that rolls

through the meadow in front of the house, or any eulogium on rural elegance, because these scenes are common to most places in the country. Nature is everywhere liberal in dispensing her beauties and her variety—and I pity those who look round and declare they see neither.

A great proportion of our happiness depends on our own choice. It offers itself to our taste, but it is the heart that gives it a relish. What at one time, for instance, we think to be humor is at another disgustful or insipid. So, unless we carry our appetite with us to the treat, we shall vainly wish to make ourselves happy. "Was I in a desert," says Sterne, "I would find wherewith in it to call forth my affections. If I could do no better, I would fatten them on some sweet myrtle, or seek some melancholy cypress to connect myself to. I would court their shade and greet them kindly for their protection. If their leaves withered, I would teach myself to mourn; and when they rejoiced, I would rejoice along with them."

I believe you could hardly find the way to the summer house, where we have enjoyed many happy hours together and which you used to call "The Temple of Apollo." It is now more elegantly furnished than it formerly was and is enriched with a considerable addition to the library and music.

In front of the avenue that leads to this place is a figure of CONTENT, pointing with one hand to the Temple, and with the other to an invitation executed in such an antique style that you would think it done either by the ancient inhabitants of the country or by the hand of a fairy. She is very particular in the characters she invites, but those whom she invites she heartily welcomes.

Rural Inscription

Come ye who loath the horrid crest,
 Who hate the fiery front of Mars;
Who scorn the mean—the sordid breast—
 Who fly Ambition's guilty cares:
Ye who are blessed with peaceful souls
 Rest here: Enjoy the pleasures round:
Here Fairies quaff their acorn bowls
 And lightly print the mazy ground.

Thrice welcome to this humble scene—
(To ye alone such scenes belong)
Peace smiles upon the fragrant green
And here the woodland sisters throng,
And fair CONTENTMENT's pleasing train,
 Whilst in the Heav'n the stars advance,
With many a maid and many a swain
Lead up the jocund, rural dance.

Thrice welcome to our calm retreat,
 Where Innocency oft hath strove,
With violet blue and woodbine sweet,
 To form the votive wreath to Love:
O! pardon then, our cautious pride—
 (Caution, a virtue rare, I ween)
For evils with the great abide,
 Which dwell not in our sylvan scene.

These are the scenes to which I have chosen to retreat; contented with the suffrage of the virtuous and the good, and inattentive to the contemptuous sneer of the giddy and the futile; for even *these* have the vanity to look with pity on those who voluntarily remove from whatever agrees with *their* ideas of pleasure. He who has no conception of the beauties of the mind will contemn a person awkward or ill-favored; and one whose store of enjoyment is drawn from affluence and abundance will be astonished at the conduct of him who finds cause to rejoice, though surrounded with inconvenience and penury. Hence we judge of the happiness of others by the standard of our own conduct and prejudices.

From this misjudging race I retire, without a sigh, to mingle in their amusements, nor yet disgusted at whatever is thought of sufficient consequence to engage their pursuits. I fly from the tumult of the town—from scenes of boisterous pleasure and riot to those of quietness and peace, "where every breeze breathes health and every sound is the echo of tranquillity." On this subject I give my sentiments to you with freedom, from a conviction that I bear the world no spleen; at the same time with a degree of deference to the judgment of others, from a conviction that I may be a little prejudiced.

I hope to be with you soon, in the mean time continue to write.

Letter VIII

WORTHY to HARRINGTON

New York

I applaud your change of sentiment: Harriot is a good girl, and your conduct is extremely praiseworthy and honorable. It is what her virtues incontestibly merit. But I advise you certainly to gain your father's approbation before you proceed so far as to be unable to return. A contrary step might terminate in the utter ruin of you both. Direct to me at Belleview, for I intend to stop there in my return to Boston.

Letter IX

HARRINGTON to WORTHY

Boston

I have had a conversation with my father on the subject of early marriages, but to no purpose. I will not be certain whether he understood my drift, but all his arguments are applicable to my situation. One must be an adept to argue with him; and interested as he thinks himself in the result of the debate, he cannot be prevailed upon to relinquish his settled opinion. I am too much chagrined to write you even the heads of our conversation. I now stand upon my old ground.

Letter X

WORTHY to MYRA

Belleview

I am very happy at present enjoying the sweets of Belleview with our excellent friend Mrs. Holmes. To dwell in this delightful retreat, and to be blessed with the conversation of this amiable woman, cannot be called solitude. The charms of nature are here beheld in the most luxuriant variety: it is here diversified with a beautiful prospect. The late Mr. Holmes planned his garden; it is elegant, but simple. My time glides off my hands most happily. I am sometimes indulging my solitary relections in contemplating the sublimity of the scenes around me—and sometimes in conversation with Eliza and the old people.

The old gentleman is a man of a most benevolent heart; he continues to preach—is assiduous in the duties of his profession and is the love and admiration of his flock. He prescribes for the health of the body, as well as that of the soul, and settles all the little disputes of his parish. They are contented with his judgment, and he is at once their parson, their lawyer, and their physician. I often read in the little building that was finished by his son. He was a man of an excellent taste, and I have paid my tribute to his memory. It is the same place that you used to admire, and perhaps I improve more of my time in it on that very account.

Letter XI

Mrs. HOLMES to MYRA

Belleview

I sit down to give you, my dear Myra, some account of the visitants of today, and their conversation. We are not always *distinguished* by such company, but perhaps it is sometimes necessary; and as it is a relaxation from thought, it serves to give us more pleasure in returning to the conversation of people of ideas.

Mrs. Bourn assumes a higher rank in life than she pretended to seven years ago. She then walked on foot; she now, by good fortune, rides in a chariot. Placed, however, in a situation with which her education does not altgether comport, she has nothing disagreeable but her over assiduity to please. This is sometimes disgusting, for one cannot feast heartily upon honey: it is an error which a candid mind easily forgives. She sometimes appears solicitious to display her mental accomplishments and desirous to improve those of her daughter; but it is merely apparent. Notwithstanding a temporary wish may arise towards the attainment of this point, a habitual vacancy nips it in the bud.

Miss Bourn is about the age of fourteen—genteel, with a tolerable share of beauty, but not striking. Her dress was elegant, but might have been adjusted to more advantage. Not altogether awkward in her manners, nor yet can she be called graceful—she has a peculiar air of *drollery* which takes her by fits; and for this reason, perhaps, she does not avail herself of every opportunity of displaying the modesty of her sex. She has seen much company; but instead of polishing her manners, it has only increased her assurance.

Thus much of the characters of our *company*. After some small chat which passed as we took a turn in the garden, we entered the Temple.

"What books would you recommend to put into the hands of my daughter?" said Mrs. Bourn, as she walked into the library. "It is a matter of some importance." "It is a matter of *more* importance," answered Worthy, "than is generally imagined; for unless a proper selection is made, one would do better never to read at all. Now, Madam, as much depends on the choice of books, care should be taken not to put those in the way of young persons which might leave on their minds any disagreeable prejudices, or which has a tendency to corrupt their morals." "As obvious as your remark is," added Mr. Holmes, "it is evidently overlooked in the common course of education. We wisely exclude those persons from our conversation whose characters are bad, whose manners are depraved, or whose morals are impure; but if they are excluded from an apprehension of contaminating our minds, how much more dangerous is the company of those books where the strokes aimed at virtue are redoubled and the poison of vice, by repeatedly reading the same thing, indelibly distains the young mind?"

"We all agree," rejoined Worthy, "that it is as great a matter of virtue and prudence to be circumspect in the selection of our books, as in the choice of our company. But, Sir, the best things may be subverted to an ill use. Hence, we may possibly trace the cause of the ill tendency of many of the novels extant."

"Most of the novels," interrupted my father, "with which our female libraries are overrun, are built on a foundation not always placed on strict morality, and in the pursuit of objects not always probable or praiseworthy. Novels not regulated on the chaste principles of true friendship, rational love, and connubial duty appear to me totally unfit to form the minds of women, of friends, or of wives."

"But, as most young people read," says Mrs. Bourn, "what rule can be *hit upon* to make study always terminate to advantage?"

"Impossible," cried Miss Bourn, "for I read as much as anybody; and, though it may afford amusement while I am employed, I do not remember a single word when I lay down the book."

"This confirms what I say of novels," cried Mr. Holmes, addressing Worthy in a jocular manner, "just calculated to kill time—to attract the attention of the reader for an hour, but to leave not one idea on the mind."

"I am far from condemning every production in the gross," replied Worthy; "general satire against any particular class or order of men, may be viewed in the same light as a satire against the species. It is the same with books. If there are corrupt or mortified members, it is hardly fair to destroy the whole body. Now I grant some novels have a bad tendency, yet there are many which contain excellent sentiments—let these receive their deserved reward, let those be discountenanced; and if it is impossible 'to smite them with an apoplexy, there is a moral certainty of their dying of a consumption.' But, as Mrs. Bourn observes, most young persons read, I will therefore recommend to those who wish to mingle instruction with entertainment, method and regularity in reading. To *dip* into *any book* burdens the mind with unnecessary lumber, and may rather be called a disadvantage than a benefit. The record of memory is so scrawled and blotted with imperfect ideas that not one legible character can be traced."

"Were I to throw my thoughts on this subject," said my good father-in-law—as he began to enter more warmly into the debates, drawing his chair opposite Worthy and raising his hand with a poetical enthusiasm—"Were I to throw my thoughts on this subject into an allegory, I would describe the human mind as an extensive plain, and knowledge as the river that should water it. If the course of the river be properly directed, the plain will be fertilized and cultivated to advantage; but if books, which are the sources that feed this river, rush into it from every quarter, it will overflow its banks; and the plain will become inundated. When, therefore, knowledge flows on in its proper channel, this extensive and valuable field, the mind, instead of being covered with stagnant waters, is cultivated to the utmost advantage and blooms luxuriantly into a general efflorescence—for a river properly restricted by high banks is necessarily progressive."

The old gentleman brought down his hand with great solemnity, and we complimented him on his poetical exertion. "I cannot comprehend the meaning of this matter," said the penetrative Miss Bourn. "I will explain it to you, my little dear," said he, with great good nature. "If you read with any design to improve your mind in virtue and every amiable accomplishment, you should be careful to read methodically, which will enable

you to form an estimate of the various topics discussed in company, and to bear a part in all those conversations which belong to your sex. You see, therefore, how necessary general knowledge is—what would you think of a woman advanced in life who has no other store of knowledge than what she has obtained from experience?"

"I think she would have a sorry time of it," answered Miss Bourn.

"To prevent it in yourself," said Mrs. Bourn to her daughter, "be assiduous to lay in a good stock of this knowledge, while your mind is yet free from prejudice and care."

"How shall I *go to work*, Madam," inquired the delicate daughter.

Mrs. Bourn turned towards Mr. Holmes, which was hint enough for the good old man to proceed.

"There is a medium to be observed," continued he, "in a lady's reading; she is not to receive everything she finds, even in the best books, as invariable lessons of conduct; in books written in an easy, flowing style, which excel in description and the luxuriance of fancy, the imagination is apt to get heated; she ought, therefore, to discern with an eye of judgment between the superficial and the penetrating, the elegant and the tawdry—what may be merely amusing and what may be useful. General reading will not teach her a true knowledge of the world.

"In books she finds recorded the faithfulness of friendship, the constancy of *true love*, and even that honesty is the best policy. If virtue is represented carrying its reward with it, she too easily persuades herself that mankind has adopted this plan. Thus she finds, when perhaps it is too late, that she has entertained wrong notions of human nature; that her friends are deceitful; that her lovers are false; and that men consult interest oftener than honesty.

"A young lady who has imbibed her ideas of the world from desultory reading, and placed confidence on the virtue of others, will bring back disappointment when she expected gratitude. Unsuspicious of deceit, she is easily deceived—from the purity of her own thoughts, she trusts the faith of mankind until experience convinces her of her error. She falls a sacrifice to her credulity, and her only consolation is the simplicity and goodness of her heart.

"The story of Miss Whitman* is an emphatical illustration of the truth of these observations. An inflated fancy, not restricted by judgment, leads too often to *disappointment* and repentance. Such will be the fate of those who become (to use her own words)

> Lost in the magic of that sweet employ,
> To build *gay scenes* and fashion *future joy.*

"With a good heart she possessed a poetical imagination and an unbounded thrift for novelty; but these airy talents, not counterpoised with judgment or perhaps serious reflection, instead of adding to her happiness, were the cause of her ruin."

"I conclude from your reasoning," said I, "and it is besides, my own opinion that many fine girls have been ruined by reading novels."

"And I believe," added Mrs. Bourn, "we may trace from hence the causes of spleen in many persons advanced in life."

"You mean old maids, Madam," cried the sagacious Miss Bourn, "like my aunt Deborah. She calls all the men deceitful, and most women, with her, are no better than they should be."

"Well said!" exclaimed Worthy, "the recollection of chagrin and former disappointment sours one's temper and mortifies the

*This young lady was of a reputable family in Connecticut. In her youth she was admired for beauty and good sense. She was a great reader of novels and romances and, having imbibed her ideas of the characters of men from those fallacious sources, became vain and coquetish, and rejected several offers of marriage in expectation of receiving one more agreeable to her fanciful idea. Disappointed in her fairy hope, and finding her train of admirers less solicitous for the honor of her hand in proportion as the roses of youth decayed, she was the more easily persuaded to relinquish that stability which is the honor and happiness of the sex. The consequences of her amour becoming visible, she acquainted her lover of her situation; a husband was proposed for her, who was to receive a considerable sum for preserving the reputation of the lady; but, having received security for the payment, he immediately withdrew. She then left her friends and traveled in the stage as far as Watertown, where she hired a young man to conduct her in a chaise to Salem. Here she wandered alone and friendless and at length repaired to the Bell Tavern, in Danvers, where she was delivered of a lifeless child, and in about a fortnight after (in July, 1788) died of a puerperal fever, aged about 35 years.

Before her death she amused herself with reading, writing and needlework and, though in a state of anxiety, preserved a cheerfulness, not so much the effect of insensibility as of patience and fortitude. She was sensible of her approaching fate as appears from the following letter, which was written in characters.

"Must I die alone? Shall I never see you more? I know that you will come, but you will come too late. This is, I fear, my last ability. Tears fall so, I know not how to write. Why did you leave me in so much distress? But I will not reproach you: all that was dear I left for you; but I do not regret it. May God forgive in both what was

heart. Disappointment will be more or less severe in proportion as we elevate our expectations; for the most *sanguine tempers* are the soonest discouraged, as the highest building is in the most danger of falling."

"It appears from what I have said," resumed Mr. Holmes, "that those books which teach us a knowledge of the world are useful to form the minds of females and ought therefore to be studied."

I mentioned Rochefoucault's maxims.

"Do they not degrade human nature?" inquired my father.

"This little book," answered Worthy, "contains much truth—and those short sketches traced by the hand of judgment present to us the leading features of mankind." "But," replied my father, "that *interest should assume all shapes* is a doctrine which, in my mind, represents a caricature rather than a living picture." "It is the duty of a painter to produce a likeness," said Worthy. "And a skillful one," cried my father, continuing the metaphor, "will bring the amiable qualities of the heart to light and throw those which disgrace humanity into the shade." "I

amiss. When I go from hence, I will leave you some way to find me; if I die, will you come and drop a tear over my grave?"

In the following poem, she, like the dying swan, sings her own elegy; and it is here added, as a sorrowful instance, how often the best and most pleasing talents, not accompanied by virtue and prudence, operate the destruction of their possessor.

The description of her unfortunate passion will remind the critical reader of the famous ode of Sappho. In genius and in misfortune, these poetical ladies were similar.

"DISAPPOINTMENT"

"With fond impatience all the tedious day
I sighed and wished the lingering hours away;
For when bright Hesper led the starry train,
My shepherd swore to meet me on the plain;
With eager haste to that dear spot I flew,
And lingered long, and then with tears withdrew;
Alone, abandoned to love's tenderest woes,
Down my pale cheeks the tide of sorrow flows;
Dead to all joys that fortune can bestow,
In vain for me her useless bounties flow;
Take back each envied gift, ye powers divine,
And only let me call Fidelio mine.

"Ah, wretch! what anguish yet thy soul must prove,
Ere thou canst hope to lose thy care in love;
And when Fidelio meets thy tearful eye,
Pale fear and cold despair his presence fly;

doubt," rejoined Worthy, "whether this is flattery will answer the purpose you aim to accomplish. You entertain a high opinion of the dignity of *human nature* and are displeased at the author who advances any thing derogatory to that dignity. Swift, in speaking of these maxims in one of his best poems, affirms

> They argue no corrupted mind
> In him—the fault is in mankind.

"As I began the subject," added I, "it shall be ended by one observation. As these maxims give us an idea of the manners and characters of men, among whom a young person is soon to appear, and as it is necessary to her security and happiness that she be made acquainted with them, they may be read to advantage."

"There is another medium," said Mr. Holmes, assenting to my observation, "to be noticed in the study of a lady. She takes up a book, either for instruction or entertainment: the medium lies in knowing when to put it down. Constant application becomes labor—it sours the temper and gives an air of thoughtfulness, and frequently of absence. By *immoderate reading* we hoard up opinions and become insensibly attached to them; this miserly conduct sinks us to affectation and disgustful pedantry; *conversation* only can remedy this dangerous evil, strengthen the

> With pensive steps, I sought thy walks again,
> And kissed thy token on the verdant plain;
> With fondest hope, through many a blissful bower,
> We gave the soul to fancy's pleasing power,
> Lost in magic of that sweet employ,
> To build gay scenes and fashions future joy,
> We saw mild peace o'er fair canaan rise,
> And shower her blessing from benignant skies;
> on airy hills our happy mansion rose,
> Built but for joy, no room for future woes;
> Sweet as the sleep of innocence, the day
> (By transport measures) lightly danced away;
> To love, to bliss, the unioned soul was given,
> And each! too happy, asked no brighter heaven

> "And must the hours in ceaseless anguish roll?
> Will no soft sunshine cheer my clouded soul?
> Can this dear earth no transient joy supply?
> Is it my doom to hope, despair and die?
> Oh! come, once more, with soft endearments come,
> Burst cold prison of the sullen tomb;
> Though favored walk, thy chosen maid attend,
> Where well known shades their pleasing branches bend;

judgment, and make reading really useful. They mutually depend upon and assist each other.

"A knowledge of history which exhibits to us in one view the rise, progress and decay of nations—which points out the advancement of the mind in society, and the improvements in the arts which adorn human nature—comes with propriety under the notice of a lady. To observe the origin of civilization—the gradual progress of society and the refinements of manners, policy, morality and religion—to observe the progression of mankind from simplicity to luxury, from luxury to effeminacy, and the gradual steps of the decline of empire, and the dissolution of states and kingdoms, must blend that happy union of instruction and entertainment which never fails to win our attention to the pursuit of all subjects.

"Poetry claims her due from the ladies. Poetry enlarges and strengthens the mind, refines the taste and improves the judgment. It has been asserted that women have no business with *satire*. Now satire is but a branch of poetry. I acknowledge, however, much false wit is sent into the world under this general title; but no critic with whom I am acquainted ever called satire false wit; for so long as vice and folly continue to predominate in the human heart, the satirist will be considered as a useful member of society. I believe Addison calls him an auxiliary to

Shed the soft poison from thy speaking eye,
And look those raptures lifeless words deny;
Still be, though late, reheard what ne'er could tire,
But, told each eve, fresh pleasures would inspire;
Still hope those scenes which love and fancy drew;
But, drawn a thousand times, were ever new.

"Can fancy paint, can words express;
Can aught on earth my woes redress;
E'en thy soft smiles can ceaseless prove
Thy truth, thy tenderness and love.
Once thou couldst every bliss inspire,
Transporting Joy, and gay Desire:
Now cold Despair her banner rears,
And Pleasure flies when she appears;
Fond Hope within my bosom dies,
And Agony her place supplies:
O, thou! for whose dear sake I bear,
A doom so dreadful, so severe,
May happy fates thy footsteps guide,
And o'er thy peaceful home preside;
Nor let Eliza's early tomb
Infect thee, with its baleful gloom." [Brown's note]

the pulpit. Suffer me to enlarge on this *new idea*. Satire is the correction of the vices and follies of the human heart; a woman may, therefore, read it to advantage. What I mean by enforcing this point is to impress the minds of females with a principle of self-correction; for among all kinds of knowledge which arise from reading, the duty of self-knowledge is a very eminent one; and it is at the same time the most useful and important.

"Our ordinary intercourse with the world will present to us in a very clear point of view the fallacious ideas we sometimes entertain of our own self-knowledge. We are blinded by pride and self love and will not observe our own imperfections, which we blame with the greatest acrimony in other people and seem to detest with the greatest abhorrence, so that it often happens, while we are branding our neighbor for some foible, or vanity, we ourselves are equally guilty.

"Ridiculous as this conduct must appear in the eyes of all judicious people, it is too frequently practiced to escape observation.

"I will drop this piece of morality, with a charge to the fair reader, that whenever she discovers a satire, ridiculing or recriminating the follies or crimes of mankind, that she look into her own heart and compare the strictures on the conduct of others with her own feeling."

Letter XII

Mrs. HOLMES to MYRA

In Continuation

My good father-in-law, being so strenuous in proving the eligibility of reading satire, had spun out what he called his *new idea* to such a metaphysical nicety that he unhappily diminished the number of his hearers; for Mrs. Bourn, to whom he directed his discourse, had taken down a book and was reading to herself, and Miss Bourn was diverting herself with the cuts in Gay's *Fables.*

A considerable silence ensued, which Worthy first broke, by

asking Mrs. Bourn what book she had in her hand. Every one's attention was alarmed at this important inquiry. Mrs. Bourn, with little difficulty, found the title page and began to read, *A Sentimental Journey through France and Italy, by Mr. Yorick.*

"I do not like the *title*," said Miss Bourn.

"Why, my dear!" apostrophized the mother, "you are mistaken; it is a very famous book."

"Why, my dear!" retorted the daughter, "it is sentimental. I abominate everything that is sentimental—it is so unfashionable too."

"I never knew before," said Mr. Holmes, "that wit was subject to the caprice of fashion."

"Why, Squire Billy," returned Miss Bourn, "who is just arrived from the center of politeness and fashion, says the bettermost geniuses never read any sentimental books; so you see sentiment is out of date."

The company rose to go out.

"Sentiment out of date!" cried Worthy, repeating the words of Miss Bourn, and taking the book from her mother, as she walked towards the door, "Sentiment out of date! Alas! poor Yorick, may thy pages never be soiled by the fingers of prejudice." He continued his address to the book as they went out, in the same *Shandean* tone: "These antisentimentalists would banish thee from the society of all books! Unto what a pitiful size are the race of *readers* dwindled. Surely these *antis* have no more to do with thee than the gods of the *Canaanites*. In character and understanding they are alike: eyes have *they*, but they see not—ears have *they*, but they hear not; neither is there any knowledge to be found in them." "It is hardly worth while to beat it into them," said my father-in-law; "so let us follow the company."

We did so. They walked towards the house, and Worthy and I brought up the rear.

I could not but remark, as we went on, that Miss Bourn had spoken the sentiments of many of her sex; "and whence," said I to Worthy, "arises this detestation of books in *some* of us females, and why are *they* enemies to anything that may be called sentiment and conversation: I grant it often happens there is such rapidity of *speeches* that one may be at a loss to distinguish the speakers; but why is there such a calm silence, should an unfortunate sentiment inadvertently—"

"I will tell you," interrupted he. "You all read, and it is from the books which engage your attention that you generally imbibe your ideas of the principal subjects discussed in company. Now the books which employ your hours of study happen to be novels, and the *subjects* contained in these novels are commonly confined to *dress, balls, visiting,* and the like *edifying* topics; does it not follow that these must be the subjects of your conversation? I will not dispute whether the novel makes the woman, or the woman makes the novel; or whether they are written to engage your attention or flatter your vanity. I believe the result will show they depend, in some measure, upon each other; and an uninformed woman, by reading them, only augments the number of her futile ideas. *The female mind*, notwithstanding, *is competent to any task,* and the accomplishments of an elegant woman depend on a proper cultivation of her intelligent powers. A barrenness—a sterility of conversation—immediately discovers where this cultivation is wanting."

"Give me leave," answered I, "to espouse the cause of this class of females. Tell me candidly, Mr. Worthy, whether the insipid flattery, perhaps sacrificed at the expense of truth, does not misguide many of us into erroneous paths? You declare we are handsome; and your conduct demonstrates you to be more solicitous for the possession of *beautiful*, than of *mental*, charms. Hence is the deluded female persuaded of the force of her fascinating powers, and vainly imagines one glance of her eye sufficient to reduce a million of hearts whenever she chooses. Her aims, therefore, are confined to the decoration of her person; and her views center solely in finishing herself in those attractive, all powerful graces, with which you declare yourselves to be enchanted. How then are they to be censured for neglecting to improve and to adorn the mind when your adulation diverts their attention to an external object?"

"I join with you," replied Worthy, "in calling it insipid flattery; and the vain coxcomb, the powdered beau, the insignificant *petit maitre*, are those who make use of it. Will women of real merit and sound sense believe what is said to *them* to be *their* real sentiments? No. There must be a congeniality in the minds of those who give and receive flattery. Has not the vain coquette as much inclination to be thought a goddess as the empty admirer to declare her so?

"Flattery has become a kind of epidemical distemper; many

run into it, perhaps, without designing it, or only through civility. There are some women who expect it—who dress to be admired and who deem it a mark of impoliteness and rudeness in men who do not pay them the tribute of compliment and adulation. A man of sense *may* comply with their expectation. He will still think them agreeable *playthings*, to divert him at an hour of relaxation; but I cannot suppose he will entertain any serious thoughts of *a more permanent connection.*

"May we not conclude these things to be productive of many evils that happen in society? Do they not frighten all sentiment from conversation, introduce affectation—pride, envy, clandestine marriages, elopements, division of families—and ultimately terminate in the *ruin* of very many innocent but inconsiderate females?"

By this time we had not into the house; our company soon after departed, leaving us at full leisure to contemplate on the many wrong ideas entertained, and fallacious steps pursued by the generality of mankind in the sentimental part of female education.

Letter XIII

WORTHY to MYRA

Belleview

A peaceful, recluse life is suited to my temper. There is something in the soft breath of Nature, in the delicacy of smiling meadows and cultivated fields, in the sublimity of an aged wood, of broken rocks, of rivers pouring along their lucid waves —to which the heart always gives a ready reception. There is something within us congenial to these scenes; they impress the mind with ideas similar to what we feel in beholding one whom we tenderly esteem.

I was making this observation to Mrs. Holmes, and she told me I was in love—"These are the very scenes," said she, "which your beloved Myra used to praise and admire, and for which

you by a secret sympathy entertain the same predilection. The piece of embroidery which she worked at an early age, and which ornaments the Temple, I have seen you gaze upon several times; you seem to trace perfection in every part of it because it was executed by the hand of Myra."

I acknowledge I have often *gazed* upon it (as Mrs. Holmes terms it) but did not recollect it to be a piece of your work. I stole an opportunity to revisit it by myself, and I instantly remembered it. I remembered when you finished it, and all the happy, inoffensive scenes of our childhood returned fresh upon my heart.

It is the work of Myra, said I to myself. Did not her fingers trace these beautiful, expanding flowers? Did not she give to this carnation its animated glow, and to this opening rose its languishing grace? Removed as I am—continued I in a certain interior language that every son of nature possesses—removed as I am, from the amiable object of my tenderest affection, I have nothing to do but to admire this offspring of industry and art. It shall yield more fragrance to my soul than all the *bouquets* in the universe.

I did not care to pursue the thought—it touched a delicate string. At first, however, I flattered myself I should gain some consolation; but I lost in every reflection.

I considered the work as coming from your hand and was delighted the more with it. A piece of steel that has been rubbed with a loadstone retains the power of attracting small bodies of iron: so the beauties of this embroidery, springing from your hands, continue to draw my attention and fill the mind with ideas of the artist.

Letter XIV

HARRINGTON to WORTHY

Boston

How incompetent is the force of words to express some peculiar sensations! Expression is feeble when emotions are exquisite.

I wish you could be here to see with what ease and dignity everything comes from the hand of Harriot. I cannot give a description equivalent to the great idea I wish to convey. You will tell me I am in love. What is love? I have been trying to investigate its nature—to strip it of its mere term and consider it as it may be supported by principle, I might as well search for the philosopher's stone.

Everyone is ready to praise his mistress—she is always described in her "native simplicity" as "an angel!" with a "placid mien," as "mild, animated" and "altogether captivating." And at length the task of description is given up as altogether "undescribable." Are not all these in themselves bare, insignificant words? The world has so long been accustomed to hear the sound of them that the idea is lost. But to the question—What is love? Unless it is answered now, perhaps it never will be. Is it not an infinitude of graces that accompany everything said by Harriot? That adorn all she does? They must not be taken severally—they cannot be contemplated in the abstract. If you proceed to a chemical analysis, their tenuous essence will evaporate: they are in themselves nothing, but the aggregate is love.

When an army composed of a great number of men moves slowly on at a distance, nobody thinks of considering a single soldier.

Letter XV

HARRINGTON to WORTHY

Boston

Am I to believe my eyes—my ears—my heart! And yet I cannot be deceived. We are generally most stupid and incredulous in what most materially concerns us. We find the greatest difficulty in persuading ourselves of the attainment of what we most ardently desire. She loves!—I say to myself; Harriot loves me, and I reverence myself.

I think I may now take upon me some share of happiness. I may say I have not lived in vain, for all my heart holds dear is mine. Joy and love encompass me—peace and tranquility are before me; the prospect is fair and promising as the gilded dawn of a summer's day. There is none to supplant me in her affection. I dread no rival, for our tempers are similar and our hearts beat in unison together.

Letter XVI

HARRINGTON to WORTHY

Boston

Love softens and refines the manners, polishes the asperities of awkwardness, and fits us for the society of gentle beings. It goes further: it mends the heart and makes us better men; it gives the faint-hearted an extraordinary strength of soul and renders them equal and frequently superior to danger and distress.

My passions you know are quick; my prejudices are some-
times obstinate. She tells me these things are wrong. This gentle
reprimand is so tempered with love that I think she commends
me. I, however, promise a reform and am much pleased with my
improvement. Harriot molds my heart into what form she
chooses.

A little party is proposed tomorrow evening, and I shall at-
tend Harriot. These elegant relaxations prevent the degeneracy
of human nature, exhilarate the spirits, and wind up this
machine of ours for another revolution of business.

Letter XVII

HARRINGTON to WORTHY

Boston

Our little party was overthrown by a strange piece of folly. A
Miss P—— was introduced, a young lady of beauty and elegant
accomplishments. The whole company were beginning to be
cheerful: business and care were disgusted at the sight of so
many happy countenances and had gone out from among us.
Jollity and good humor bade us prepare for the dance. Un-
happily at this juncture a lady and gentleman were engaged in a
conversation concerning Miss P—— and one of them repeated the
words, "a mechanic's daughter." It is supposed the word "me-
chanic" was repeated scornfully. She heard it—thought herself
insulted—and indignantly retired. Disorder and confusion im-
mediately took place, and the amusement was put an end to for
the evening.

I wish people would consider how little time they have to
frolic here—that they would improve it to more advantage, and
not dispute for any precedence or superiority but cultivate good
nature and sociability. "A mechanic"—and pray whence this
distinction!

Inequality among mankind is a foe to our happiness; it even
affects our little parties of pleasure. Such is the fate of the

human race: one order of men lords it over another. Upon what grounds its right is founded I could never yet be satisfied.

For this reason, I like a democratic government better than any other kind of government; and, were I a Lycurgus, no distinction of rank should be found in my commonwealth.

In my tour through the United States, I had an opportunity of examining and comparing the different manners and dispositions of the inhabitants of the several republics. Those of the Southern states, accustomed to a habit of domineering over their slaves, are haughtier, more tenacious of honor, and indeed possess more of an aristocratic temper than their sisters of the confederacy. As we travel to the northward, the nature of the Constitution seems to operate on the minds of the people. Slavery is abolished. All men are declared free and equal; and their tempers are open, generous and communicative. It is the same in all those countries where the people enjoy independence and equal liberty. Why then should those distinctions arise which are inimical to domestic quietude? Or why should the noisy voice of those who seek distinction so loudly re-echo in the ears of peace and jollity as to deafen the sound of the music? For while we are disputing, who shall lead off the dance? Behold! the instrument gets out of tune—a string snaps—and where is our chance for dancing?

Letter XVIII

HARRINGTON to WORTHY

Boston

My beloved has left me for a while; she has attended Mrs. Francis in a journey to Rhode Island. And here am I—anxious—solitary—alone!

No thoughts but thoughts of Harriot are permitted to agitate me. She is in my view all the day long; and when I retire to rest, my imagination is still possessed with ideas of Harriot.

Letter XIX

HARRINGTON to HARRIOT

Boston

If a wish, arising from the most tender affection, could transport me to the object of my love, I persuade myself that you would not be troubled with reading this letter.

You must expect nothing like wit or humor, or even common sense, from me; wit and humor are flown with you, and your return only can restore them. I am sometimes willing to persuade myself that this is the case: I think I hear the well known voice; I look around me with the ecstacy of Orpheus, but that look breaks the charm; I find myself alone, and my Eurydice vanished to the shades.

I hope you will not permit yourself to grow envious of the beauties of Rhode Island. Of the force of their charms I am experimentally acquainted. Wherever fortune has thrown me, it has been my happiness to imagine myself in love with some divine creature or other; and after all it is but truth to declare that the passion was seated more in fancy than in the heart; and it is justice to acknowledge to you that I am now more provident of my passion, and never suffer the excursion of fancy, except when I am so liberal as to admit the united *beauty* of the Rhode Island ladies in competition with yours.

Where there are handsome women, there will necessarily be fine gentlemen; and should they be smitten with your *external graces*, I cannot but lament their deplorable situation when they discover how egregiously they have been cheated. What must be his disappointment, who thought himself fascinated by beauty, when he finds he has unknowingly been charmed by reason and virtue!

But this you will say contains a sentiment of jealousy and is but a transcript of my apprehensions and gloomy anxieties. When will your presence, like the return of the sun in the spring

which dispels glooms and reanimates the face of nature, quiet these apprehensions. If it be not in a short time, I shall proceed on a journey to find you out; until then I commit you to the care of your guardian angel.

Letter XX

HARRINGTON to HARRIOT

Boston

Last night I went on a visit to your house: it was an adventure that would have done honor to the *Knight of La Mancha.* The moon ascended a clear, serene sky; the air was still; the bells sounded the solemn hour of midnight. I sighed—and the reason of it I need not tell you. This was, indeed, a pilgrimage; and no *Musselman* ever traveled barefooted to *Mecca* with more sincere devotion.

Your absence would cause an insufferable *ennui* in your friends, were it not for the art we have in making it turn to our amusement. Instead of wishing you were of our party, you are the goddess to whose honor we perform innumerable *heathenish* rites. Libations of wine are poured out, but not a guest presumes to taste it until he implores the name of Harriot; we hail the new divinity in songs and strew around the flowers of poetry. You need not, however, take to yourself any extraordinary addition of vanity on this occasion, as your absence will not cause any repining:

"Harriot, our goddess and our grief no more."

But to give you *my* opinion on this important matter, I must descend to plain truth and acknowledge I had rather adore you a *present* mortal, than an *absent* divinity; and therefore I wish for your return with more religious ardor than a devout disciple of the false prophet for the company of the *houris.*

Thanks to the power of imagination for one fanciful interview. Methought I somewhere unexpectedly met you, but I was

soon undeceived of my imaginary happiness. I awoke, repeating these verses:

> Though sleep her sable pinions spread,
> My thoughts still run on you;
> And visions hovering o'er my head,
> Present you to my view.
>
> By Fancy's magic pencil dressed,
> I saw my Delia move;
> I clasped her to my anxious breast,
> With tears of joy and love.
>
> Methought she said, "Why thus forlorn?
> Be all thy care resigned."
> I woke and found my Delia gone,
> But still the tear behind.

Letter XXI

HARRIOT to MYRA

Rhode Island

We arrived here in safety, but our journey is not without incident—an incident which exhibits a melancholy picture of the wickedness and depravity of the human heart.

When we came to the house of Mrs. Martin, who, I suppose you know, is cousin to Mrs. Francis, we were not a little astonished at the evident traces of distress in her countenance; all her actions were accompanied with an air of solemnity, and her former gaiety of heart was exchanged for sad, serious thoughtfulness. She, however, put on a face of vivacity upon our being introduced, but her cheerfulness was foreign to the feeling of her heart.

Mr. Martin was equally agitated; he endeavored to dispossess himself of an *uncommon* weight of remorse, but in vain. All his dissimulation could not conceal his emotion, nor his art abate the continual upbraidings of conscious guilt.

Mrs. Francis was anxious to inquire the cause of this extraordinary change, but wisely forebore adding to the distress of her friend by desiring her to explain it, in a manner too precipitate. She was in a short time made acquainted with the particulars of the story, which is not more melancholy than uncommon.

Sometime after the marriage of the Martins, the beautiful Ophelia, sister to Mrs. Martin, returned from an European visit to her friends in Rhode Island. Upon her arrival, she received a polite offer from her brother-in-law of an elegant apartment at his house in town, which was cheerfully accepted. Fatal acceptation. He had conceived a passion for Ophelia and was plotting to gratify it. By a series of the most artful attentions, suggested by a diabolic appetite, he insinuated himself into her affection: he prevailed upon the heart of the unsuspicious Ophelia and triumphed over her innocence and virtue.

This incestuous connection has secretly subsisted until the present time—it was interrupted by a symptom which rendered it necessary for Ophelia to retire into the country where she delivered a child, at once the son and nephew of Martin.

This event was a severe mortification to the proud spirit of Shepherd, the father of Ophelia. His resentment to his daughter was implacable, and his revenge of the injury from Martin not to be satiated. The blaze of family dispute raged with unquenchable fury; and poor Ophelia received other punishment from the hand of a vindictive father than bare recrimination.

The affection of Martin now became changed to the vilest hatred.

Thus doomed to suffer the blackest ingratitude from her seducer on the one hand and to experience the severity of paternal vengeance on the other—and before her the gloomy prospect of a blasted reputation—what must be the situation of the hapless Ophelia! Hope, the last resort of the wretched, was forever shut out. There was no one whom she dared implore by the tender name of father, and he who had seduced her from her duty and her virtue was the first to brand her with the disgraceful epithets of undutiful and unchaste.

Perhaps it was only at this time that she became fully sensible of her danger; the flattery and dissimulation of Martin might have banished the idea of detection and glossed over that of criminality. Now she awoke from her dream of insensibility; she was like one who had been deluded by an *ignis fatuus* to the

brink of a precipice, and there abandoned to his reflection to contemplate the horrors of the sea beneath him into which he was about to plunge.

Whether from the promises of Martin, or the flattery of her own fancy, is unknown; but it is said she expected to become his wife, and made use of many expedients to obtain a divorce of Martin and her sister: But this is the breath of rumor. Allowing it to be truth, it appears to be the last attempt of despair; for such unnatural exertions, with the compunction attending them, represent a gloomy picture of the struggle between sisterly affection and declining honor. They however proved unavailable, and her efforts to that end may with propriety be deemed a wretched subterfuge.

In the meanwhile the rage of Shepherd was augmenting. Time, instead of allaying, kindled the flame of revenge in the breast of the old man. A sense of the wounded honor of his family became every day more exquisite; he resolved to call a meeting of the parties, in which the whole mystery should be developed: Ophelia should confront her seducer, and a thorough enquiry and explication be brought about.

Ophelia exercised all her powers to prevent it; she entreated her father to consent to her desire, but her tears and entreaties were vain. To this earnest desire of is daughter, Shepherd opposed the honor of his family. She replied that such a procedure would publish its disgrace and be subversive of his intention: that she hoped to live retired from the world, and that it was in his power to accept her happy repentance. In extenuating, she wished not to vindicate her errors, but declared herself to be penetrated with a melancholy sense of her misconduct and hoped her penitence might expiate her guilt. She now beheld in the most glaring colors the dangers to which she had been exposed, and acknowledged the effects of her temerity had impressed her mind with sincere contrition. All persons, continued she, are not blessed with the like happiness of resisting temptation; she entreated her father, therefore, to believe her misfortunes proceeded from credulity and not from an abandoned principle—that they arose more from situation than a depraved heart. In asking to be restored to the favor and protection of a parent, she protested she was not influenced by any other motive than a wish to demonstrate the sincerity of her repentance and to establish the peace and harmony of the family.

Ophelia now became melancholy, and her intentions visibly bent on the *manner of her death*. As the time drew nigh, her sensibility became more exquisite. What was before distress, she now averred to be horror. Her conduct bordered upon insanity.

The day was appointed to bring to a settlement this unhappy business: the time of hearing arrived—the parties met—the presence of Ophelia was necessary—she was missing—the unfortunate Ophelia died by her own hand.

Mrs. Shepherd entered the apartment of her daughter: she beheld her pale and trembling—she saw the vial and the cup with the remains of the poison—she embraced her lost child. "My Ophelia! my daughter! return, return to life."

At this crisis entered the father. He was mute. He beheld his daughter struggling with the pangs of dissolution. He was dumb with grief and astonishment.

The dying Ophelia was conscious of the distress of her parents, and of her own situation. She clasped her mother's hand and, raising her eye to heaven, was only heard to articulate, "Let my crime be forgotten with my name. O fatal! fatal poison!"

Adieu! my dear Myra. This unhappy affair has worked me into a fit of melancholy. I can write no more. I will give you a few particulars in my next. It is impossible to behold the effects of this horrid catastrophe and not be impressed with feelings of sympathetic sorrow.

Letter XXII

HARRIOT to MYRA

Rhode Island

How frail is the heart! How dim is human foresight! We behold the gilded bait of temptation and know not until taught by experience, that the admission of one error is but the introduction of calamity. One mistake imperceptibily leads to another, but the consequences of the whole bursting suddenly

on the devoted head of an unfortunate wanderer becomes intolerable. How acute must be that torture which seeks an asylum in suicide! O Seduction! how many and how miserable are the victims of thy unrelenting vengeance. Some crimes, indeed, cease to afflict when they cease to exist; but Seduction opens the door to a dismal train of innumerable miseries.

You can better imagine the situation of the friends of the unfortunate Ophelia than I can describe it.

The writings she left were expressive of contrition for her past transaction, and an awful sense of the deed she was about to execute. Her miserable life was insupportable; there was no oblation but in death—she welcomed death, therefore, as the pleasing harbinger of relief to the unfortunate. She remembered her once loved seducer with pity and bequeathed him her forgiveness. To say she felt no agitation was not just, but that she experienced a calmness unknown to a criminal was certain. She hoped the rashness of her conduct would not be construed to her disadvantage, for she died in charity with the world. She felt like a poor wanderer about to return to a tender parent and flattered herself with the hopes of a welcome, though unbidden, to return. She owned the way was dark and intricate, but lamented she had no friend to enlighten her understanding or unravel the mysteries of futurity. She knew there was a God who will reward and punish; she acknowledged she had offended him and confessed her repentance. She expatiated on the miserable life she had *suffered*; not that she feared detection, that was impossible; but that she had be,n, doing an injury to a sister who was all kindness to her. She prayed her sister's forgiveness—even as she herself forgave her seducer; and that her crime might not be called ingratitude, because she was always sensible of her obligation to that sister. She requested her parents to pardon her and acknowledged she felt the pangs of a bleeding heart at the shock which must be given to the most feeling of mothers. She entreated her sisters to think of her with pity and died with assurance that her friends would so far revere her memory as to take up one thing or another and say this belonged to poor Ophelia.

O my friend! what scenes of anguish are here unfolded to the survivors. The unhappy Shepherd charged Martin with the seduction and murder of his daughter. What the termination of this most horrible affair will be is not easy to foresee.

Letter XXIII

HARRIOT to MYRA

Rhode Island.

Whatever may be the other causes (if there were any besides her seduction) which drove the unhappy Ophelia temerariously to end her existence, it certainly becomes us, my dear friend, to attend to them—and to draw such morals and lessons of instruction from each side of the question as will be a mirror by which we may regulate our conduct and amend our lives. A prudent pilot will shun those rocks upon which others have been dashed to pieces and take example from the conduct of others less fortunate than himself. It is the duty of the moralist, then, to deduce his observations from preceeding facts in such a manner as may directly improve the mind and promote the economy of human life.

This may be an apology for sending you the arguments of Martin in answer to Shepherd, who in his rage and grief had called him the murderer of his child.

He reminded Shepherd of his obstinacy in *persisting* in an explanatory meeting and refusing to grant Ophelia's request in suffering the affair to subside. "Your proud spirit," said he, "would not hearken to the gentle remonstrance of your daughter. Your heart was closed to every conciliatory proposition. Though she expressed a propensity to fly from the eye of the world, she had hitherto appeared lulled in a kind of happy insensibility; yet the approaching time of explanation was terrible; it renewed the story and torture of all her misfortunes, and the idea filled her with grief and dismay. Had you been as willing to receive her, as she to return to you, happy would it have been for both; but your pride was the cause of additional calamities. When the time arrived—but why shall we harrow up our souls with the reiteration of her sorrowful exit?

"From these circumstances," said Martin, "you cannot accuse

me as the *immediate* cause of Ophelia's death; the facts are as I have stated them. Thus was a straying but penitent child driven to despair and suicide by a severe use of paternal power, and a vain attempt to resent an injury for which it was impossible the accused party could make compensation."

Notwithstanding the plausibility of Martin's plea, I have little hesitation in my mind to charge him with the *remote cause* of the miserable end of Ophelia.

How far parental authority may be extended is a question which I shall not determine; I must, however, think it depends upon the combination of circumstances. The duty of a child to her parents will be in proportion to the attention paid to her education. Instead of the usual pains bestowed by many partial parents upon the vain parade of forming the manners of a child and burdening the mind with the *necessity* of the douceurs and the graces, would it not often be happier for both to take a small share of thought to kindle *one spark of grace* in the heart?

Happy the parents who have bestowed upon their children such an education as will enable them, by a principle of mediocrity, to govern them without extorting obedience and to reclaim them without exercising severity.

Letter XXIV

HARRIOT to MYRA

Rhode Island.

Mrs. Francis is not altogether satisfied with her journey to this part of the country. She does not delight to brood over sorrow. She flies from the house of mourning to scenes of dissipation congenial to her temper and disposition—and, like the rest of the world, bears the misfortunes of her friends with a most Christian fortitude.

The melancholy aspect of affairs here will therefore shorten our visit; so you may expect us at Boston in a few days.

My faithful lover (with whom I will certainly make you acquainted in a short time) continues to write to me in very passionate and sentimental strains. His last letter proves him to be *a tolerable maker of rhymes*, and I enclose it* for your *entertainment.*

*See Letter XX. [Brown's note.]

Letter XXV

MYRA to HARRIOT

(Written before she had received the preceding.)

Boston

Your sorrowful little history has infected me with grief. Surely there is no human vice of so black a die, so fatal in its consequences—or which causes a more general calamity, than that of *seducing* a female from the path of honor. This idea has been improved by my brother on the hint of your favor—as an acknowledgment for which I enclose you his production.

The Court of Vice

An Apologue

VICE on a solemn night of state,
In all her pomp of terror fate,
Her voice in deep, tremendous tone,
Thus issued from her ebon throne:
"This night at our infernal court,
Let all our ministers resort.
Who most annoys the human race
At our right hand shall take his place,
Raised on a throne—advanced in fame—
Ye crimes now vindicate your claim."

Eager for praise, the hideous host
All spoke, aspiring to the post.

PRIDE said, to gain his private ends,
He sacrificed his dearest friends;
Insulted all with manners rude,
And introduced ingratitude.
'Twas he infused *domestic* hate
And party spirit in the *state*;
Hoped they'd observe his mystic plan,
Destroyed all confidence in man;
And justified his high pretentions
By causing envy and dissensions.

INTEMPERANCE loud demanded the place
He'd long deceived the human race;
None could such right as he maintain,
Disease and death were in his train.

THEFT next appeared to claim the station,
Ever constant in his dark vocation;
He thought the place might well repay
The *crime* who labored night and day.

FRAUD owned (though loath to speak in his praise)
He gained his point by secret ways;
His voice in cities had been heard
And often in senates been preferred!
Yet much derision had he borne,
Treated by honest fools with scorn;
His influence on the western shore,
Was not so great as heretofore:
He owned each side alike failed,
Complained how sadly he was railed,
Cursed by the name in every street,
Of Paper, Tender, Rogue and Cheat:
Yet if some honor should requite
His labor—things might still go right.

MURDER before the footstool stood,
With tattered robe stained in blood.
"And who," he cried, with daring face,
"Denies my title to the place?
My watchful eyes mankind survey
And single out the midnight prey;

Not cowardlike I meet the foe
With footsteps insecure and slow,
Or cause his death by languid strife—
Boldly this dagger ends his life.
Give back, ye crimes, your claims resign,
For I demand the post as mine."

AVARICE declared his love of gold;
His nation or himself he sold;
He taught the sin of PRIDE betimes,
Was foster-father of all *crimes*:
He pawned his life; he staked his soul,
And found employment for the whole:
Acknowledged that he gain'd his wealth
By FRAUD, by MURDER and by STEALTH:
On one so useful in her cause,
VICE well might lavish due applause.

The haggard host bowed low the head,
The *Monster* rose, and thus she said:
"Ye *ministers* of VICE, draw near,
For fame no longer persevere;
No more your various parts disclose,
Men *see and hate you all as foes*.
One yet remains among your crew;
Then rise, SEDUCTION! claim your due.
Your baleful presence quickly parts
The tie that holds the happiest hearts;
You *rob* what *wealth* can never repay;
Like Judas with a kiss *betray*:
Hence come the starving, trembling train
Who prostitute themselves for gain,
Whose languid visages impart
A smile, while anguish gnaws the heart;
Whose steps decoy unwary youth
From honor, honesty, and truth,
Which followed until too late to mend,
In ruin, and the gallows end.
Be thine the post. Besides, who knows
Where all thy consequences close?
With thee, SEDUCTION! are allied
HORROR, DESPAIR and SUICIDE.
You wound—but the *devoted* heart
Feels not alone the poignant smart:
YOU wound—the electric pain extends
To fathers, mothers, sisters, friends.

MURDER may yet delight in blood
And deluge round the crimson flood;
But sure his merits rank above
Who murders in the mask of love."

Letter XXVI

MYRA to Mrs. HOLMES

Boston

In one of my former letters I acquainted you that I suspected my brother to be in love; and now, Madam, I am enabled to tell you with whom—the amiable Harriot.

Harriot attended Mrs. Francis in her journey to Rhode Island; and our young hero has, in her absence, been dreaming of his mistress; and, in a letter to her he has written a description of his visionary interview. Harriot, with whom I maintain a constant correspondence, and who keeps no secret from me, enclosed the verses in her last letter. It was then I discovered the handwriting of Master Harrington.

I was a little mortified that the young man had kept me in ignorance of his amour all this time, and this morning I determined upon a little innocent revenge. "Tommy," said I, as he entered the room, "here is a piece of poetry, written by an acquaintance of mine. I want your judgment on it." "Poetry or rhyme," answered he, advancing towards me, and casting his eye on it. He took the letter and began to read. "Why do you blush, young man?" said I, "Harriot is a fine girl."

This produced an *eclaircissement*; and as the matter must remain secret, for a certain weighty reason, I am to be the *confidante*.

I must acknowledge to you, Mrs. Holmes, there is a certain *un je ne sais quoi* in my amiable friend that has always interested me in her favor. I have an affection for her which comes from the heart—an affection which I do not pretend to account for. Her dependence on Mrs. Francis hurts me; I do not think this

lady is the gentle, complaisant being that she appears to be in company. To behold so fine a girl in so disagreeable a situation might at first attract my commiseration and esteem, and a more intimate knowledge of her virtues might have ripened them into love. Certain it is, however, that whom I admire as a friend, I could love as a sister. In the feelings of the heart there can be no dissimulation.

Please tell Mr. Worthy that he may continue to write, and that I will condescend to read his letters.

Letter XXVII

WORTHY to MYRA

Belleview

I am just returned from a melancholy excursion with Eliza. I will give you the history of it. We generally walk out together but we this time went further than usual. The morning was calm and serene: all nature was flourishing, and its universal harmony conspired to deceive us in the length of the way.

While we were pursuing our walk, our ears were struck with a plaintive, musical voice singing a melancholy tune. "This," said Mrs. Holmes, "must be Fidelia—the poor distracted girl was carried off by a ruffian a few days before her intended marriage, and her lover in despair threw himself into the river." Eliza could say no more, for Fidelia resumed her melancholy strain in the following words:

> Tall rose the lily's slender frame,
> It shed a glad perfume;
> But ah! the cruel spoiler came,
> And nipped its opening bloom.
>
> Curse on the cruel spoiler's hand
> That stole thy bloom and fled;
> Curse on his hand—for thy true lover
> Is numbered with the dead.

Poor maiden! like the lily frail,
 'Twas all in vain you strove;
You heard the stranger's tender tale—
 But where was thy true love?

Thou wast unkind and false to him,
 But he did constant prove;
He plunged headlong in the stream.
 Farewell, farewell, my love!

'Twas where the river rolls along,
 The youth all trembling stood;
Oppressed with grief, he cast himself
 Amidst the cruel flood.

White over his head the billows foam,
 And circling eddies move;
Ah! there he finds a watery tomb—
 Farewell, farewell, my love!

We advanced towards the place from whence the sound issued; and Fidelia, who heard our approach, immediately rose from the ground. "I was tired," she said, "and sat down here to rest myself."

She was dressed in a long white robe, tied about the waist with a pink ribbon; her fine brown hair flowed loosely round her shoulders. In her hand she held a number of wild flowers and weeds, which she had been gathering. "These," she cried, "are to make a nosegay for my love." "He hath no occasion for it," said Eliza. "Yes! where he lives," cried Fidelia, "there are plenty—and flowers that never fade too. I will throw them into the river, and they will swim to him; they will go straight to him." "And what will he do with them?" I asked. "O!" said the poor girl as she looked wistfully on them, and sorted them in her hand, "he loves everything that comes from me—he told me so." "He will be happy to receive them," cried Eliza. "Where he is," said Fidelia, "is happiness—and happy are the flowers that bloom there—and happy shall I be, when I go to him. Alas! I am very ill now." "He will love you again," said Eliza, "when you find him out." "He was very kind," cried she, tenderly; "he delighted to walk with me over all these fields—but now, I am obliged to walk alone." Fidelia drew her hand across her cheek, and we wept with her. "I must go," she said; "I must go," and she turned abruptly from us and left us with great precipitation.

Letter XXVIII

WORTHY to MYRA

Belleview

My melancholy meditations led me yesterday to the same place where I had seen the distracted Fidelia; and walking down the hill, I again beheld her by the side of a beautiful spring. Before I could come up to the place, she was gone. She went hastily over the field—I followed her. After a few minutes' walk, I overtook her; and we both went on together towards a small neat farm house. An old man was sitting at the door; he gave a sigh as she passed by him to go in. I asked him if she was his daughter. "Alas!" said he, "my poor child; she has been in this state of affliction for near a twelve month." I inquired what cause produced the loss of her senses. He looked down sorrowfully—the question awakened the gloomy sensations of past evils, the recollection of which was painful, and opened wounds afresh that were not yet healed. "She has lost her lover," cried the old man. "The youth was the son of one of our neighbors—their infancy was marked by a peculiar attachment to each other. When the young people danced together, Fidelia was always the partner of Henry. As they grew up their mutual tenderness ripened into passionate affection. They were engaged to each other, and Henry saved all his little stock of money to begin the world by himself. All the town beheld them with pleasure—they wished them success and happiness—and from their knowledge of both their characters were led to hope they would one day become good members of society. But these hopes are blasted, and they now bestow the bitterest curses on the wretch who has crushed their expectations—who has deprived Fidelia of her senses and caused the death of her lover.

"The gay Williams comes among us, and participates in our domestic pastimes. He singles out Fidelia and is assiduous in his attentions to her. Her little heart is lifted up, but her prudence rises superior to her vanity. Henry observes the operations of Williams and thinks he sees in him a powerful rival. The unhappy youth becomes melancholy: he sickens with jealousy. The pleas-

ures of our country are forgotten by him—his thoughts are con-
tinually employed on his Fidelia. To complete the measure of his
promised happiness, he wishes to call her his own. He declares the
desire of his soul. Fidelia pledges her faith. He now sees the ac-
complishment of all his wishes in reversion—his heart leaps for joy.
As the little paraphernalia is preparing, the ruffian hand of the Se-
ducer dashes the cup of joy from their lips. Fidelia suddenly disap-
pears. Williams—the ungrateful Williams—betrays her to a carriage
he had prepared, and she is hurried off. Henry stands astonished—
wild with grief and dismay; he appears senseless and confounded.

"When the heart is elevated by strong expectation, disappoint-
ment and misfortune come with redoubled force. To receive pain,
when we look for pleasure, penetrates the very soul with accumu-
lated anguish."

The old man paused. He endeavored to hide a tear that was
stealing down his cheek and to check the violence of his passion.

I asked him how long his daughter was missing. "Not long," he
answered; "the young men, enraged at the insult, arm themselves
and pursue the robber—they overtake him. Williams is wounded in
the scuffle and is carried away bleeding by his servant. My daugh-
ter is regained—we thank Heaven for her restoration. She inquired
for her Henry. Alas! Henry is no more! The object of his love had
flown from him, and with her all the light of his soul. Darkness
and grief had encompassed him: he had no resource, no consola-
tion, no hope. She whom his soul loved was stolen, was wrested
from his embrace. Who was there to administer relief? Who was
there to supply her loss? Not one. The light of his reason now be-
came clouded. He was seized by despair; and urged forward by the
torments of disappointed love, he plunged into the river—to close
his sorrows with his life.

"The loss of Fidelia's senses followed this tragic event.

"She hears the fate of her lover and becomes petrified. The idea
of her sorrows—her own agitation and care for her person—are lost
in the reflection of her lover's death. A while she raved—but she is
now somewhat restored, and, as you see, the poor maniac strays
about the fields harmless and inoffensive."

The old man proceeded to inform me of the death of his wife—
the idea of one misfortune aroused in him that of another, or
rather there was a gradual progression in them and consequently
a connection. He told me she did not long survive the death of
Henry. "O Charlotte!" he cried, "thou wast kind and cheerful—

very pleasant hast thou been unto me. I will not cease to regret thy loss, till I meet thee in a better world.

"Our hearts," continued the old man, addressing me, "are loosened from their attachment to this world by repeated strokes of misfortune. Wisely is it ordered thus. Every calamity severs a string from the heart, until one scene of sorrow on the back of another matures us for eternity. Thus are our affections estranged from this scene of misery. The cord that detains the bird is severed in two—and it flies away.

"Formerly as I sat in this place—in the mild shade of the evening—when I had returned from my labor and took Fidelia on my knee, how often have I rendered thanks to Heaven for the happiness I enjoyed, and implored his power to make my child such another as Charlotte. This sweet remembrance yet swells and agitates my heart; and in the midst of the distress which surrounds me, I feel a consolation in tracing to you a feeble sketch of the happy times that are passed."

The old man was sensibly affected: he delighted to dwell on what his child had been—he thought of those times—and he sighed when he contrasted them with the present.

"In her disordered state," continued he, "she knows me not as a father. I spread my morsel before her, and she flies from it. She forgets the sound of my voice—she is no longer unto me as a daughter. She who hath so often said she would support me with her arm and lead me about, when I should be old and decrepit—to her I call, but she returns me no answer. Is not the cause of my woe a melancholy instance of the baleful art of the seducer? She is deprived of her reason and knows not the weight of her misery; and I am doubly burdened with her affliction and the accumulated misfortune of immature decrepitude."

"Seduction is a crime," I observed, "that nothing can be said to palliate or excuse."

"And woe to him," added the old man, "who shall endeavor to extenuate it. *They have taken away my staff,*" continued he, raising a look of imploring mercy to Heaven, while a trembling tear rolled from his swollen eye; "*They have taken away my staff in my old age.*"

Freely did my heart share in the sorrows of the good old man. When I left him, I prayed Heaven to compassionate his distress; and as I bent my pensive step towards Belleview, I had leisure to animadvert on the fatal tendency of seduction.

Letter XXIX

Mrs. HOLMES to MYRA

Belleview

I am sometimes mortified to find the books which I recommend to your perusal are not always applicable to the situation of an *American* lady. The general observations of some *English* books are the most useful things contained in them, the principal parts being chiefly filled with local descriptions, which a young woman here is frequently at a loss to understand.

I send you a little work entitled "A Lady of Quality's Advice to her Children" which, though not altogether free from this exception, is highly worthy of your attention. A parent who is represented struggling with the distress of a lingering illness bequeaths a system of education to her offspring. I do not recommend it to you as a novel, but as a work that speaks the language of the heart and that inculcates the duty we owe to ourselves, to society and the Deity.

Didactic essays are not always capable of engaging the attention of young ladies. We fly from the labored precepts of the essayist to the sprightly narrative of the novelist. Habituate your mind to remark the difference between truth and fiction. You will then always be enabled to judge of the propriety and justness of a thought and never be misled to form wrong opinions by the meretricious *dress* of a pleasing tale. You will then be capable of deducing the most profitable lessons of instruction, and the design of your *reading* will be fully accomplished.

Hence you will be provided with a key to the characters of men: to unlock these curious cabinets is a very useful, as well as an entertaining employment. Of those insidious gentlemen, who plan their advances towards us on the *Chesterfieldian* system, let me advise you to beware. A prudent commander would place a double watch, if he apprehended the enemy were more disposed to take the fort by secrecy and undermining than by an open assault.

I cannot but smile sometimes to observe the ridiculous figure of some of our young gentlemen, who affect to square their conduct by his Lordship's principles of politeness. They never tell a story unless it be very short—they talk of decorum and the *etiquette*—they detest everything vulgar or common—they are on the rack if an old man should let fall a proverb—and a thousand more trifling affectations, the ridicule of which arises not so much from their putting on this foreign dress as from their ignorance or vanity in pretending to imitate those rules which were designed for an English nobleman. Unless, therefore, they have a prospect of being called by Congress to execute some foreign negotiation, they ought certainly to be minding their business.

This affectation of fine breeding is destructive to morals. Dissimulation and insincerity are connected with its tenets and are mutually inculcated with the art of pleasing.

A person of this character grounds his motives for pleasing on the most selfish principle. He is polite not for the honor of obliging you; he endeavors to make you believe but that he himself might be obliged. Suspect him, therefore, of insincerity and treachery, one who sacrifices truth to complaisance and advises you to the pursuit of an object which would tend to his advantage.

Always distinguish the man of sense from the coxcomb. Mr. Worthy is possessed of a good understanding and an exact judgment. If you are united with him, let it be the study of your life to preserve his love and esteem. His amiable character is adorned with modesty and a disposition to virtue and sobriety. I never anticipate your future happiness, but I contemplate this part of his character with pleasure. But remember the fidelity of a wife alone will not always secure the esteem of a husband; when her personal attractions do not continue to delight his eye, she will flatter his judgment. I think you are enabled to perform this, because you are solicitous to supply your mind with those amiable qualities which are more durable than beauty. When you are no longer surrounded with a flattering circle of young men and the world shall cease to call you beautiful, your company will be courted by men of sense who know the value of your conversation.

I am pleased with the conduct of some agreeable girls, and the return of civility and attention they often make to the conceited compliments of a certain class of beaux. These ladies wisely consider them as the butterflies of a day, and therefore generally scorn *to break them on a wheel!*

When you are in company, where the vain and thoughtless endeavor to show their ingenuity by ridiculing particular orders of men, your prudence will dictate to you not to countenance their abuse. The book I have just mentioned intimates that "there are a great many things done and said in company which a woman of virtue will neither see nor hear." To discountenance levity is a sure way to guard against the encroachment of temptation; to participate in the mirth of a buffoon is to render yourself equally ridiculous. We owe to ourselves a *detestation* of folly, and to the world the appearance of it. I would have you avoid coquetry and affectation, and the observance of my maxims will never make you a prude. Pretend, therefore, should a vain youth throw out illiberal sarcasms against mechanics, lawyers. ministers, virtue, religion, or any serious subject, not to comprehend the point of his wit.

I have seldom spoken to you on the importance of religion and the veneration due to the characters of the clergy. I always supposed your good sense capable of suggesting their necessity and eligibility. The ministers of no nation are more remarkable for learning and piety than those of this country. The fool may pretend to scorn, and the irreligious to contemn, but every person of sense and reflection must admire that sacred order, whose business is to inform the understanding and regulate the passions of mankind. Surely, therefore, that class of men will continue to merit our esteem and affection, while virtue remains upon earth.

I am always pleased with the reasonable and amiable light in which the clergy are placed by the author of the *Guardian.* "The light," says he. "in which these points should be exposed to the view of one who is prejudiced against the names, Religion, Church, Priest, or the like, is to consider the Clergy as so many Philosophers, the Churches as Schools, and their Sermons as Lectures for the improvement and information of the audience. How would the heart of Tully or Socrates have rejoiced, had they lived in a nation where the law had made provisions for philosophers to read lectures of philosophy, every seventh day, in several thousands of schools, erected at the public charge, throughout the whole country, at which lectures, all ranks and sexes, without distinction, were obliged to be present, for their general improvement!"

You may, perhaps, think this letter too serious, but remember that virtue and religion are the foundation of education.

Letter XXX

Mrs. HOLMES to MYRA

Belleview

You will observe, my dear friend, that most of the letters I have written to you of late on female education are confined to the subject of study. I am sensible of the ridicule sometimes levelled at those who are called learned ladies. Either these ladies must be uncommonly pedantic, or those who ridicule them uncommonly ignorant. Do not be apprehensive of acquiring that title or sharing the ridicule, but remember that the knowledge which I wish you to acquire is necessary to adorn your many virtues and amiable qualifications. This ridicule is evidently a *transatlantic* idea, and must have been imbibed from the source of some *English* novel or magazine. The *American* ladies of this class, who come within our knowledge, we know to be justly celebrated as ornaments to society and an honor to the sex. When it is considered how many of our countrywomen are capable of the talk, it is a matter of regret that *American* literature boasts so few productions from the pens of the ladies.

Self-complacency is a most necessary acquirement, for the value of a woman will always be commensurate to the opinion she entertains of herself. A celebrated *European* wit, in a letter to a lady, concenters much good advice in one short rule of conduct: "REVERENCE THYSELF."

I was this morning reading Swift's letter to a very young lady on her marriage. Although this famous writer is not celebrated for delicacy or respect towards us, yet I wish some of his observations contained less truth. If you are in company, says this writer, when the conversation turns on the manners and customs of remote nations, or on books in verse or prose, or on the nature and limits of virtue and vice, it is a shame for a

lady not to relish such discourses, not to improve by them and endeavor by reading and information to have her share in those entertainments, rather than turn aside, as is the usual custom, and consult with the woman who sits next her about a new cargo of fans.

He then descends to particulars and insists on the necessity of orthography. Is it not a little hard, continues he, that not one gentleman's daughter in a thousand should be brought to read or understand her own natural tongue, or be judge of the easiest books that are written in it, as any one may find who can have the patience to hear them mangle a play or a novel?

If there be any of your acquaintance to whom this passage is applicable, I hope you will recommend the study of Mr. Webster's *Grammatical Institute* as the best work in our language to facilitate the knowledge of grammar. I cannot but think Mr. Webster intended his valuable book for the benefit of his countrywomen; while he delivers his *rules* in a pure, precise, and elegant style, he *explains* his meaning by *examples* which are calculated to inspire the female mind with a thirst for emulation and a desire of virtue.

No subject has been more exhausted than that of education. Many *Utopian* schemes have been delineated, and much speculation employed. When I peruse these labors, and am persuaded the intention of their authors is to promote our welfare, I feel myself prompted to a prudent and amiable demeanor; and I suppose every woman of reason and reflection feels the same inclination to virtue, and the same sensations of gratitude in reading the works of those writers, the characteristics of whom are sentiment, morality and benevolence.

What books do you read, my dear? We are now finishing Barlow's *Vision of Columbus,* and we shall begin upon Dwight's *Conquest of Canaan* in a few days. It is very agreeable to read with one who points out the beauties of the author as we proceed. Such an one is Worthy. Sometimes Mr. Holmes makes one of our party, and his notes and references to the ancient poets are very entertaining. Worthy is delighted with the ease and freedom with which we live here. We have little concerts, we walk, we ride, we read, we have good company: this is Belleview in all its glory!

Adieu, my dear—I shall continue this subject no longer,

though I flatter myself you would receive my hints with satisfaction because you must be persuaded I love you and so interest myself in your welfare. I need not add that I think your conduct worthy of you. You are such a good girl that I know not in what to direct you; for you leave me no room for advice—continue to anticipate the desires of my heart and to secure the high opinion you have there obtained.

Letter XXXI

Mrs. HOLMES to MYRA

Belleview

If the affair of your brother and Harriot be serious, and matrimony is really on the tapis, do not fail to make me *previously* acquainted with it. I very much doubt the evidence of the verses—they weigh in my mind—and he is easily excused for sending them to so fine a girl as Harriot.

Your observations on her dependence on Mrs. Francis do honor to your heart. Virtue does not consist in affluence and independence, nor can it be reflected on us by the glory of our connections. Those who pride themselves on it make but an indifferent figure; for in the estimation of all sensible people, true merit is personal.

However, my dear friend, as one who wishes for your welfare and the happiness of your family, I advise you to discourage the proposed connection. And if you cannot undertake this disagreeable talk with a *certainty of success,* do not fail to acquaint me of it *speedily.*

Letter XXXII

HARRINGTON to WORTHY

Boston

What ails my heart? I feel a void here. Yet I verge towards my happiness, for a few days makes Harriot mine. Myra says I had *better not marry her*. What could prompt her to use such an expression? *Better not marry her*. She has repeated it several times—and with too much eagerness. I give no heed to it, and yet why should it affect me in this manner? Is it an artifice to fathom the depth of my love? Such schemes are my utter aversion—it disturbs me—I hate such artifice. You cannot imagine how it touches my heart.

Letter XXXIII

Mrs. HOLMES to MYRA

Belleview

It is the duty of friends to be interested in all the concerns of one another—to join in their joys and to avert the stroke of danger. It is the duty of a sentinel to give the alarm at the approach of what he may think such; and if the result does not prove to be a real evil, he has but performed his duty, and the action is meritorious.

If your exertions to countermine the connection of your brother with Harriot should prove ineffectual (and do not fail to acquaint me with it either way), *I have a tale to unfold* which may possibly forbid the bans.

Letter XXXIV

HARRINGTON to WORTHY

Boston

I find my temper grow extremely irritable—my sensibility is wounded at the slightest neglect—I am very tenacious of everything and of everybody.

A party was made yesterday to go on the water; I was omitted, and the neglect hurt me. I inquired the cause, and what think you is the answer? "I am no company—I am asked a question and return nothing to the point—I am absent—I am strangely altered within a few days—I am thinking of a different subject when I ought to be employed in conversation—I am extravagant in my observations—I am no company."

They would persuade me that I am little better than a mad man. I have no patience with their nonsensical replies. Such wiseacres do not deserve my pity.

Letter XXXV

MYRA to Mrs. HOLMES

Boston

Your letter is filled with such ambiguous expressions that I am utterly at a loss to discover your meaning.

I have, however, founded him on the article of marriage; and the result is that he loves Harriot most passionately. And on account of my father's aversion to early marriages, he will marry her privately in a few days.

The oftener I read your letter, the more I am perplexed and astonished: "*You have a tale to unfold.*" For Heaven's sake, then unfold it, before it is too late. And as you dread the consequence of keeping it secret by disclosing it to me, you will prevent the mischief you so much deprecate. I am all impatience.

Letter XXXVI

HARRINGTON to WORTHY

Boston

I have just left Harriot—but how have I left her? In tears. I wish I had not gone. Mrs. Francis had entrusted Harriot with some trifling commission. It was not done—she had not had time to perform it. Harriot was reprimanded. Yes, by Heaven! This Mrs. Francis had the insolence to reprimand Harriot in my presence. I was mortified—I walked to the window—my heart was on fire—my blood boiled in my veins. It is impossible to form an idea of the disorder of my nerves; Harriot's were equally agitated. Mrs. Francis saw our confusion and retired; she left me so completely out of temper that I was forced to follow her example. I kissed away the tear from the cheek of Harriot and withdrew to my chamber.

Here let me forget what has passed: my irritability will not permit it—my feelings are too easily set in motion to enjoy long quietness—my nerves are delicately strung; they are now out of tune, and it is a hard matter to harmonize them.

I feel that I have a soul, and every man of sensibility feels it within himself. I will relate a circumstance I met with in my late travels through South Carolina. I was always susceptible to *touches of nature.*

I had often remarked a female slave pass by my window to a spring to fetch water. She had something in her air superior to those of her situation—a fire that the damps of slavery had not extinguished.

As I was one day walking behind her, the wind blew her tattered handkerchief from her neck and exposed it to my sight—I asked her the cause of the scar on her shoulder. She answered composedly, and with an earnestness that proved she was not ashamed to declare it. "It is the mark of the whip," said she, and went on with the history of it, without my desiring her to proceed. "My boy of about ten years old was unlucky enough to break a glass tumbler—this crime was immediately inquired into. I trembled for the fate of my child, but I was thought to be guilty. I did not deny the charge and was tied up. My former good character availed nothing. Under every affliction, we may receive consolation; and during the smart of the whip, I rejoiced—because I shielded with my body the lash from my child; and I rendered thanks to the best of beings that I was allowed to suffer for him."

"Heroically spoken!" said I, "may He whom you call the best of beings continue you in the same sentiments. May thy soul be ever disposed to sympathize with thy children, and with thy brethren and sisters in calamity. Then shalt thou feel every circumstance of thy life afford thee satisfaction; repining and melancholy shall fly from thy bosom. All thy labors will become easy—all thy burdens light, and the yoke of slavery will never gall thy neck."

I was sensibly relieved as I pronounced these words, and I felt my heart glow with feelings of exquisite delight as I anticipated the happy time when the sighs of the slave shall no longer expire in the air of freedom. What delightful sensations are those in which the heart is interested! In which it stoops to enter into the little concerns of the most remote ramification of Nature! Let the vain, the giddy, and the proud pass on without deigning to notice them; let them cheat themselves of happiness. These are circumstances which are important only to a sentimental traveler.

Hail *Sensibility!* Sweetener of the joys of life! Heaven has implanted thee in the breasts of his children to soothe the sorrows of the afflicted, to mitigate the wounds of the stranger who falleth in our way. *Thou* regardest with an eye of pity those whom *wealth* and *ambition* treat in terms of reproach. Away, ye seekers of power—ye boasters of wealth. Ye are the Levite and the Pharisee who restrain the hand of charity from the indigent and turn with indignation from the way-worn son of misery. But *Sensibility* is the good Samaritan who taketh him by the hand and consoleth him and poureth wine and oil into his wounds. Thou

art a pleasant companion—a grateful friend—and a *neighbor* to
those who are destitute of shelter.

From thee! Author of Nature! from thee, thou inexhaustible
spring of love supreme, floweth this tide of affection and sym-
pathy—thou whose tender care extendeth to the least of thy
creation, and whose eye is not inattentive even though a sparrow
fall to the ground.

Letter XXXVII

Mrs. HOLMES to MYRA

Belleview, 12 o'clock at night

I cannot rest. This affair lies so heavy on my mind that sleep
flies from my eyelids. Your brother *must* discontinue his addresses
to Harriot. With what should I not have to upbraid myself it,
through my remissness, your brother marries his sister!

Great God! of what materials hast thou compounded the
hearts of thy creatures! Admire, O my friend! the operation of
nature—and the power of sympathy!

Harriot is your sister! I dispatch the bearer at this late hour
to confide in your bosom the important secret.

Letter XXXVIII

MYRA to Mrs. HOLMES

Boston

Accept my warmest acknowledgment, my good friend, for
your kindness. Your letter sufficiently explains your former
anxiety; it has removed all ambiguities.

Your servant entered hastily with the letter and gave it to me
with evident tokens of its containing a matter of importance.

My father was present. I broke it open, not without agitation; I read it, but the shock was too severe. It fell from my hands, and I sunk into the chair.

My fainting was not of any duration. I opened my eyes and found my father supporting me. The idea of Harriot was still engraven deeply in my heart. I inquired for my sister: the tear rolled down his cheek—it was a sufficient answer to my inquiry. He said nothing—there was no necessity of his saying a word.

Could I ask him to explain your letter? No—my heart anticipated his feeling. The impropriety struck me at once. "*You have a tale to unfold*." Do not delay to unfold it.

Letter XXXIX

Mrs. HOLMES to MYRA

Belleview

I readily undertake to give you a sketch of the history of Harriot. Her mother's name was Maria Fawcet; her person I yet recollect, and forgive me if I drop a tear of pity at the recital of her misfortunes.

My mother and Mrs. Holmes were remarkable friends; and the intimacy, you know, was maintained between the two families. I was on a visit with my mother when the destiny of Maria led her to Belleview. I was frequently there during her illness and was with her in her last moments.

It was the custom of Mrs. Holmes to walk in the garden towards the close of the day. She was once indulging her usual walk, when she was alarmed by the complaints of a woman which came from the road. Pity and humanity were ever peculiar characteristics of my amiable parent. She hastened to the place from whence the sound issued and beheld a young woman, bathed in tears, sitting upon the ground. She inquired the cause of her distress with that eager solicitude to relieve, which a sight so uncommon would naturally occasion. It was sometime before the distressed woman could return an intelligible answer, and

then she with difficulty proceeded: "Your goodness, Madam, is unmerited. You behold a stranger, without home—without friends—whose misery bears her down to an untimely grave. Life truly is a blessing. But my life is become burdensome; and were the Almighty this moment to command me to 'the world of spirits, methinks I could gladly obey the summons and rejoice in the stroke which bade me depart from sorrow and the world."

"Moderate your grief, my dear woman; repine not at the will of Providence, nor suffer yourself to despair, however severe your misfortunes," said Mrs. Holmes.

The unfortunate woman was at length prevailed on to accompany Mrs. Holmes into the house; she partook of some refreshment and retired to sleep. In a few days she appeared to be better, but it was a temporary recovery; she then told her story, with frequent interruptions, in substance as follows:

HISTORY of MARIA

"I date the rise of my misfortunes," said Maria, "at the beginning of my acquaintance with the Honorable Mr. Harrington. But for his solicitations I might still have lived in peace—a sister would not have had occasion to blush at the sound of my name, nor had a mother's pillow been steeped in tears, too fondly prone to remember a graceless but repenting child. We lived happily together in the days of my father; but when it pleased Providence to remove him, we no longer asserted our pretentions to that rank of life which our straitened finances were unable to continue. A young woman in no eligible circumstances has much to apprehend from the solicitations of a man of affluence. I am now better persuaded of this truth than I ever was before. This was my unhappy situation: I always entertained a predilection for Mr. Harrington—he urged his passion with protestations of sincerity and affection—he found my heart too slightly guarded —he strove—he triumphed.

"—Must I proceed!

"A smiling female was the offspring of our illicit connection. Ah! my little Harriot!" continued Maria, as she wiped away a tear from her eye, "mayest thou enjoy that happiness which is denied to thy mother.

"Our amour was not fated to last long. I discovered his gay temper to be materially altered. He was often times thoughtful

and melancholy, and his visits became suddenly shorter and less frequent.

"I afterwards thought this change of conduct owing to jealousy, for he once asked me if a gentleman had called upon me. I persisted in avowing my abhorrence of his ungenerous suspicion. He left me abruptly, and I saw nothing of him after.

"A stroke so unexpected fell heavy on my heart; it awakened me to the state of misery into which my imprudence had hurried me. What recompense would I expect from my seducer? He had been married two years. From the inflexibility of his temper I had little to hope; and I formed a determination of leaving town, for I had now indubitable testimony of his affection being estranged from me. Half frantic, I immediately set out, but whither I knew not. I walked with precipitation until Providence directed me to your hospitable door. To your goodness, Madam, I am indebted for prolonging my existence *a few days:* for amidst the kindness and civilities of those around me, I feel myself rapidly verging towards the grave. I prepare myself for my approaching fate and daily wait the stroke of death with trembling expectation."

She wrote to Mr. Harrington about a week before her decease. I transcribe the letter:

"The Hon. Mr. Harrington:

"To the man for whom my bleeding heart yet retains its wonted affection, though the author of my guilt and misery, do I address my feeble complaint. O! Harrington, I am verging to a long eternity; and it is with difficulty I support myself while my trembling hand traces the dictates of my heart. Indisposed as I am, and unable as I feel to prosecute this talk, I however collect all my powers to bid you a long a final farewell.

"O! Harrington, I am about to depart—for why should I tarry here? In bitter tears of sorrow do I weep away the night, and the returning day but augments the anguish of my heart by recalling to view the sad sight of my misfortunes. And have I not cause for this severe anguish, at once the sorrow and disgrace of my family? Alas! my poor mother! Death shall expiate the crime of thy daughter, nor longer raise the blush of indigna tion on thy glowing cheek. Ought I not, therefore, to welcome the hand of death?

"But what will become of my poor helpless infant, when its

mother lies forgotten in the grave? Wilt thou direct its feet in the path of virtue and rectitude? Wilt thou shelter it from the rude blasts of penury and want? Open your heart to the solicitude of a mother—of a mother agonizing for the future welfare of her child. Let me entreat you to perform this request—by the love which you professed for thy Maria, by her life which you have sacrificed.

"And wilt thou not drop a tear of pity in the grave of thy Maria? I know thy soul is a soul of sensibility, but my departure shall not grieve thee. No, my Harrington, it shall not wrest a sigh from thy bosom. Rather let me live and defy the malice and misery of the world. But can tenderness—can love atone for the sacrifices I have made? Will it blot out my errors from the book of memory? Will love be an excuse for my crime, or hide me from the eye of the malignant? No, my Harrington, it will not. The passion is unwarrantable. Be it thine, gentle Amelia -be it thine to check the obtruding sigh and wipe away the tear from his face; for thou art his wife, and thy soul is the seat of compassion. But, for me—

"Farewell!—farewell forever!

Maria"

She survived but a short time and frequently expressed a concern for her child. But Mrs. Holmes quieted her fears by promising to protect it. She accordingly made inquiry after it. It is the same Harriot who was educated by her order and whom she afterwards placed in the family of Mrs. Francis.

The assurances of my mother were like balm to the broken-hearted Maria—"I shall now," said she, "die in peace."

The following is a copy of a letter written by the Rev. Mr. Holmes to the Hon. Mr. Harrington:

Belleview

"Sir:

"We have a scene of distress at our house peculiarly pathetic and affecting, and of which you perhaps are the sole author. You have had a criminal connection with Miss Fawcet. You have turned her upon the world inhumanly; but chance—rather let me say, Providence—hath directed her footsteps to my dwelling where she is kindly entertained, and will be so as long as she

remains in this wilderness world, which is to be, I fear, but a short time. And shall she not, though she hath been decoyed from the road that leadeth to peace, be entitled to long life and happiness? Shall she not, if she return with tears of repentance and contrition, be entitled to our love and charity? Yes—this is my doctrine. If I behold any child of human nature distressed and forlorn, and in real want of the necessities of life, must I restrain or withhold the hand of charity? Must I cease to recall the departing spirit of them who are ready to perish, until I make diligent inquiry into their circumstances and character? Surely, my friend, it is a duty incumbent on us by the ties of humanity and fellow feeling and by the duty imposed on us by our holy religion, equally to extend the hand of relief to *all the necessitous* however they may be circumstanced in the great family of mankind.

"The crime of Maria is not the blackest in the annals of human turpitude; but however guilty she might have been, the tears of penitence do certainly make atonement therefor.

"Thus much have I thought proper to say in vindication of my conduct—in sheltering under my roof a poor wanderer who hath strayed, but not wantonly, and who hath now happily returned.

"One would imagine there was little necessity of making such a vindication to you; but my sentiments always flow from the abundance of my heart, and I am willing the whole world should judge of those which influence my conduct. Now, though some men, who charity is contracted and who may be denominated *prudes in virtue,* might deem wrongfully of my attention to the calamity of this frail woman, yet let me appeal to the hearts and understandings of all men; and these in particular, if I have erred, whether it be not an error on the side of humanity. Would to God such amiable errors were more frequent! Inasmuch, my friend, as there is joy in heaven over one sinner that repenteth, I may say with assurance that I have felt an emanation of this heavenly joy animate my heart, in beholding this woman delighting to steer her course heavenward.

"From the unhappy condition of Maria, I have been led to reflect on the mischievous tendency of seduction. Methinks I view the distressing picture in all its horrid colors.

"Behold the youthful virgin arrayed in all the delightful

charms of vivacity, modesty and sprightliness. Behold even while she is rising in beauty and dignity, like a lily of the valley, in the full blossom of her graces, she is cut off suddenly by the rude hand of the seducer. Unacquainted with his baseness and treachery, and too ready to repose confidence in him, she is deluded by the promises and flattery of the man who professes the greatest love and tenderness for her welfare. But did she understand the secret villainy of his intentions, would she appear thus elate and joyous? Would she assent to her ruin? Would she subscribe her name to the catalogue of infamy? Would she kiss the hand of the atrocious dastard, already raised to give the final wound to her reputation and peace?

"O! Why there not an adequate punishment for this crime, when that of a common traitor is marked with its deserved iniquity and abhorrence!

"Is it necessary to depict the state of this deluded young creature after her fall from virtue? Stung with remorse and frantic with despair, does she not fly from the face of day and secrete her conscious head in the bosom of eternal forgetfulness? Melancholy and guilt transfix her heart, and she sighs out her miserable existence—the prey of poverty, ignominy and reproach! Lost to the world, to her friends, and to herself, she blesses the approach of death in whatever shape he may appear, that terminates a life no longer a blessing to its possessor or a joy to those around her.

"Behold her stretched upon the mournful bier! Behold her silently descend to the grave! Soon the wild weeds spring afresh round the *little hillock,* as if to shelter the remains of betrayed innocence—and the friends of her youth shun even the spot which conceals her relics.

"Such is the consequence of seduction, but it is not the only consequence. Peace and happiness fly the nuptial couch which is unattended by love and fidelity. The mind no longer enjoys its quiet, while it ceases to cherish sentiments of truth and gratitude. The sacred *ties* of connubial duty are not to be violated with impunity; for though a violation of those ties may be overlooked by the eye of justice, the heart shall supply a *monitor,* who will not fail to correct those who are hardy enough to burst them asunder.

W. Holmes"

To this letter ·Mr. Harrington returned the following answer.

"Hon. Mr. Harrington to the Rev. Mr. Holmes:

"Permit me, my ever honored friend, to return you thanks for your late favors. Need I add an acknowledgment for your liberality? No, your heart supplies a source of pleasure which is constantly nourished by your goodness and universal charity.

"The picture you have exhibited of a ruined female is undoubtedly just, but that the rude *spoiler* has his share of remorse is equally so. The conclusion of your letter is a real picture of the situation of my heart.

"Perhaps you were always ignorant of the real motives that influenced me, and gave a particular bias to my conduct. At an early period of my life, I adopted a maxim that *the most necessary learning was a knowledge of the world,* the pursuit of which, quadrating with a volatility of disposition, presented a variety of scenes to my heated imagination. The *eclat* of my companions gratifying my vanity and increasing the gale of passion, I became insensibly hurried down the stream of dissipation. Here I saw mankind in every point of view: from the acme of the most consummate refinement, to the most abject stage of degradation. I soon became a ready proficient in the great school of the world, but an alteration of conduct was soon after necessary. I was compelled to it, not so much from the world's abhorrence of a dissolute course of life as the dictates of my own heart. It was, indeed, my policy to flatter the world and exhibit a fair outside, for I was in love with Amelia. My licentious amour with Maria was secret: she was affectionate and tender—her manners were pleasing. Still I was unhappy.

"My career of dissipation, however alluring it struck my vitiated fancy, left little satisfaction on the mind. Reflection had its turn; and the happiness I had promised myself in a connection with the amiable Amelia, I fully enjoyed in our marriage. A course of uninterrupted tranquility ensued, but it was of short duration. The volatility of my temper, and the solicitude of my old associates, induced me at subsequent periods to fall again into my old vagaries. The taverns frequently found me engaged in meannesses derogatory to the character of a gentleman. These things I perceived affected the soul of Amelia—she was all meekness, gentleness and compassion, and she never once upbraided me with my illiberal conduct.

But let concealment, like a worm in the bud,
Feed on her damask cheek.

"Blessed be that power who has implanted within us that con-
sciousness of reproach, which springs from gentleness and love!
Hail sensibility! Ye eloquent *tears of beauty*! that add dignity to
human nature by correcting its foibles. It was these that corrected
my faults when recrimination would have failed of success; it was
these that opened every avenue of contrition in my heart, when
words would have dammed up every sluice of repentance.

"It was now I appeared fully sensible that my conduct had
hitherto been a course of disorder; that systems of reformation,
however well planned, had been overturned by the breath of adu-
lation before they had been thoroughly carried into execution;
that I had been drifting upon a sea of inconsistency, without
exercising my judgment. I was like a ship without a rudder, buffet-
ted on the bosom of the ocean, the sport of winds and waves.

"The criminality of my connection with Maria appeared with
the most aggravated circumstances; it stung me with remorse. I
instantly determined, however severe the conflict, to tear her
from my bosom—to see her no more. But how was I to inform
her of it? In what manner was I to bring about such a talk?
Maria must be sacrificed to the happiness of Amelia. This was all
I had to perform—it was a short lesson, but it was a hard one
for me to execute.

"With this determination, however, I entered the apartment of
Maria. Duty to Amelia and gratitude to Maria interchangably
agitated me. The contention was dubious; but duty prevailed,
and I adhered to my former resolution. Yet how was I to tell
her *this would be the last visit*? Conscious she had ever acted in
conformity to my wishes, how could I accuse her without ac-
cusing myself? I threw out a few inconsiderate and ungrateful
hints of jealousy and left the room abruptly. The feelings of
Maria must have been injured; but however her sensibility was
affected, mine was doubly so. I felt for her—I felt for our in-
fant, and these feelings were added to the afflictions which had
already burst upon my devoted head. A few days' consideration,
however, convinced me of the impropriety and ingratitude of
my behavior to Maria. I hastened to tell her of it—to place her
in a situation that should screen her from penury and malice
and to make provision for the child—but she was not to be

found. I was informed that she had suddenly disappeared and that a countryman had by her order called and taken away the child but a few hours before. This information burst upon my head like the voice of sudden thunder. I stood motionless, but my agitation was too violent to be of any long duration.

A natural tear I shed, but wiped it soon.

"It was your goodness, and the humanity of your family, that sheltered the wretched Maria and provided for the helpless Harriot. Your feelings are your reward.

"From all the variegated scenes of my past life, I daily learn some new lesson of humanity. Experience hath been my tutor. I now take a retrospect of my past conduct with deliberation, but not without some serious reflection: like a sailor escaped from shipwreck, who sits safely on the shore and views the horrors of the tempest; but as the gale subsides and the waves hide their heads in the bosom of the deep, he beholds with greater concern the mischief of the storm and the dangers he hath escaped. From what innate principle does this arise, but from *God within the mind*! I assert it for the honor of human nature that no man, however dissolute, comes back to the hour of reflection and solemn thoughtfulness—when the actions that are passed return upon the mind, and this *internal monitor* sits in judgment upon them and gives her verdict of approbation or dislike.

"He who listens to its call views his character in its proper light. I have attended to its cry, and I see my deformity. I recall my misspent time, but in vain; I reflect on the misery of Maria, and I curse my temertiy; I reflect on the state into which I have plunged a once happy female, and I am eager to apply a speedy remedy, but this is vain also. Can I restore her that virtue—that inno cence—that peace of which I have unmanfully robbed her? Let us leave the melancholy subject.

"I will not so far supersede the fruit of your benevolence, as to presume to offer you any recompense, than my sincere prayers for your happiness.

J. Harrington"

The disorder of Maria was fatal and rapid. But I hasten to the last scene of her life; it has, though I was young, made an impression on my mind that time cannot efface. I went to her as she was seated on the bed—virtue and harmony were blended in her aspect;

she was serene and composed. Her mien, while it expressed a consciousness of superior worth and dignity, exhibited in one view a striking picture of the grandeur of the human soul: patient, though afflicted—of a spirit broken and borne down by severe distress, yet striving to surmount all and aspire to heaven. In what words shall I paint to you, my dear Myra, her heroism and greatness of mind? "Weep not for me," said she, perceiving my emotion. "Death has nothing shocking to me—I have familiarized myself to his terrors—I feel the gradual decay of mortality; and waiting with confidence in the father of mercy, I am prepared to resign this mortal breath. I resign it in firm assurance of the soul's blessed immortality. Death I view as freeing me from a world which has lost its relish—as opening new scenes of happiness. But a few moments," continued she, clasping my hand, "and the scene of life is closed forever. Heaven opens on my soul—I go where all tears shall be wiped away—I welcome death as the angel of peace." She uttered these words with a placid smile of resignation; her head sunk down on the pillow, and the next minute she was an angel.

"Soul of the universe!" exclaimed my father-in-law; "there flew the gentlest spirit that ever animated human dust. Great were thy temptations—sincere thy repentance. If some human infirmity fell to thy lot, thy tears, dear shade, have washed out thy guilt forever!"

Letter XL

Mrs. HOLMES to MYRA

Belleview

Having presented you with several observations on seduction, I think it will not be *mal apropos* to consider the question in another point of view and discover how a woman may be accessary to her own ruin. It is hardly worthwhile to contend about the difference between the meaning of the terms accessary and principal. The difference, in fact, is small; but when a woman,

by her imprudence, exposes herself, she is accessary; for though her heart may be pure, her conduct is a tacit invitation to the seducer.

Educated in the school of luxury and pride, the female heart grows gradually torpid to the fine feelings of sensibility. The blush of modesty wears off; the charms of elegant simplicity fade by degrees; the continual hurry of dissipation supersedes the improvement of serious reflection. Reflection is a kind of relaxation from frolicking—it encourages the progress of virtue and upholds the heart from sinking to depravity.

We may lay it down as a principle, that *that conduct which will bear the test of reflection and which creates a pleasure in the mind from a consciousness of acting right is virtuous; And that she whose conduct will not bear this test is necessarily degenerating and is assenting to her destruction.*

Let a lady be liberal or even magnificent, according to her circumstances or situation in life; but let the heart remain uncorrupt. Let her not be contaminated by wealth, ambition or splendor. She may then take a happy retrospect of her conduct—her heart cannot upbraid her—and the suffrage of her own mind is a convincing proof that she has not strayed from the path of virtue.

Happy they who can thus reflect—who can recall to view the scenes that are passed and behold their actions with reiterated satisfaction. They become ambitious of excelling in everything virtuous, because they are certain of securing a continual reward. For as a mighty river fertilizes the country through which it passes and increases in magnitude and force until it empty itself into the ocean, so virtue fertilizes or improves the heart and gathers strength and vigor by continual progression until it centers in the consummation of its desires.

Dazzled by the glitter of splendor, and unmindful of the real charms of economy and simplicity, the female heart sighs for the enjoyment of fashion and flutters to join the motley train of pleasure. But how is it deluded by empty deceptions! It is like the fruit which sprang up in the infernal regions, beautiful to the eye, but which left upon the taste bitter ashes. A great quantity of this kind of fruit presents itself to my rashly-judging sex; and it frequently happens that their hearts have as little inclination to resist the temptation as our general parent to refuse the fatal apple.

We do not rouse to our aid fortitude to enable us to sur-

mount the temptation, but yield ourselves to a kind of volun-
tary slavery. Hence it is observable that a woman is often
unhappy in the midst of pleasures and petulant without cause;
that she is trifling in matters of the highest importance; that the
most momentous concern is considered futile, as whim and
caprice may chance to dictate.

The progress of female luxury, however slow it may appear,
unless timely checked, works with infallible and destructive ad-
vances. The rule we at first adopted might perhaps answer this
check; for by the examination there recommended, we behold
the dangers of a continuation of such conduct. Ruin and con-
tempt, the invariable concommitants of vice and immorality,
proclaim their denunciations on a prosecution of it.

Let us examine the gradual steps and the consequence of
female luxury. A desire to be admired is the first. Behold a
woman surrounded by her worshippers, receiving the sacrifice of
adulation. What was given her at first as compliment, she now
demands as her due. The first desire still predominating, she
attaches herself to the votaries of pride, who direct their feet in
the paths of extravagance and irreligion. Thus sunk into effemi-
nacy and meanness, *she forfeits her virtue rather than her pride.*
Thus terminates the career of a woman, whose mind is debili-
tated and whose life is expended in the pursuit of vanity.

It is said of some species of American serpents that they have
the power of charming birds and small animals, which they destine
for their prey. The serpent is stretched underneath a tree: it looks
steadfastly on the bird—their eyes meet to separate no more—the
charm begins to operate—the fascinated bird flutters and hops
from limb to limb until, unable any longer to extend its wings, it
falls into the voracious jaws of its enemy. This is no ill emblem of
the fascinating power of pleasure. Surrounded with temptation
and embarrassed in her circumstance, a woman of dissipation
becomes less tenacious of her honor—and falls an easy prey to the
fascinating power of the seducer.

Having traced to you, my dear Myra, the rise, advancement and
termination of pleasure and pride in the female heart, it appears
almost unnecessary to remark that this conduct cannot bear the
test of reflection and serious examination. We may, however, ob-
serve on the contrary, that a woman who advances a few steps
often hurries on still further to prevent thought. This bars the way
to a return to that conduct which can give pleasure on recollec-

tion. She behaves to herself as the populace did formerly to women suspected of witchcraft. They were tied neck and heels and thrown into the river: if they swam they were hung for witches; if they sank they were acquitted of the crime but drowned in the experiment. So when we only suspect our hearts of an error, we plunge still deeper into the sea of dissipation to prevent the trial of that conduct which impartial reason and judgment would approve.

Notwithstanding, I give this instance as an encouragement for virtue; yet in all those I have mentioned is a woman *accessary* to her ruin.

Do not imagine, my dear Myra, that I mean to argue against all pleasure. Many of us set out on a principle of false delicacy and destructive rivalship; we cannot behold a fine woman without wishing to appear finer. A laudable emulation in the conduct of all women is extremely praiseworthy—it stimulates them in the line of their duty and increases vivacity and good humor. Amibition, thus directed and pursued, I beg leave to designate a female virtue, because it is productive of the most happy consequences.

But it sometimes happens that particular virtues loose themselves in their neighboring vices, and this laudable emulation degenerates into destructive rivalship.

A genteel, handsome woman deservedly shares the esteem and admiration of all men; but why should this esteem and admiration, justly paid to merit, give us disquiet? The answer is ready. That desire to be admired, so predominant in all females, by degrees works itself into the ruling passion and precludes from the mind the particular virtue of emulation; for why a woman who merits the love of the world should draw on her the disapprobation of many of her own sex can be accounted for, by no other principle, than the mean, pitiful passion of envy.

This may possible give rise to defamation. It is astonishing how this practice prevails among a *few* persons—because it is known by experience to prove subversive of its very intention. The arrows of envy recoil upon herself.

How foolish must that woman appear who depreciates the merit of another that she may appear unrivalled. She raises up the dikes of ill nature and inundates the land with a flood of scandal, but unhappily drowns herself in the event.

I leave it to the result of your observation, my dear Myra,

whether the woman who is first to develop her stores of defamation and, through false emulation, the first to traduce a woman of real merit and virtue is not also the first who becomes a scandal to herself, and consequently the first that is contemned.

How opposite are the pursuits and rewards of her who participates in every rational enjoyment of life, without mixing in those scenes of indiscretion which give pain on recollection! Whose chemical genius leads her to extract the poison from the most luxuriant flowers and to draw honey even from the weeds of society. She mixes with the world seemingly indiscriminantly; and because she would secure to herself that satisfaction which arises from a consciousness of acting right, she views her conduct with an eye of scrutiny. Though her temper is free and unrestrained, her heart is previously secured by the precepts of prudence. For prudence is but another name for virtue. Her manners are unruffled; and her disposition is calm, temperate, and dispassionate, however she may be surrounded by the temptations of the world.

Letter XLI

HARRINGTON to WORTHY

Boston

Pray that the sun of Thursday may rise propitious—that it may gild the face of nature with joy. It is the day that beholds thy friend united in the indissoluble bands of Hymen.

> Let this auspicious day be ever sacred,
> No mourning, no misfortune happen on it;
> Let it be marked for triumphs and rejoicings;
> Let happy lovers ever keep it holy;
> Choose it to bless their hopes and crown their wishes.

It is the day that gives me Harriot forever.

Letter XLII

The Hon. Mr. HARRINGTON to the Rev. Mr. HOLMES

Boston

You very well know of my amour with Maria and that a daughter was the offspring of that illicit connection. That sixteen years have elapsed since, by your goodness, she has lived with Mrs. Francis and, let me add, daily improving in beauty and every amiable accomplishment. But how shall we be able—how shall we pretend to investigate the great springs by which we are actuated or account for the operation of sympathy. My son, who has been at home about eight weeks, has accidentally seen her and, to complete the triumph of nature, has loved her. He is now even upon the point of marrying—shall I proceed!—*of marrying his sister!* A circumstance seemingly fortuitous has discovered this important affair. I fly to prevent incest. Do not upbraid me with being the author of my own misfortunes. "This comes of your libertinism," you will say; "this comes of your adultery!" Spare your reflections, my friend—my heart is monitor enough. I am strangely agitated!

Letter XLIII

The Hon. Mr. HARRINGTON to the Rev. Mr. HOLMES

Boston

My heart failed me! Twenty times have I attempted to break the matter to my son—and twenty times have I returned from the task. I have engaged a friend to acquaint him how nearly

connected he already is with the object of his love. This is a
new and to me a sorrowful instance of the force of sympathy.
My grief is insupportable—my affliction is greater than I can
bear—it will bring down my grey hairs with sorrow to the grave.

Letter XLIV

HARRINGTON to WORTHY

Boston

All my airy schemes of love and happiness are vanished like a
dream. Read this, and pity your unfortunate friend.

"To Mr. T. Harrington

"Sir:

"You are about to marry a young lady of great beauty and
accomplishments. I beg you to bestow a few serious thoughts on
this important business. Let me claim your attention, while I
disclose an affair which materially concerns you. Harriot must
not be your wife. You know your father is averse to your early
connecting yourself in marriage with any woman. The duty we
owe a parent is sacred, but this is not the only barrier to
your marriage. The ties of consanguinity prevent it: she is
your *sister*. Your father, or Miss Harrington, will inform you
more particularly. It is sufficient for me to have hinted it in
time. I am, with the most perfect esteem and sincere wishes for
your happiness, your

"Unknown Friend."

The gloom of melancholy in the faces of the family but too
well corroborated this intelligence; so I asked no questions. They
read in my countenance that I had received the letter, and my
sister put into my hand *The History of Maria*. I concealed my

emotion while I read the account. "It is a pitiful tale," said I, as I returned it and walked out of the room to give vent to the agitation of my heart.

I have not yet seen Harriot—Myra has run to greet her with the new title of *sister*. Adieu! my friend—little happiness is left for me in this world.

Letter XLV

MYRA to Mrs. HOLMES

Boston

In what words shall I describe to you, my dear friend, the misery that has suddenly overwhelmed us! It is impossible to communicate the distressed situation of Harriot. Expression is inadequate to give you an idea of our meeting; I called her my friend—my sister. She always loved me, but joy and affection gave way to passion. Her speech refused its office.

> Sorrow in all its pomp was there,
> Mute and magnificent without a tear.

She had gained a sister—she had lost a lover. A burst of joy would suddenly break from her, but it was of short duration and was succeeded by pangs of exquisite distress. Nature was unable to support it, and she fainted under the weight of the severe conflict. Her constitution at best is feeble; her present illness is therefore attended with more danger. Unless a speedy alternation should take place, the physician has little hopes of her recovery. Heaven preserve us!

Letter XLVI

HARRINGTON to WORTHY

Boston

I have seen her—I pressed her to my heart—I called her my love—my *sister*. Tenderness and sorrow were in her eyes. How am I guilty, my friend? How is this transport a crime? My love is the most pure, the most holy. Harriot beheld me with tears of the most tender affection. "Why," said she, "why, my friend, my dear Harrington, have I loved! In what manner have I been culpable? *How was I to know you were my brother?* Yes! I might have known it—how else could you have been so kind—so tender—so affectionate!" Here was all the horror of conflicting passions, expressed by gloomy silence—by stifled cries—by convulsions—by sudden floods of tears. The scene was too much for my heart to bear—I bade her adieu. My heart was breaking—I tore myself from her and retired.

What is human happiness? The prize for which all strive, and so few obtain. The more eagerly we pursue it, the farther we stray from the object: Wherefore I have determined within myself that we increase in misery as we increase in age. If there are any happy, they are those of thoughtless childhood.

I then viewed the world at a distance in perspective. I thought mankind appeared happy in the midst of pleasures that flowed round them. I now find it a deception, and I am tempted sometimes to wish myself a child again. Happy are the dreams of infancy, and happy their harmless pursuits. I saw the *ignis fatuus* and have been running after it, but now I return from the search. I return and bring back disappointment. As I reflect on these scenes of infantine ignorance, I feel my heart interested and become sensibly affected. However futile these feelings may appear as I communicate them to you, they are feelings I venture to assert which everyone must have experienced who is possessed of a heart of sensibility.

Letter XLVII

HARRINGTON to WORTHY

Boston

I no longer receive satisfaction from the enjoyments of the world. Society is distasteful to me. My favorite authors I have entirely relinquished. In vain I try to forget myself, or seek for consolation. My repose is interrupted by distressing visions of the night—my thoughts are broken—I cannot even think regularly.

Harriot is very weak; there is no hope of her life.

Letter XLVIII

HARRINGTON to WORTHY

Boston

My dear friend, I have a great desire to see you. I wish you could come home speedily. I must be short—I have some serious business to do.

Farewell!

P.S. They say life is a blessing, and it is our duty to improve and enjoy it; but when life becomes insupportable and we find no blessing in it, have we not a right to resign it?

Letter XLIX

The Hon. Mr. HARRINGTON to the Rev. Mr. HOLMES

Boston

Accumulated sorrows continue to break over my devoted head. Harriot is at times deprived of her reason, and we have no expectation of her recovery. My son is deeply affected—he seems strangely disordered.

Revolving in my mind all these things, and the unhappy affair that led to them, the whole train of my past life returned fresh upon my mind. Pained with the disagreeable picture and oppressed with the weight of my affliction, I sank down to sleep: these circumstances had so strongly impressed my imagination that they produced the following dream. My blood is chilled with horror as I write.

Methought I suddenly found myself in a large open field, waste and uncultivated—here I wandered in a solitary manner for some time. Grief seized my heart at the awful appearance of the place, and I cried aloud: "How long shall I travel here, alone and friendless? A dusky mist swims before my sight, and the obscure horizon seems only to enclose this dismal wild!" Having advanced a few steps, I thought a light at a distance appeared to my doubtful view. Faint with fatigue, I approached it and had the satisfaction to behold a person of the most benign aspect—a quiet serenity was painted on his brow, and happiness ineffable beamed from his divine countenance. Joy leaped in my bosom, and in the ecstacy of passion I endeavored to clasp the blessed spirit to my heart; but it vanished in my embrace.

"Teach me, blessed shade," said I, with a trembling voice, "teach me to find the habitations of men. What do I here? Why am I doomed to explore the barren bosom of this baleful desert?" "*This*," returned the spirit in a voice which, while it commanded veneration and love, struck awe and terror into my soul, "*This* is not the habitation of the sons of mortality; it is

the place appointed to receive the souls of all men, after they have resigned the bodies they animated on earth. Those who have violated the laws of reason, humanity, and religion, and have dishonored their God, here meet the punishment due to their crimes.

"Attend me, therefore, and view the condition of those thoughtless souls, who a few days ago were upon earth immersed in pleasure, luxury and vice. Regardless of futurity, and unprepared for their eternal summons to another world, they persisted in the delight of their own eyes in opposition to the divine law and were deaf to the voice of reclaiming virtue. These, the sons of folly and riot, are smitten by the angel of death while they are yet drinking of the bowl of vice—while the words of blasphemy yet dwell upon their tongues. And when their unhappy spirits sink to these infernal regions, their surviving companions rehearse their funeral panegyrics—the praise of one is that he could drink the longest; the merit of another is that he could sing a good song; a third secures his fame by being excellent in mimicry and buffoonery. How unhappy must he be who leaves no other testimony of his usefulness behind him!

"How different is the fate of the good man. While upon earth his life is employed in the cause of virtue. The happiness he bestows on those around him is reflected with tenfold reward; and when he takes rank in that happy place, where there is fullness of joy and leaves the world of mankind, what numbers are joined in the general concern for his loss. The aged, while they prepare for the same journey, delight to dwell on his good actions; the virgin strews flowers on his grave; the poet consumes the midnight oil to celebrate his virtues."

There was so much benignity in every word and action of my attendant that I found myself imperceptibly attached to him. My attention to his discourse had prevented me from observing the progress we had made, for we had arrived at a place encircled with high walls. A great gate, at the command of my guide, instantly flew open. "Follow me," said he. I tremblingly obeyed.

My ears were instantaneously filled with the faint cries of those here doomed to receive the rewards of their demerits. Looking earnestly forward, I beheld a group of unhappy wretches. I observed a person who was continually tormenting them. He held in one hand a whip, the lashes of which were

composed of adders and the stings of scorpions; and in the other a large mirror which, when he held up to the faces of the tormented, exhibited their crimes in the most flagrant colors and forced them to acknowledge the justness of their punishment. "These," said my guide, "who are scourged with a whip of scorpions, and who start with horror at the reflection of their deeds upon earth, are the souls of the gambler—the prodigal—the duelist, and the ingrate.

"Those whom you see yonder," continued he, "those wasted, emaciated spirits, are the souls of the envious: they are doomed to view the most beautiful fruit which they can never taste, and behold pleasures which they can never enjoy. This punishment is adjudged them because most of those vile passions, by which men suffer themselves to be ruled, bring real evil for promised good.

"For this reason the all-wise Judge hath ordered the same passions still to inflame those ghosts, with which they were possessed on earth. Observe yon despicable crew! Behold the sin of avarice! Those sordid ghosts are the souls of misers. They eye their delightful bags with horrid pleasure and with a ghastly smile brood over their imaginary riches. Unable to carry their wealth about with them, they are confined to one spot and in one position. This infernal joy is the source of their tortures, for behold them start at every sound and tremble at the flitting of a shade. Thus are they doomed to be their own tormentors—to pore over their gold with immortal fear, apprehension, and jealousy and to guard their ideal wealth with the tears of care and the eyes of eternal watchfulness.

"Behold here," continued my guide, "the miserable division of suicides!" "Unhappy they!" added I, "who, repining at the ills of life, raised the sacrilegious steel against their own bosoms! How vain the reiterated wish to again animate the breathless clay—to breathe the vital air—to behold the cheering luminary of Heaven!" "Upbraid me not, O my father!" cried a voice. I looked up and thought my son appeared among them; but immediately turning from so shocking a spectacle, I suddenly beheld my once loved Maria. "O delight of my youth! do I behold thee once more! Let me hide my sorrows in thy friendly bosom." I advanced towards her, but she flew from me with scorn and indignation. "O speak! Maria! speak to

me!" She pointed with her finger to a group of spirits and was out of sight in a moment.

"Let me," said my conductor, "prepare you for a more dreadful sight." The increasing melancholy, and affecting gloom of the situation, forboded something terrifying to my soul. I looked toward the place where Maria had pointed and saw a number of souls remote from any division of the unhappy. In their countenances were depicted more anguish, sorrow and despair. I turned my head immediately from this dreadful sight, without distinguishing the nature of their torments. Quivering with horror, I inquired who they were. "These," answered my guide with a sigh, "are the miserable race of seducers. Repentance and shame drive them far from the rest of the accursed. Even the damned look on them with horror and thank fate their crimes are not of so deep a die."

He had hardly finished, when a demon took hold of me and furiously hurried me in the midst of this unhappy group. I was so terrified that it immediately roused me from my sleep.

Even now, while I write to you, my good friend, my hand trembles with fear at the painful remembrance —

'Twas but a dream, but then
So terrible, it shakes my very soul.

Letter L

HARRIOT to HARRINGTON

Boston

Must I then forget the endearments of the lover and call you by the name of brother? But does our friendship remain upon this foundation? Is this all that unites us? And has there subsisted nothing more tender—a sentiment more voluntary in our hearts? My feelings affirm that there has. At the hour of our first interview I felt the passion kindle in my breast. Insensible

of my own weakness, I indulged its increasing violence and delighted in the flame that fired my reason and my senses. Do you remember our walks, our conversations, our diversions? The remembrance of these things fill my mind with inconceivable torture; they seem to reproach me with unmerited criminality. I deprecate, I detest all these scenes of gaiety and frivolity; yet I have preserved my innocence and my virtue. What then have I to deprecate, what have I to detest?

Alas! how have we been forming schemes of happiness, and mocking our hearts with unsubstantial joys. Farewell! farewell! ye gilded scenes of imagination. How have we been deluded by visionary prospects and idly dwelt upon that happiness which was never to arrive. How fleeting have been the days that were thus employed—when anticipation threw open the gates of happiness and we vainly contemplated the approach of bliss; when we beheld in reversion the pleasures of life and fondly promised ourselves one day to participate in them; when we beheld in the magic mirror of futurity the lively group of loves that sport in the train of joy. We observed in transports of delight the dear delusion and saw them, as it were, in bodily form pass in review before us, as the fabled hero views the region of pre-existent spirits and beholds a race of men yet to be born.

Such was our hope, but even this fairy anticipation was not irrational. We were happy in idea, nor was the reality far behind. And why is the vision vanished? O! I sink, I die, when I reflect—when I find in my Harrington a brother—I am penetrated with inexpressible grief. I experience uncommon sensations. I start with horror at the idea of incest—of ruin—of perdition.

How do I lament this fatal discovery that includes the termination of a faithful love! I think of him to whom I have resolved to be eternally constant—and ah! how often have I resolved it in my heart. I indulge, in idea, the recollection of his caresses, of his protestations, and of his truth and sincerity. I become lost in a wilderness, and still I travel on and find myself no nearer an escape. I cherish the dear idea of a lover. I see the danger and do not wish to shun it, because to avoid it is to forget it. And can I, at one stroke, erase from my mind the remembrance of all in which my heart used to delight? Ah! I have not the fortitude—I have not the virtue, to

"forget myself to marble." On the contrary, I strive no longer to remember our present connection. I endeavor to forget. I curse the idea of a brother—my hand refuses to trace the word; and yet

> —The name appears
> Already written; blot it out, my tears!

Ah, whence this sorrow that invests my soul! this gloom that darkens! this fire of impassioned grief that involves all my thoughts! why do I rave, and why do I again abandon myself to despair! Come, O Harrington! be a friend, a protector, a brother —be him on whom I could never yet call by the tender, the endearing title of *parent*. I will reverence him in whom all the charities of life are united. I will be dutiful and affectionate to you, and you shalt be unto me as a father. I will bend on the knee of respect and love and will receive your blessing.

Why did you go away so soon? Why leave me when I was incapable of bidding you adieu? When you pressed my cheek with the kiss of love, of fraternal affection, what meant its conscious glow? What meant the ebullition of my veins, the disorder of my nerves, the intoxication of my brain, the blood that mantled in my heart? My hand trembled, and every object seemed to swim before my doubtful view. Amidst the struggle of passion, how could I pronounce the word—how could I call you by the title of brother. True, I attempted to articulate the sound, but it died upon my tongue; and I sank motionless into your arms.

Allied by birth, and in mind, and similar in age—and in thought still more intimately connected—the sympathy which bound our souls together at first sight is less extraordinary. Shall we any longer wonder at its irresistible impulse? Shall we strive to oppose the *link of nature* that draws us to each other? When I reflect on this, I relapse into weakness and tenderness and become a prey to warring passions. I view you in two distinct characters: if I indulge the idea of one, the other becomes annihilated; and I vainly imagine I have my choice of a brother or—

I am for a while calm—but alas! how momentary is that calmness; I dwell with rapture on what fancy has represented. But is the choice regulated by virtue? Is it prompted by reason? I recollect myself and endeavor to rouse my prudence and fortitude; I abhor my conduct and wish for obscurity and forgetful-

ness. Who can bear the torment of fluctuating passion? How deplorable is the contest? The head and the heart are at variance; but when nature pleads, how feeble is the voice of reason? Yet, when reason is heard in her turn, how criminal appears every wish of my heart? What remorse do I experience? What horrors surround me? Will my feeble frame, already wasted by a lingering decline, support these evils? Will the shattered, frail bark outride the tempest; and will the waves of affliction beat in vain? Virtue, whose precepts I have not forgotten, will assist me—if not to *surmount,* at least to *suffer* with fortitude and patience.

Oh! I fear, I fear my decaying health. If I must depart, let me beseech you to forget me. I know the strength of your passion, and I dread the fatal consequences my departure may occasion you.

Once more let me intreat you, my dear friend, to arm yourself with every virtue which is capable of sustaining the heaviest calamity. Let the impetuosity of the lover's passion be forgotten in undisturbed quietness of the brother's affection, and may all the blessings that life can supply be yours. Seek for content and you will find it, even though we should never meet again in this world.

Letter LI

MYRA to Mrs. HOLMES

Boston

The curtain is dropped, and the scene of life is forever closed. *The lovely Harriot is no more.*

She is fit to appear in Heaven, for her life was a scene of purity and innocence. If there is any consolation to be felt by a survivor, it is the reflection of the amiable qualities of the deceased. My heart shall not cease to cherish her idea, for she was beautiful without artifice and virtuous without affectation.

> See! there all pale and dead she lies;
> Forever flow my streaming eyes.
> There dwelt the fairest, the lovliest mind,
> Faith, sweetness, wit together joined.
> Dwelt faith and wit and sweetness there?
> O! view the change, and drop a tear.

My brother is exceedingly agitated. He will never support this disastrous stroke. Nothing can attract his attention——nothing can allay his grief. But it is the affliction of reason and not of weakness. God grant that it prove not fatal to him.

Letter LII

HARRINGTON to WORTHY

Boston

She is gone—she is dead—she who was the most charming, the most gentle, is gone. You may come—you may desire to behold all that was lovely—but your eyes will not see her.

Yes! I raved—I was distracted—but now I am calm and dispassionate. I am smooth as the surface of a lake. I shall see her again.

When our spirits are disencumbered of this load of mortality, and they wing their flight to the celestial regions, shall we not then know those who were dear to us in this world? Shall we not delight in their society, as we have done in this state of existence? Yes—certainly we shall—we shall find them out in Heaven. There alone is happiness—there shall I meet her—there our love will not be a crime. Let me indulge this thought: it gives a momentary joy to my heart; it removes the dark mist that swims before my eyes. It restores tranquility. But the more I reflect on this thought—the more I long to be there—the more I detest this world and all it contains. I sigh to fly away from it.

Letter LIII

HARRINGTON to WORTHY

Boston

Ingratitude is a predominant principle in the conduct of man. The perfidious [ingrate] who owes to me his reputation and fortune, and with whom I intrusted a great part of my property, has deceived me. This affair will materially retard my business.

To be unfortunate in trade is not worth a sigh—to receive inattention and incivility does not merit a frown. But *ingratitude*—it is this that cuts to the quick. Yet I freely give him my pity; for what man, who considered for a moment the inconsistency of the human heart, would hurl the thunderbolt of indignation at the head of an ingrate? What an important little thing is man! He contrives to overreach his neighbor and mount to the enjoyment of riches, ambition and splendor; but he remembers not the period of enjoyment—that his life is a day and his space a point!

Naturalists inform us of insects whose term of existence is confined to a few hours. What is the business and importance of such a life?

Would not a being, whose *circle of living* is the immensity of ages, inquire with equal propriety: "What is the importance of *man*? What actions can he perform? What happiness can he enjoy, whose insignificant life is circumscribed to seventy years?" In this point of view I behold the tinsel, the vanity and noise of the world, and the little plots and cunning artifices of mankind to cheat and ruin one another.

Ingratitude, then, is constitutional and inseparable from human nature; but it ought not to fill us with surprise, because it is no new discovery. It has ever been invariably the characteristic of man. Is not the page of antiquity distained with the blood of those who ought to have received honor and adoration? Behold the brilliant race of the world's benefactors:

consider their benevolent actions, and regard their ungrateful return. These benefactors—who have been sent from heaven to inform and entertain mankind, to defend the world from the arm of tyranny, and to open the gates of salvation—have been despised, and banished, and poisoned and crucified.

Behold the support of the Roman power, the invincible Belisarius who protected his country from the ravage of the Huns and displayed the Roman eagle in every quarter of the globe! Behold him fall a sacrifice to malice, to faction and ingratitude! Behold him cast out by the country he had defended, and for which he had wasted his life to protect and honor, and left alone to deplore his unfortunate condition when he was old and blind and naked and miserable!

Unfortunate is the man who trusts his happiness to the precarious friendship of the world. I every day become more of a misanthrope and see nothing to increase my desire of living but your esteem and affection. I want advice, but I am too proud to let the world know I am weak enough to be under obligation to any one else.

That you may never want friends or advice is the sincere prayer of [your friend Harrington.]

Letter LIV

HARRINGTON to WORTHY

Boston

All the scenes of my past life return fresh upon my memory. I examine every circumstance as they pass in review before me. I see nothing to cause any disagreeable or unwelcome sensations—no terror upbraids me—no reproaching conscience stings my bosom as I reflect on the actions that are past. With her I expected happiness. I have expected a vain thing, for there is none. She is gone—gone into a far country. She is preparing a place for me—a place of unutterable bliss. But ah! an immeasurable gulf lies between us. Who can tell the distance that

separates us? What labor—what toil—what pain must be endured in traversing the thorny paths that lead to her blessed abode?. And will she not receive me into those happy regions with as much joy—with as sincere a welcome—if I cut short my journey? And will not the Eternal Dispenser of Good pardon the awful deed that frees me from this world of misery—the deed by which I obtrude myself into his divine presence?

Why must I wait the lingering hand of the grisly messenger to summon me to the world above?

Letter LV

HARRINGTON to WORTHY

Boston

Am I a child that I should weep? I have been meditating on the cause of my calamities. Why did my father love Maria—or rather, why did I love their Harriot? Curse on this tyrant custom that dooms such helpless children to oblivion or infamy! Had I known her to have been my sister, my love would have been regular. I should have loved her as a sister: I should have marked her beauty—I should have delighted in protecting it. I should have observed her growing virtues—I should have been happy in cherishing their growth. But alas! she is gone, and I cannot stay. I stand on the threshold of a vast eternity.

Letter LVI

HARRINGTON to WORTHY

Boston

I am determined to quit this life. I feel much easier since my determination. The step must not be taken with rashness. I must be steady—calm—collected. I will endeavor to be so.

Her eager solicitation—the anxiety she always expressed for me. When I think she is no more, it wrings my heart with grief and fills my eyes with tears.

I must go.

The idea chills me—I am frozen with horror—cold damps hang on my trembling body. My soul is filled with a thousand troubled sensations. I must depart—it must be so. My love for thee, O Harriot! is dearer than life. Thou hast first set out—and I am to follow.

Were it possible that I *could live* with her, should I be happy? Would her presence restore peace and tranquility to my disordered mind? Ah no! it never would *here*—it *never* would. I will fly to the place where she is gone. Our love will there be refined—it will be freed from all criminality. I will lay my sorrows before her—and she shall wipe away all tears from my eyes.

When the disembodied spirit flies above—when it leaves behind the senseless clay and wings its flight—it matters not with me what they do with his remains.

Cover his head with a clod or a stone;
It is all one—it is all one!

Letter LVII

HARRINGTON to WORTHY

Boston

The longer I live—and the more I see of the misery of life—the more my desire of living is extinguished. What I formerly esteemed trifles and would not deign to term misfortunes now appear with a formidable aspect. Though I once thought them harmless and innoxious to my peace, they assume new terrors every day. But is not this observation general? It is. It is thus every son of human nature gradually wishes for death, and neglects to seek for and improve those conforts which by diligent search there is a possibility of attaining.

Am I to reason from analogy? I know what has been—the afflictions I have felt. But what is the prospect before me? The path is darkened by mists—

Puzzled in mazes, and perplexed with errors.

Who is there hardy enough to try its difficulties? Is not the view horrible! My pains and anxieties have been severe—those, which, if I live, I shall suffer, may be yet more so. This idea sinks me to despair.

As a thing becomes irksome to us, our detestation is always increased. Whatever object is disagreeable, we pine and sicken until it is moved out of sight. Life growing upon one in this manner—increasing in horrors—with continual apprehension of death—a certainty of surviving every enjoyment, and no prospect of being delivered from suspense—it is intolerable. He will assuredly be tempted to terminate the business with his own hand.

Letter LVIII

WORTHY to HARRINGTON

Belleview

You argue as if your reason were perverted. Let your mind be employed, and time will wear out these gloomy ideas; for it is certainly a truth that *the love of life increases with age.* Your letters, therefore, are predicated on the most erroneous principles.

Remember the story of the old man who had been buried in a dungeon the greater part of his life and who was liberated at an advanced age. He viewed, once more, the light of the sun and the habitations of men. He had come into a new order of beings, but found their manners distasteful. In the midst of the sunshine of the world, he remembered the prison where he had wasted his life; and he sighed to be again immured within its walls.

Such is our passion for life: we love it because we know it, and our attachment becomes the more riveted the longer we are acquainted with it. Our prison grows familiar—we contemplate its horrors. But however gloomy the walls that surround us, there is not one but sets a full value on his dreary existence. There is not one but finds his partiality for his dungeon increase in proportion to the time he hath occupied it. For among the race of human beings confined to this narrow spot, how few are they who are hardy enough to break their prison?

Let us watch over all we do with an eye of scrutiny. The world will not examine the causes that give birth to our actions. They do not weigh the motives of them—they do not consider those things which influence our conduct. But as that conduct is more or less advantageous to society, they deem it madness or wisdom, or folly or prudence. Remember this.

Letter LIX

HARRINGTON to WORTHY

Boston

You are egregiously mistaken, argue as you will. My perceptions are as clear as any one's The burden that is at first heavy and inconvenient galls us as we proceed; it soon becomes intolerable, we sink under its weight and lie gasping in the public way long before night.

As to the world—who strives to please it will be deservedly rewarded. He will reap his labor for his pains. Let it judge of my conduct. I despise its opinion. *Independency of spirits* is my motto—I think for myself.

Letter LX

HARRINGTON to WORTHY

Boston

How vain is the wish that sighs for the enjoyment of worldly happiness. Our imagination dresses up a phantom to impose on our reason: as Pygmalion loved the work of his own hand, so do we fall in love with the offspring of our brain. But our work eludes our embrace; we find no substance in it—and then fall a weeping and complain of disappointment. Miserable reasoners are we all.

Why should I mourn the loss of Harriot any longer? Such is my situation: in the midst of anxiety and distress, I complain of what cannot be remedied. I lament the loss of that which is irretrievable. So on the sea-beat shore, the hopeless maid, unmindful of the storm, bewails her drowned lover.

Letter LXI

WORTHY to HARRINGTON

Belleview

I thank you for your letters, but I wish you had something better for the subject of them. The sad repetition of your feelings and sorrows pains me exceedingly. I promise to be with you soon—perhaps before you can receive this letter.

Whatever concerns my friend most sensibly affects me. You, Harrington, are the friend of my heart, and nothing has so much grieved me as the story of your misfortunes.

It is a maxim well received, and seems to be admitted an article in the moral creed of mankind, "that the enjoyments of life do not compensate the miseries." Since then we are born to suffer, and pain must attend us in all the stages of our journey, let us philosophically welcome our companion. The most eligible plan we can adopt is to be contented in the condition that Providence hath assigned us. Let us trust that our burden will not be heavier than we can bear. When we adopt this plan, and are sensible we have this trust, our lesson is complete. We have learned all—we are arrived to the perfection of sublunary happiness.

Do not think I am preaching to you a mere sermon of morality. Let me impress your mind with the folly of repining, and the blessing of a contented mind.

Let me entreat you not to puzzle your brain with vain speculations. If you are disposed to argue, do not put foolish cases that never existed; take the light of facts and reason from them.

When we are surrounded with the miseries of life—the baseness of false friends—the malice of enemies; when we are enveloped in those anxious fears—the result of too much sensibility: then human nature feels a degree of oppression which, without a manly exertion of reason and this practical philosophy, would

be intolerable. I have heard you mention St. Evremond as a philosopher of this kind. Arm yourself with his prudence and fortitude. He, though in exile—though reduced almost to penury, and laboring under the disadvantages of a bad constitution—lived to be a very old man; he established a course of rational pleasures. For when the mind is employed, we regret the loss of time; we become avaricious of life.

When misfortunes come upon us without these consolations, it is hard, I acknowledge, to buffet the storm. It is then human frailty is most apparent. There is nothing left to hope. Reason is taken from the helm of life. And nature—helpless, debilitated nature—lost to herself and every social duty—splits upon the rocks of despair and suicide. We have seen several examples of this. By exploring and therefore shunning the causes, let us avoid the catastrophe.

The pensive and melancholy will muse over the ordinary accidents of life and swell them, by the power of imagination, to the heaviest calamities. Hence we find a treacherous friend will sensibly affect some men, and a capricious mistress will destroy a real lover. Hence people in misfortune frequently construe the slightest inattention into neglect and insult and deem their best friends false and ungrateful. The sting of ingratitude deeply pierces the heart of sensibility.

The passions and affections which govern mankind are very inconsistent. Men confined to the humble walks of life sigh for the enjoyment of wealth and power, which when obtained become loathsome. The mind unaccustomed to such an easy situation is discontented and longs to be employed in those things in which it was formerly exercised.

The greatest rulers and potentates become unhappy—they wish for the charms of solitude and retirement, which when attained become more irksome than their former condition. Charles the Fifth of Spain resolved to taste the pleasures of a recluse life by abdicating the throne; he soon found his imagination had deceived him and repented of the step he had taken. This lazy life, when compared to the business and grandeur of a court, became tasteless and insipid. "The day," says a historian, "he resigned his crown to his son was the very day in which he repented making his such a present."

It is a great art to learn to be happy in the state in which we are placed. I advise you to mingle in the concerns of your

acquaintances; be cheerful and undisturbed and give yourself not up to those gloomy ideas which tend only to make you more wretched. If such obtrude themselves, avoid being alone. I had rather be a dupe to my imagination than sacrifice an hour's easiness to my sensibility or understanding. Determine to be happy, and you will be so.

God be with you!

Letter LXII

HARRINGTON to WORTHY

Boston

When we seek for diversion in any place, and there is nothing to be found that we wish, it is certainly time to depart.

Tomorrow I go. There is nothing here that can calm the tumult of my soul—I fly from the sight of the human countenance—I fly from the face of day. I fly from books—books that could always cheer me in a melancholy moment are now terrifying. They recall scenes to my recollection that are past—pleasant scenes that I am never more to enjoy. They present pictures of futurity—of gloomy futurity. I just opened a book, and these are the words that I read: "The time of my fading is near, and the blast that shall scatter my leaves. Tomorrow shall the traveler come, he that saw me in my beauty shall come; his eyes will search the field, but they will not find me."

These words pierce me to the quick—they are a dismal prospect of my approaching fate.

Tomorrow I shall go. But ah! whither?

O! my friend, when we find nothing we desire in this world, it is time to depart. To live is a disgrace—to die is a duty.

Letter LXIII

WORTHY to Mrs. HOLMES

Boston

I arrived in town last evening. You desired me to write you a statement of affairs as I should find them here—and of my marriage with the amiable Myra. I promised to obey, but how little do we know of the termination or consequence of the most probable event!

I saw my beloved. Her eyes were yet heavy and smarting with weeping for the death of Harriot—and *this*, once the house of joy and cheerfulness, is turned into the house of mourning. My unfortunate friend had just then fallen into a calm sleep, and it was impossible to see him. It was what I very much desired, but it was the wish of the family that I should desist for the pesent. He had not slept the evening before; he had been heard walking across his chamber all the night, with little intermission, oftentimes talking to himself in a passionate tone of voice.

This melancholy account deeply affected me and I parted from my beloved, praying Heaven to give her consolation and to be the support of my disordered friend.

It is with difficulty I bring myself to the serious and painful employment of being the informer of unwelcome tidings. My heart feels the wound—vainly it tells me my friend is no more. My hand reluctantly traces—my friend, my Harrington, is no more.

Early this morning I was surprised with a visit from a gentleman whom I had formerly seen at Myra's. It was the same neighbor who informed Harrington of his affinity to Harriot. He found a difficulty in his utterance: he told me, with trembling lips, my young friend Harrington was dead. "He has killed

himself," said I. He asked me if I had heard the news—I told him my heart presaged it.

When any uncommon event happens to us, we often have a presentiment of it. The circumstances of his death are these: at midnight the gentleman heard the report of the pistol and went into the house—he found the unhappy youth weltering in his blood—few signs of life remained—the ball had entered his brain—the surgeon came, but in a few hours he was cold. A few friends were requested to attend; and this gentleman had called upon me, by desire of Myra.

It is not possible to describe the distress of the family and connections. I shall leave it to your imagination.

A letter that he had written for me laid unsealed upon the table, and *The Sorrows of Werter* was found lying by its side. I send you the letter—it appears to have been written at intervals and expresses the disorder and agitation of his mind.

Letter LXIV

HARRINGTON to WORTHY

Harriot is dead—and the world to me is a dreary desert. I prepare to leave it. The fatal pistol is charged—it lies on the table by me, ready to perform its duty—but that duty is delayed till I take my last farewell of the best of friends.

Your letter is written with the impetuosity of an honest heart; it expresses great sincerity and tenderness.

I thank you for all your good advice—it comes too late. O Worthy! she is dead—she is gone—never to return, never again to cheer my heart with her smiles and her amiable manners. Her image is always before me—and can I forget her? No! She is continually haunting my mind, impressing the imagination with ideas of excellence. But she is dead—all that delighted me is become torpid—is descended into the cold grave.

```
—  —  —  —  With thee
```
Certain my resolution is to die;
How can I live without thee—how forego
Thy converse sweet, and love so dearly joined,
To live again in these wild woods forlorn?
```
—  —  —  —  —  —  —  —  —
—  —  —  —  —  loss of thee
```
Will never from my heart—no! no!—I feel
The link of nature draw me.
```
—  —  —  —  —  From thy state
```
Mine never shall be parted, bliss or woe.

Thou hast set out on a long journey—but you shall not go alone—I hasten to overtake thee. My resolution is not to be diverted—is not to be shaken—I will not be afraid. I am inexorable.

I have just seen my father—he is dejected—sullen grief is fixed on his brow. He tells me I am very ill. I looked at Myra—she wiped her face with her handkerchief—perhaps they did not imagine this was the last time they were to behold me.

She mentioned the name of Worthy, but my thoughts were differently engaged. She repeated your name, but I took no heed of it. Take her, my Worthy—Myra is a good girl—take her—comfort her. Let not my departure interrupt your happiness; perhaps it may for a short time. When the grass is grown over my grave, lead her to it in your pensive walks. Point to the spot where my ashes are deposited. Drop one tear on the remembrance of a friend, of a brother—but I cannot allow you to be grieved—grieve for me! Wretch that I am—why do I delay?

—I wish I could be buried by the side of her; then should the passenger who knows the history of our unfortunate loves say: "Here lies Harrington and his Harriot—in their lives they loved, but were unhappy—in death they sleep undivided." Guardian spirits will protect the tomb which conceals her body —the body where every virtue delighted to inhabit.

Do not judge too rashly of my conduct—let me pray you to be candid. I have taken advantage of a quiet moment and written an epitaph. If my body were laid by hers, the inscription would be pertinent. Let no one concerned be offended at the moral I have chosen to draw from our unfortunate story.

—My heart sinks within me—the instrument of death is before me—farewell! farewell! My soul sighs to be freed from its confinement. Eternal Father! accept my spirit. Let the tears of sorrow blot out my guilt from the book of thy wrath.

Letter LXV

WORTHY to Mrs. HOLMES

Boston

We have surmounted the performance of the last scene of our tragedy, with less difficulty and distress than I imagined. Great numbers crowded to see the body of poor Harrington; they were impressed with various emotions, for their sympathizing sorrow could not be concealed. Indeed a man without sensibility exhibits no sign of a soul. I was struck with admiration at the observations of the populace, and the justness of the character they drew of the deceased. "Alas!" said one, "poor youth, thou art gone. Thou wast a promising genius, of violent passions; thou wast possessed of a too nice sensibility, and a dread of shame. It is only such an one who would take the trouble to kill himself. Ah! poor well-natured, warm-hearted, hot-headed youth—how my heart bleeds for you! We consider thee as the dupe of nature, and the sacrifice of seduction." The old father hears this, and becomes overwhelmed with shame and sorrow.

The jury which sat upon the body of our friend, after mature consideration, brought in their verdict suicide. The rigor of the law was not executed; the body was privately taken away, and I saw it deposited by the side of his faithful Harriot.

I send you enclosed a copy of the Monumental Inscription, as it was written by Harrington. I found it with many loose papers. It contains the story of our unfortunate friends, and a profitable moral is deduced from it.

Though a few weeks begin to spread a calm over our passions,

yet the recollection of our misfortunes will sometimes cause a momentary agitation, as the ocean retains its swell after the storm subsides.

Monumental Inscription

Thou who shalt wander over these humble plains,
Where one kind grave their hapless dust contains,
O pass not on—if merit claim a tear.
Or dying virtue cause a sigh sincere.
Here rest their heads, consigned to parent earth,
Who to one common father owed their birth,
Unknown this union. Nature still presides,
And sympathy unites, whom Fate divides.
They see—they love—but heaven their passion tries,
Their *love* sustains it, but their *mortal* dies.
Stranger! contemplate well before you part
And take this serious counsel to thy heart:
Does some fair female of unspotted fame,
Salute thee, smiling, with a father's name,
Bid her detest the fell seducer's wiles,
Who smiles to win—and murders as he smiles.
If ever wandering near this dark recess,
Where guardian spirits round the ether press,
Where, on their urn, celestial care descends,
Two lovers come, whom fair success attends:
"Over the pale marble shall they join their heads,
And drink the falling tears each other sheds,
Then sadly say, with mutual pity moved,
O! may we never love as these have loved."

THE END

THE

COQUETTE

OR, THE

HISTORY OF ELIZA WHARTON

A

NOVEL

FOUNDED ON FACT

THE COQUETTE

OR

THE HISTORY OF ELIZA WHARTON

LETTER I

To Miss Lucy Freeman.

New Haven

An unusual sensation possesses my breast—a sensation which I once thought could never pervade it on any occasion whatever. It is *pleasure*, pleasure, my dear Lucy, on leaving my paternal roof. Could you have believed that the darling child of an indulgent and dearly-beloved mother would feel a gleam of joy at leaving her? But so it is. The melancholy, the gloom, the condolence which surrounded me for a month after the death of Mr. Haly had depressed my spirits and palled every enjoyment of life. Mr. Haly was a man of worth—a man of real and substantial merit. He is, therefore, deeply and justly regretted by *his* friends. He was chosen to be a future guardian and companion for me and was, therefore, beloved by *mine*. As their choice, as a good man, and a faithful friend, I esteemed him; but no one acquainted with the disparity of our tempers and dispositions, our views and designs, can suppose my heart much engaged in the alliance. Both nature and education had instilled into my mind an implicit obedience to the will and desires of my parents. To them, of course, I sacrificed my fancy in this affair, determined that my reason should concur with theirs and on that to risk my future happiness. I was the more encouraged, as I saw from our first acquaintance his declining health and expected that the event would prove as it has. Think not, however, that I rejoice in his death. No, far be it from me; for though I believe that I never felt the passion of love for Mr. Haly, yet a

habit of conversing with him, of hearing daily the most virtuous, tender, and affectionate sentiments from his lips, inspired emotions of the sincerest friendship and esteem.

He is gone. His fate is unalterably and, I trust, happily fixed. He lived the life, and died the death, of the righteous. O that my last end may be like his! This event will, I hope, make a suitable and abiding impression upon my mind, teach me the fading nature of all sublunary enjoyments and the little dependence which is to be placed on earthly felicity. Whose situation was more agreeable, whose prospects more flattering, than Mr. Haly's? Social, domestic, and connubial joys were fondly anticipated, and friends and fortune seemed ready to crown every wish; yet, animated by still brighter hopes, he cheerfully bade them all adieu. In conversation with me but a few days before his exit, "There is," said he, "but one link in the chain of life undissevered; that, my dear Eliza, is my attachment to you. But God is wise and good in all his ways; and in this, as in all other respects, I would cheerfully say, His will be done."

You, my friend, were witness to the concluding scene; and, therefore, I need not describe it.

I shall only add on the subject that if I have wisdom and prudence to follow his advice and example, if his prayers for my temporal and eternal welfare be heard and answered, I shall be happy indeed.

The disposition of mind which I now feel I wish to cultivate. Calm, placid, and serene, thoughtful of my duty, and benevolent to all around me, I wish for no other connection than that of friendship.

This letter is all an egotism. I have even neglected to mention the respectable and happy friends with whom I reside, but I will do it in my next. Write soon and often; and believe me sincerely yours,

Eliza Wharton.

LETTER II

To Miss Lucy Freeman.

New Haven

Time, which effaces every occasional impression, I find gradually dispelling the pleasing pensiveness which the melancholy event, the subject of my last letter, had diffused over my mind. Naturally cheerful, volatile, and unreflecting, the opposite disposition I have found to contain sources of enjoyment which I was before unconscious of possessing.

My friends here are the picture of conjugal felicity. The situation is delightful—the visiting parties perfectly agreeable. Everything tends to facilitate the return of my accustomed vivacity. I have written to my mother and received an answer. She praises my fortitude and admires the philosophy which I have exerted under what she calls my heavy bereavement. Poor woman! she little thinks that my heart was untouched; and when that is unaffected, other sentiments and passions make but a transient impression. I have been, for a month or two, excluded from the gay world and, indeed, fancied myself soaring above it. It is now that I begin to descend and find my natural propensity for mixing in the busy scenes and active pleasures of life returning. I have received your letter—your moral lecture rather; and be assured, my dear, your monitorial lessons and advice shall be attended to. I believe I shall never again resume those airs which you term *coquettish*, but which I think deserve a softer appellation as they proceed from an innocent heart and are the effusions of a youthful and cheerful mind. We are all invited to spend the day tomorrow at Colonel Farington's, who has an elegant seat in this neighborhood. Both he and his lady are strangers to me; but the friends by whom I am introduced will procure me a welcome reception. Adieu.

Eliza Wharton.

LETTER III

To Miss Lucy Freeman.

New Haven

Is it time for me to talk again of conquests? Or must I only enjoy them in silence? I must write to you the impulses of my mind, or I must not write at all. You are not so morose as to wish me to become a nun, would our country and religion allow it. I ventured yesterday to throw aside the habiliments of mourning and to array myself in those more adapted to my taste. We arrived at Colonel Farington's about one o'clock. The colonel handed me out of the carriage and introduced me to a large company assembled in the hall.

My name was pronounced with an *emphasis*, and I was received with the most flattering tokens of respect. When we were summoned to dinner, a young gentleman in a clerical dress offered me his hand and led me to a table furnished with an elegant and sumptuous repast, with more gallantry and address than commonly fall to the share of students. He sat opposite me at table; and whenever I raised my eye, it caught his. The ease and politeness of his manners, with his particular attention to me, raised my curiosity and induced me to ask Mrs. Layton who he was. She told me that his name was Boyer; he was descended from a worthy family; he had passed with honor and applause through the university where he was educated; he had since studied divinity with success and now had a call to settle as a minister in one of the first parishes in a neighboring state.

The gates of a spacious garden were thrown open at this instant, and I accepted with avidity an invitation to walk in it. Mirth and hilarity prevailed; and the moments fled on downy wings while we traced the beauties of art and nature, so liberally displayed and so happily blended in this delightful retreat. An enthusiastic admirer of scenes like these, I had rambled some way from the company, when I was followed by Mrs. Layton to offer her condolence on the supposed loss which I had sustained in the death of Mr. Haly. My heart rose against the woman, so ignorant of human nature as to think such conversation accept-

able at such a time. I made her little reply and waved the subject, though I could not immediately dispel the gloom which it excited.

The absurdity of a custom authorizing people at a first interview to revive the idea of griefs which time has lulled, perhaps obliterated, is intolerable. To have our enjoyments arrested by the empty compliments of unthinking persons for no other reason than a compliance with fashion is to be treated in a manner which the laws of humanity forbid.

We were soon joined by the gentlemen, who each selected his partner; and the walk was prolonged.

Mr. Boyer offered me his arm, which I gladly accepted, happy to be relieved from the impertinence of my female companion. We returned to tea; after which the ladies sang and played by turns on the pianoforte, while some of the gentlemen accompanied with the flute, the clarinet, and the violin, forming in the whole a very decent concert. An elegant supper, and half an hour's conversation after it, closed the evening; then we returned home, delighted with our entertainment, and pleased with ourselves and each other. My imagination is so impressed with the festive scenes of the day that Morpheus waves his ebon wand in vain. The evening is fine beyond the power of description; all nature is serene and harmonious, in perfect unison with my present disposition of mind. I have been taking a retrospect of my past life and, a few juvenile follies excepted which I trust the recording angel has blotted out with a tear of charity, find an approving conscience and a heart at ease. Fortune, indeed, has not been very liberal of her gifts to me; but I presume on a large stock in the bank of friendship which, united with health and innocence, gives me some pleasing anticipations of future felicity. Whatever my fate may be, I shall always continue your

Eliza Wharton.

LETTER IV

To Mr. Selby.

New Haven

You ask me, my friend, whether I am in pursuit of truth or a lady. I answer, Both. I hope and trust they are united and really expect to find truth and the virtues and the graces besides, in a fair form. If you mean by the first part of your question whether I am searching into the sublimer doctrines of religion—to these I would by no means be inattentive; but, to be honest, my studies of that kind have been very much interrupted of late. The respectable circle of acquaintances with which I am honored here has rendered my visits very frequent and numerous. In one of these I was introduced to Miss Eliza Wharton—a young lady whose elegant person, accomplished mind, and polished manners have been much celebrated. Her fame has often reached me; but, as the Queen of Sheba said to Solomon, the half was not told me. You will think that I talk in the style of a lover. I confess it; nor am I ashamed to rank myself among the professed admirers of this lovely fair one. I am in no danger, however, of becoming an enthusiastic devotee. No, I mean I act upon just and rational principles. Expecting soon to settle in an eligible situation, if such a companion as I am persuaded she will make me may fall to my lot, I shall deem myself as happy as this state of imperfection will admit. She is now resident at General Richman's. The general and his lady are her particular friends; they are warm in her praises. They tell me, however, that she is naturally of a gay disposition. No matter for that; it is an agreeable quality, where there is discretion sufficient for its regulation. A cheerful friend, much more a cheerful wife, is peculiarly necessary to a person of a studious and sedentary life. They dispel the gloom of retirement and exhilarate the spirits depressed by intense application. She was formerly addressed by the late Mr. Haly of Boston. He was not, it seems, the man of her choice; but her parents were extremely partial to him and wished the connection to take place. She, like a dutiful child, sacrificed her own inclination to their pleasure so far as to acquiesce in his visits. This she more easily accomplished as his

health, which declined from their first acquaintance, led her to suppose, as the event has proved, that he would not live to enter into any lasting engagements. Her father, who died some months before him, invited him to reside at his house for the benefit of a change of air, agreeably to the advice of his physicians. She attended him during his last illness with all the care and assiduity of a nurse and with all the sympathizing tenderness of a sister.

I have had several opportunities of conversing with her. She discovers an elevated mind, a ready apprehension, and an accurate knowledge of the various subjects which have been brought into view. I have not yet introduced the favorite subject of my heart. Indeed, she seems studiously to avoid noticing any expression which leads towards it; but she must hear it soon. I am sure of the favor and interest of the friends with whom she resides. They have promised to speak previously in my behalf. I am to call, as if accidentally, this afternoon just as they are to ride abroad. They are to refer me to Miss Wharton for entertainment till their return. What a delightful opportunity for my purpose! I am counting the hours—nay, the very moments. Adieu. You shall soon again hear from your most obedient

J. Boyer.

LETTER V

To Miss Lucy Freeman.

New Haven

These bewitching charms of mine have a tendency to keep my mind in a state of perturbation. I am so pestered with these admirers! Not that I am so very handsome neither; I don't know how it is, I am certainly very much the taste of the other sex. Followed, flattered, and caressed, I have cards and compliments in profusion. But I must try to be serious; for I have, alas! one serious lover. As I promised you to be particular in my writing, I suppose I must proceed methodically. Yesterday we had a party to dine. Mr. Boyer was of the number. His attention was immediately engrossed; and I soon perceived that every word, every action, and every look was studied to gain my approba-

tion. As he sat next me at dinner, his assiduity and politeness were pleasing; and as we walked together afterwards, his conversation was improving. Mine was sentimental and sedate—perfectly adapted to the taste of my gallant. Nothing, however, was said particularly expressive of his apparent wishes. I studiously avoided every kind of discourse which might lead to this topic. I wish not for a declaration from anyone, especially from one whom I could not repulse and do not intend to encourage at present. His conversation, so similar to what I had often heard from a similar character, brought a deceased friend to mind and rendered me somewhat pensive. I retired directly after supper. Mr. Boyer had just taken leave.

Mrs. Richman came into my chamber as she was passing to her own. "Excuse my intrusion, Eliza," said she. "I thought I would just step in and ask you if you have passed a pleasant day."

"Perfectly so, madam; and I have now retired to protract the enjoyment by recollection." "What, my dear, is your opinion of our favorite, Mr. Boyer?" "Declaring him your favorite, madam, is sufficient to render me partial to him; but to be frank, independent of that, I think him an agreeable man." "Your heart, I presume, is now free." "Yes, and I hope it will long remain so." "Your friends, my dear, solicitous for your welfare, wish to see you suitably and agreeably connected." "I hope my friends will never again interpose in my concerns of that nature. You, madam, who have ever known my heart, are sensible that, had the Almighty spared life in a certain instance, I must have sacrificed my own happiness or incurred their censure. I am young, gay, volatile. A melancholy event has lately extricated me from those shackles which parental authority had imposed on my mind. Let me then enjoy that freedom which I so highly prize. Let me have the opportunity, unbiased by opinion, to gratify my natural disposition in a participation of those pleasures which youth and innocence afford." "Of such pleasures, no one, my dear, would wish to deprive you; but beware, Eliza! Though strewed with flowers, when contemplated by your lively imagination, it is after all a slippery, thorny path. The round of fashionable dissipation is dangerous. A phantom is often pursued, which leaves its deluded votary the real form of wretchedness." She spoke with an emphasis and, taking up her candle, wished me a good night. I had not power to return the com-

pliment. Something seemingly prophetic in her looks and expressions cast a momentary gloom upon my mind, but I despise those contracted ideas which confine virtue to a cell. I have no notion of becoming a recluse. Mrs. Richman has ever been a beloved friend of mine; yet I always thought her rather prudish. Adieu.

<div align="right">Eliza Wharton.</div>

LETTER VI

To Miss Lucy Freeman.

<div align="right">New Haven</div>

I had scarcely seated myself at the breakfast table this morning when a servant entered with a card of invitation from Major Sanford, requesting the happiness of my hand this evening at a ball given by Mr. Atkins, about three miles from this. I showed the billet to Mrs. Richman, saying, "I have not much acquaintance with this gentleman, madam; but I suppose his character sufficiently respectable to warrant an affirmative answer." "He is a gay man, my dear, to say no more; and such are the companions we wish when we join a party avowedly formed for pleasure." I then stepped into my apartment, wrote an answer, and dispatched the servant. When I returned to the parlor, something disapprobating appeared in the countenances of both my friends. I endeavored, without seeming to observe, to dissipate it by chitchat; but they were better pleased with each other than with me and, soon rising, walked into the garden and left me to amuse myself alone. My eyes followed them through the window. "Happy pair!" said I. "Should it ever be my fate to wear the hymeneal chain, may I be thus united! The purest and most ardent affection, the greatest consonance of taste and disposition, and the most congenial virtue and wishes distinguish this lovely couple. Health and wealth, with every attendant blessing, preside over their favored dwelling and shed their benign influence without alloy." The consciousness of exciting their displeasure gave me pain, but I consoled myself with the idea that it was ill-founded.

"They should consider," said I, "that they have no satis-

faction to look for beyond each other; there every enjoyment is centered; but I am a poor solitary being who need some amusement beyond what I can supply myself. The mind, after being confined at home for a while, sends the imagination abroad in quest of new treasures; and the body may as well accompany it, for aught I can see."

General Richman and lady have ever appeared solicitous to promote my happiness since I have resided with them. They have urged my acceptance of invitations to join parties though they have not been much themselves of late, as Mrs. Richman's present circumstances render her fond of retirement. What reason can be assigned for their apparent reluctance to this evening's entertainment is to me incomprehensible; but I shall apply the chemical powers of friendship and extract the secret from Mrs. Richman tomorrow, if not before. Adieu. I am now summoned to dinner, and after that I shall be engaged in preparation till the wished-for hour of hilarity and mirth engrosses every faculty of your

<div align="right">Eliza Wharton.</div>

LETTER VII

To Mr. Selby.

<div align="right">New Haven</div>

Divines need not declaim, nor philosophers expatiate, on the disappointments of human life. Are they not legibly written on every page of our existence? Are they not predominantly prevalent over every period of our lives?

When I closed my last letter to you, my heart exulted in the pleasing anticipation of promised bliss; my wishes danced on the light breezes of hope; and my imagination dared to arrest the attention of, and even claim a return of affection from, the lovely Eliza Wharton. But imagination only it has proved, and that dashed with the bitter ranklings of jealousy and suspicion.

But to resume my narrative. I reached the mansion of my friend about four. I was disagreeably struck with the appearance of a carriage at the door, as it raised an idea of company which might frustrate my plan; but still more disagreeable were my

sensations when, on entering the parlor, I found Major Sanford evidently in a waiting posture. I was very politely received; and when Eliza entered the room with a brilliance of appearance and gaiety of manner which I had never before connected with her character, I rose, as did Major Sanford, who offered his hand and led her to a chair. I forgot to sit down again but stood transfixed by the pangs of disappointment. Miss Wharton appeared somewhat confused but, soon resuming her vivacity, desired me to be seated, inquired after my health, and made some commonplace remarks on the weather; then, apologizing for leaving me she gave her hand again to Major Sanford, who had previously risen and reminded her that the time and their engagements made it necessary to leave the good company; which, indeed, they both appeared very willing to do. General Richman and lady took every method in their power to remove my chagrin and atone for the absence of my fair one; but ill did they succeed. They told me that Miss Wharton had not the most distant idea of my visiting there this afternoon, much less of the design of my visit; that for some months together she had been lately confined by the sickness of Mr. Haly, whom she attended during the whole of his last illness; that this confinement had eventually increased her desire of indulging her natural disposition for gaiety. She had, however, they said, an excellent heart and reflecting mind, a great share of sensibility, and a temper peculiarly formed for the enjoyments of social life. "But this gentleman, madam, who is her gallant this evening—is his character unexceptionable? Will a lady of delicacy associate with an immoral, not to say profligate, man?" "The rank and fortune of Major Sanford," said Mrs. Richman, "procure him respect; his specious manners render him acceptable in public company, but I must own that he is not the person with whom I wish my cousin to be connected even for a moment. She never consulted me so little on any subject as that of his card this morning. Before I had time to object, she dismissed the servant; and I forbore to destroy her expected happiness by acquainting her with my disapprobation of her partner. Her omission was not design; it was juvenile indiscretion. We must, my dear sir," continued she, "look with a candid eye on such eccentricities. Faults, not foibles, require the severity of censure." "Far, madam, be it from me to censure any conduct which as yet I have observed in Miss Wharton; she has too great an interest in my heart to admit of that."

We now went into more general conversation. Tea was served, and I soon after took leave. General Richman, however, insisted on my dining with him on Thursday, which I promised. And here I am again over head and ears in the hypo—a disease, you will say, peculiar to students. I believe it is peculiar to lovers; and with that class I must now rank myself, though I did not know, until this evening, that I was so much engaged as I find I really am. I knew, indeed, that I was extremely pleased with this amiable girl; that I was interested in her favor; that I was happier in her company than anywhere else; with innumerable other circumstances, which would have told me the truth had I examined them. But be that as it may, I hope and trust that I am, and ever shall be, a reasonable creature and will not suffer my judgment to be misled by the operations of a blind passion.

I shall now lay aside this subject; endeavor to divest even my imagination of the charmer; and return, until Thursday, to the contemplation of those truths and duties which have a happy tendency to calm the jarring elements which compose our mortal frame. Adieu.

<div align="right">J. Boyer.</div>

LETTER VIII

To Mr. Charles Deighton.

<div align="right">New Haven</div>

We had an elegant ball last night, Charles; and what is still more to the taste of your old friend, I had an elegant partner: one exactly calculated to please my fancy—gay, volatile, apparently thoughtless of everything but present enjoyment. It was Miss Eliza Wharton—a young lady whose agreeable person, polished manners, and refined talents have rendered her the toast of the country around for these two years; though for half that time she has had a clerical lover imposed on her by her friends; for I am told it was not agreeable to her inclination. By this same clerical lover of hers she was for several months confined as a nurse. But his death has happily relieved her; and she now returns to the world with redoubled luster. At present she is a visitor to Mrs. Richman, who is a relation. I first saw her on a

party of pleasure at Mr. Frazier's, where we walked, talked, sang, and danced together. I thought her cousin watched her with a jealous eye; for she is, you must know, a prude; and immaculate—more so than you or I—must be the man who claims admission to her society. But I fancy this young lady is a coquette; and if so, I shall avenge my sex by retaliating the mischiefs she meditates against us. Not that I have any ill designs, but only to play off her own artillery by using a little unmeaning gallantry. And let her beware of the consequences. A young clergyman came in at General Richman's yesterday while I was waiting for Eliza. He was much more cordially received by the general and his lady than was your humble servant; but I lay that up.

When she entered the room, an air of mutual embarrassment was evident. The lady recovered her assurance much more easily than the gentleman. I am just going to ride and shall make it in my way to call and inquire after the health of my dulcinea. Therefore, adieu for the present.

<div align="right">Peter Sanford.</div>

LETTER IX

To Miss Lucy Freeman.

<div align="right">New Haven</div>

I am not so happy today in the recollection of last evening's entertainment as I was in the enjoyment.

The explanation which I promised you from Mrs. Richman yesterday I could not obtain. When I went down to dinner, some friends of General Richman's had accidentally dropped in, which precluded all particular conversation. I retired soon to dress and saw Mrs. Richman no more till I was informed that Major Sanford waited for me. But I was surprised, on going into the parlor, to find Mr. Boyer there. I blushed and stammered, but I know not why; for certain I am that I neither love nor fear the good man yet, whatever I may do some future day. I would not be understood that I do not respect and esteem him, for I do both. But these are calm passions, which soothe rather than agitate the mind. It was not the consciousness of any

impropriety of conduct, for I was far from feeling any. The entertainment for which I was prepared was such as virtue would not disapprove; and my gallant was a man of fortune, fashion, and, for aught I knew, of unblemished character.

But Mr. Boyer was much more disconcerted than myself. Indeed, he did not recover his philosophy while I stayed. I believe, by some hints I have received since, that he had some particular views in which he was disappointed.

Our ball had every charm which could render a ball delightful. My partner was all ease, politeness, and attention; and your friend was as much flattered and caressed as vanity itself could wish. We returned to General Richman's about two. Major Sanford asked leave to call and inquire after my health this morning, and I am now expecting him. I rose to breakfast. The late hour of retiring to rest had not depressed, but rather exhilarated, my spirits. My friends were waiting for me in their parlor. They received me sociably, inquired after my health, my last evening's entertainment, the company, &c.; when, after a little pause, Mrs. Richman said, "And how do you like Major Sanford, Eliza?" "Very well indeed, madam; I think him a finished gentleman. Will you, who are a connoisseur, allow him that title?" "No, my dear; in my opinion he falls far below it, since he is deficient in one of the great essentials of the character; and that is *virtue*." "I am surprised," said I; "but how has he incurred so severe a censure?" "By being a professed libertine; by having but too successfully practised the arts of seduction; by triumphing in the destruction of innocence and the peace of families." "O, why was I not informed of this before? But perhaps these are old affairs—the effects of juvenile folly—crimes of which he may have repented and which charity ought to obliterate." "No, my dear, they are recent facts—facts which he dares not deny—facts for which he ought to be banished from all virtuous society. I should have intimated this to you before; but your precipitate acceptance of his invitation deprived me of an opportunity until it was too late to prevent your going with him; and we thought it best to protract your enjoyment as long as possible, not doubting but your virtue and delicacy would, in future, guard you against the like deception."

"Must I, then, become an avowed prude at once and refuse him admission if he call in compliance with the customary forms?" "By no means. I am sensible that even the false maxims

of the world must be complied with in a degree. But a man of Major Sanford's art can easily distinguish between a forbidding and an encouraging reception. The former may, in this case, be given without any breach of the rules of politeness." Astonished and mortified, I knew not what further to say. I had been so pleased with the man that I wished to plead in his favor; but virtue and prudence forbade. I therefore rose and retired. He is this moment, I am told, below stairs; so I must bid.you adieu until the next post.

<div align="right">Eliza Wharton.</div>

LETTER X

To Miss Lucy Freeman.

<div align="right">New Haven</div>

Upon closing my last letter, I walked down and found Major Sanford alone. He met me at the door of the parlor and, taking my hand with an air of affectionate tenderness, led me to a seat and took one beside me. I believe the gloom of suspicion had not entirely forsaken my brow. He appeared, however, not to notice it; but, after the compliments of the day had passed, he entered into an easy and agreeable conversation on the pleasures of society—a conversation perfectly adapted to my taste and calculated to dissipate my chagrin and pass the time imperceptibly. He inquired the place of my native abode; and, having informed him, he said he had thoughts of purchasing the seat of Captain Pribble in that neighborhood for his residence; and could he be assured of my society and friendship, his resolution would be fixed. I answered his compliment only by a slight bow. He took leave, and I retired to dress for the day, being engaged to accompany my cousin to dine at Mr. Lawrence's—a gentleman of fortune and fashion in this vicinity. Mr. Lawrence has but one daughter, heiress to a large estate, with an agreeable form, but a countenance which to me indicates not much soul. I was surprised in the afternoon to see Major Sanford alight at the gate. He entered with the familiarity of an old acquaintance and, after accosting each of the company, told me, with a low bow, that he did not expect the happiness of seeing me again so soon.

I received his compliment with a conscious awkwardness. Mrs. Richman's morning lecture still rang in my head: and her watchful eye now traced every turn of mine and every action of the Major's. Indeed, his assisuity was painful to me; yet I found it impossible to disengage myself a moment from him, till the close of the day brought our carriage to the door; then he handed me in and, pressing my hand to his lips, retired.

What shall I say about this extraordinary man? Shall I own to you, my friend, that he is pleasing to me? His person, his manners, his situation: all combine to charm my fancy and, to my lively imagination, strew the path of life with flowers. What a pity, my dear Lucy, that the graces and virtues are not oftener united! They must, however, meet in the man of my choice; and till I find such a one, I shall continue to subscribe my name

Eliza Wharton.

LETTER XI

To Mr. Charles Deighton.

New Haven

Well, Charles, I have been maneuvering today a little revengefully. That, you will say, is out of character. So baleful a passion does not easily find admission among those softer ones which you well know I cherish. However, I am a mere Proteus and can assume any shape that will best answer my purpose.

I called this afternoon, as I told you I intended, at General Richman's. I waited some time in the parlor alone before Eliza appeared: and when she did appear, the distant reserve of her manners and the pensiveness of her countenance convinced me that she had been vexed, and I doubted not but Peter Sanford was the occasion. Her wise cousin, I could have sworn, had been giving her a detail of the vices of her gallant and warning her against the dangers of associating with him in future. Notwithstanding, I took no notice of any alteration in her behavior, but entered with the utmost facetiousness into a conversation which I thought most to her taste. By degrees she assumed her usual vivacity; cheerfulness and good humor again animated her countenance. I tarried as long as decency would admit. She having

intimated that they were to dine at my friend Lawrence's, I caught at this information and determined to follow them and tease the jealous Mrs. Richman by playing off all the gallantry I was master of in her presence.

I went and succeeded to the utmost of my wishes—as I read in the vexation visible in the one, and the ease and attention displayed by the other. I believe, too, that I have charmed the eye at least of the amiable Eliza. Indeed, Charles, she is a fine girl. I think it would hurt my conscience to wound her mind or reputation. Were I disposed to marry, I am persuaded she would make an excellent wife; but that, you know, is no part of my plan, so long as I can keep out of the noose. Whenever I do submit to be shackled, it must be from a necessity of mending my fortune. This girl would be far from doing that. However, I am pleased with her acquaintance and mean not to abuse her credulity and good nature, if I can help it.

<div align="right">Peter Sanford.</div>

LETTER XII

To Miss Lucy Freeman.

<div align="right">New Haven</div>

The heart of your friend is again besieged. Whether it will surrender to the assailants or not, I am unable at present to determine. Sometimes I think of becoming a predestinarian and submit implicitly to fate, without any exercise of free will; but, as mine seems to be a wayward one, I would counteract the operations of it, if possible.

Mrs. Richman told me this morning that she hoped I should be as agreeably entertained this afternoon as I had been the preceding; that she expected Mr. Boyer to dine and take tea and doubted not but he would be as attentive and sincere to me, if not as gay and polite, as the gentleman who obtruded his civilities yesterday. I replied that I had no reason to doubt the sincerity of the one or the other, having never put them to the test; nor did I imagine I ever should. "Your friends, Eliza," said she, "would be very happy to see you united to a man of Mr. Boyer's worth, and so agreeably settled as he has a prospect of

being." "I hope," said I, "that my friends are not so weary of my company as to wish to dispose of me. I am too happy in my present connections to quit them for new ones. Marriage is the tomb of friendship. It appears to me a very selfish state. Why do people in general, as soon as they are married, center all their cares, their concerns, and pleasures in their own families? Former acquaintances are neglected or forgotten; the tenderest ties between friends are weakened or dissolved; and benevolence itself moves in a very limited sphere." "It is the glory of the marriage state," she rejoined, "to refine by circumscribing our enjoyments. Here we can repose in safety.

> The friendships of the world are oft
> Confed'racies in vice, or leagues in pleasure:
> Ours has the purest virtue for its basis;
> And such a friendship ends not but with life.

True, we cannot always pay that attention to former associates which we may wish; but the little community which we superintend is quite as important an object, and certainly renders us more beneficial to the public. True benevolence, though it may change its objects, is not limited by time or place. Its effects are the same and, aided by a second self, are rendered more diffusive and salutary."

Some pleasantry passed, and we retired to dress. When summoned to dinner, I found Mr. Boyer below. If what is sometimes said be true, that love is diffident, reserved, and unassuming, this man must be tinctured with it. These symptoms were visible in his deportment when I entered the room. However, he soon recovered himself, and the conversation took a general turn. The festive board was crowned with sociability, and we found in reality "the feast of reason and the flow of soul." After we rose from table, a walk in the garden was proposed—an amusement we are all peculiarly fond of. Mr. Boyer offered me his arm. When at a sufficient distance from our company, he begged leave to congratulate himself on having an opportunity, which he had ardently desired for some time, of declaring to me his attachment and of soliciting an interest in my favor; or, if he might be allowed the term, affection. I replied, "That, sir, is indeed laying claim to an important interest. I believe you must substitute some more indifferent epithet for the present." "Well, then," said he, "if it must be so, let it

be esteem or friendship." "Indeed, sir," said I, "you are entitled to them both. Merit has always a share in that bank; and I know of none who has a larger claim on that score than Mr. Boyer." I suppose my manner was hardly serious enough for what he considered a weighty cause. He was a little disconcerted but, soon regaining his presence of mind, entreated me with an air of earnestness to encourage his suit, to admit his adresses, and, if possible, to reward his love. I told him that this was rather a sudden affair to me and that I could not answer him without consideration. "Well, then," said he, "take what time you think proper; only relieve my suspense as soon as may be. Shall I visit you again tomorrow?" "O, not so soon," said I; "next Monday, I believe, will be early enough. I will endeavor to be at home." He thanked me even for that favor, recommended himself once more to my kindness; we walked towards the company, returned with them to the house, and he soon took leave. I immediately retired to write this letter, which I shall close without a single observation on the subject until I know your opinion.

<div align="right">Eliza Wharton.</div>

LETTER XIII

To Miss Eliza Wharton.

<div align="right">Hartford</div>

And so you wish to have my opinion before you know the result of your own.

This is playing a little too much with my patience; but, however, I will gratify you this once, in hopes that my epistle may have a good effect. You will ask, perhaps, whether I would influence your judgment. I answer: No, provided you will exercise it yourself; but I am a little apprehensive that your fancy will mislead you. Methinks I can gather from your letters a predilection for this Major Sanford. But he is a rake, my dear friend; and can a lady of your delicacy and refinement think of forming a connection with a man of that character? I hope not; nay, I am confident you do not. You mean only to exhibit a few more girlish airs before you turn matron; but I am persuaded, if you wish to lead down the dance of life with regularity, you will not find a more excellent partner than Mr. Boyer.

Whatever you can reasonably expect in a lover, husband, or friend, you may perceive to be united in this worthy man. His taste is undebauched, his manners not vitiated, his morals uncorrupted. His situation in life is, perhaps, as elevated as you have a right to claim. Forgive my plainness, Eliza. It is the task of friendship, sometimes, to tell disagreeable truths. I know your ambition is to make a distinguished figure in the first class of polished society, to shine in the gay circle of fashionable amusements, and to bear off the palm amidst the votaries of pleasure. But these are fading honors, unsatisfactory enjoyments, incapable of gratifying those immortal principles of reason and religion which have been implanted in your mind by nature, assiduously cultivated by the best of parents, and exerted, I trust, by yourself. Let me advise you, then, in conducting this affair—an affair big, perhaps, with your future fate—to lay aside those coquettish airs which you sometimes put on; and remember that you are not dealing with a fop, who will take advantage of every concession, but with a man of sense and honor, who will properly estimate your condescension and frankness. Act then with that modest freedom, that dignified unreserve, which bespeak conscious rectitude and sincerity of heart.

I shall be extremely anxious to hear the process and progress of this business. Relieve my impatience as soon as possible, and believe me yours with undissembled affection.

<div style="text-align: right">Lucy Freeman.</div>

LETTER XIV

To Miss Lucy Freeman.

<div style="text-align: right">New Haven</div>

I have received, and read again and again, your friendly epistle. My reason and judgment entirely coincide with your opinion; but my fancy claims some share in the decision, and I cannot yet tell which will preponderate. This was the day fixed for deciding Mr. Boyer's cause. My friends here gave me a long dissertation on his merits. Your letter, likewise, had its weight; and I was candidly summoning up the *pros* and *cons* in the garden, whither I had walked (General Richman and lady having

rode out), when I was informed that he was waiting in the
parlor. I went immediately in (a good symptom, you will say)
and received him very graciously. After the first compliments
were over, he seemed eager to improve the opportunity to enter
directly on the subject of his present visit. It is needless for me
to recite to you, who have long been acquainted with the whole
process of courtship, the declarations, propositions, protesta-
tions, entreaties, looks, words, and actions of a lover. They are,
I believe, much the same in the whole sex, allowing for their
different dispositions, educations, and characters; but you are
impatient, I know, for the conclusion. You have hastily perused
the preceding lines and are straining your eye forward to my
part of the farce, for such it may prove after all. Well, then, not
to play too long with the curiosity which I know to be excited
and actuated by real friendship, I will relieve it. I think you
would have been pleased to have seen my gravity on this impor-
tant occasion. With all the candor and frankness which I was
capable of assuming, I thus answered his long harangue, to
which I had listened without interrupting him: "Self-knowledge,
sir, that most important of all sciences, I have yet to learn. Such
have been my situations in life, and the natural volatility of my
temper, that I have looked but little into my own heart in
regard to its future wishes and views. From a scene of constraint
and confinement, ill-suited to my years and inclination, I have
just launched into society. My heart beats high in expectation of
its fancied joys. My sanguine imagination paints, in alluring
colors, the charms of youth and freedom, regulated by virtue
and innocence. Of these I wish to partake. While I own myself
under obligations for the esteem which you are pleased to pro-
fess for me and, in return, acknowledge that neither your person
nor manners are disagreeable to me, I recoil at the thought of
immediately forming a connection which must confine me to
the duties of domestic life and make me dependent for happi-
ness, perhaps, too, for subsistence, upon a class of people who
will claim the right of scrutinizing every part of my conduct
and, by censuring those foibles which I am conscious of not
having prudence to avoid, may render me completely miserable.
While, therefore, I receive your visits and cultivate towards you
sentiments of friendship and esteem, I would not have you con-
sider me as confined to your society or obligated to a future
connection. Our short acquaintance renders it impossible for me

to decide what the operations of my mind may hereafter be. You must either quit the subject or leave me to the exercise of my free will, which, perhaps, may coincide with your present wishes." "Madam," said he, "far is the wish from me to restrain your person or mind. In your breast I will repose my cause. It shall be my study to merit a return of affection, and I doubt not but generosity and honor will influence your conduct towards me. I expect soon to settle among a generous and enlightened people, where I flatter myself I shall be exempt from those difficulties and embarrassments to which too many of my brethren are subject. The local situation is agreeable, the society refined and polished; and if, in addition, I may obtain that felicity which you are formed to bestow in a family connection, I shall be happy indeed."

He spoke with emphasis. The tear of sensibility sparkled in his eye. I involuntarily gave him my hand, which he pressed with ardor to his lips; then, rising he walked to the window to conceal his emotion. I rang the bell and ordered tea, during and after which we shared that social converse which is the true zest of life and in which I am persuaded none but virtuous minds can participate. General Richman and lady returned with the shades of the evening. The penetrating eye of my cousin traced in *our* countenances the progress of the cause, and the smile of approbation animated *hers*. Mr. Boyer asked the favor of my company to ride tomorrow morning, which was granted. He tarried to supper and took his leave. I retired immediately to my chamber, to which I was followed by Mrs. Richman. I related to her the conversation and the encouragement which I had given to Mr. Boyer. She was pleased, but insisted that I should own myself somewhat engaged to him. This, I told her, I should never do to any man before the indissoluble knot was tied. "That," said I, "will be time enough to resign my freedom." She replied that I had wrong ideas of freedom and matrimony, but she hoped that Mr. Boyer would happily rectify them.

I have now, my dear friend, given you an account of my present situation and leave you to judge for yourself concerning it. Write me your opinion, and believe me ever yours,

Eliza Wharton.

LETTER XV

To Miss Eliza Wharton.

Hartford

I congratulate you, my dear Eliza, on the stability of your conduct towards Mr. Boyer. Pursue the system which you have adopted, and I dare say that happiness will crown your future days. You are indeed very tenacious of your freedom, as you call it; but that is a play about words. A man of Mr. Boyer's honor and good sense will never abridge any privileges which virtue can claim.

When do you return to embellish our society here? I am impatient to see you, and likewise this amiable man. I am much interested in his favor. By the way, I am told that Major Sanford has been to look at the seat of Captain Pribble, which is upon sale. It is reported that he will probably purchase it. Many of our gentry are pleased with the prospect of such a neighbor. "As an accomplished gentleman," say they, "he will be an agreeable addition to our social parties; and as a man of property and public spirit, he will be an advantage to the town." But from what I have heard of him, I am far from supposing him a desirable acquisition in either of these respects. A man of a vicious character cannot be a good member of society. In order to that, his principles and practice must be uncorrupted; in his morals, at least, he must be a man of probity and honor. Of these qualifications, if I mistake not, this gallant of yours cannot boast. But I shall not set up for a censor. I hope neither you nor I shall have much connection with him. My swain interests himself very much in your affairs. You will possibly think him impertinent, but I give his curiosity a softer name. Should I own to you that I place great confidence in his integrity and honor, you would, perhaps, laugh at my weakness; but, my dear, I have pride enough to keep me above coquetry or prudery and discretion enough, I hope, to secure me from the errors of both. With him I am determined to walk the future round of life. What folly, then, would it be to affect reserve and distance relative to an affair in which I have so much interest! Not that I am going to betray your secrets—these I have no right to divulge; but I must

be the judge what may, and what may not, be communicated. I am very much pressed for an early day of consummation, but I shall not listen to a request of that kind till your return. Such is my regard for you, that a union of love would be imperfect if friendship attended not the rites. Adieu.

<div style="text-align: right">Lucy Freeman.</div>

LETTER XVI

To Miss Lucy Freeman.

<div style="text-align: right">New Haven</div>

We go on charmingly here, almost as soft and smooth as your ladyship. It seems to me that love must stagnate if it have not a light breeze of discord once in a while to keep it in motion. We have not tried any yet, however. We had a lovely tour this forenoon, were out three long hours, and returned to dinner in perfect harmony.

Mr. Boyer informed me that he should set out tomorrow morning for his future residence and soon put on the sacred bands. He solicited an epistolary correspondence, at the same time, as an alleviation of the care which that weighty charge would bring on his mind. I consented, telling him that he must not expect anything more than general subjects from me.

We were somewhat interrupted in our confidential intercourse in the afternoon by the arrival of Major Sanford. I cannot say that I was not agreeably relieved. So sweet a repast, for several hours together, was rather sickening to my taste. My inamorato looked a little mortified at the cheerful reception which I gave the intruder and joined not so placidly in the social conversation as I could have wished.

When Mr. Boyer, after the Major took leave, pressed me to give him some assurance of my constancy, I only reminded him of the terms of our engagement. Seeing me decided, he was silent on the subject and soon bade me an affectionate adieu, not expecting, as he told me, the pleasure of a personal interview again for two or three months.

Thus far we have proceeded in this sober business. A good beginning, you will say. Perhaps it is. I do not, however, feel

myself greatly interested in the progress of the negotiation. Time may consolidate my affections and enable me to fix them on some particular object. At present the most lively emotions of my heart are those of friendship, that friendship which I hope you will soon participate with your faithful

Eliza Wharton.

LETTER XVII

To Mr. Selby.

New Haven

I have succeeded in my addresses to the lovely Eliza Wharton —as far, at least, as I had any reason to expect from our short acquaintance. I find the graces of her person and mind rise in my esteem, and I have already enjoyed in her society some of the happiest hours of my life. She is kind, affable, and condescending; yet I must own that I have not been able to infuse into her bosom the ardor which I feel in my own. I know that the native modesty of the sex would restrain the discovery; but there is an animation of countenance, which betrays the sensations of the heart, that I find wanting in hers on this occasion.

I have just taken leave of my fair and propose returning to-morrow morning to take upon me the solemn charge which lies with such weight upon my mind that I need every support, both human and divine. Eliza has promised to correspond with me. From this I anticipate a source of pleasure which alone can atone for her absence.

J. Boyer.

LETTER XVIII

To Mr. Charles Deighton.

New Haven

Do you know, Charles, that I have commenced lover? I was always a general one, but now I am somewhat particular. I shall

be the more interested. as I am likely to meet with difficulties; and it is the glory of a rake, as well as of a Christian, to combat obstacles. This same Eliza, of whom I have told you, has really made more impression on my heart than I was aware of, or than the sex, take them as they rise, are wont to do. But she is besieged by a priest—a likely lad though. I know not how it is; but they are commonly successful with the girls, even the gayest of them. This one, too, has the interest of all her friends, as I am told. I called yesterday at General Richman's and found this pair together, apparently too happy in each other's society for my wishes. I must own that I felt a glow of jealousy, which I never experienced before, and vowed revenge for the pain it gave me, though but momentary. Yet Eliza's reception of me was visibly cordial; nay, I fancied my company as pleasing to her as that which she had before. I tarried not long, but left him to the enjoyment of that pleasure which I flatter myself will be but shortlived. O, I have another plan in my head—a plan of necessity, which, you know, is the mother of invention. It is this: I am very much courted and caressed by the family of Mr. Lawrence, a man of large property in this neighborhood. He has only one child—a daughter, with whom I imagine the old folks intend to shackle me in the bonds of matrimony. The girl looks very well; she has no soul, though, that I can discover; she is heiress, nevertheless, to a great fortune, and that is all the soul I wish for in a wife. In truth, Charles, I know of no other way to mend my circumstances. But lisp not a word of my embarrassments for your life. Show and equipage are my hobby horse; and if any female wishes to share them with me and will furnish me with the means of supporting them, I have no objection. Could I conform to the sober rules of wedded life and renounce those dear enjoyments of dissipation in which I have so long indulged, I know not the lady in the world with whom I would sooner form a connection of this sort than with Eliza Wharton. But it will never do. If my fortune or hers were better, I would risk a union; but as they are, no idea of the kind can be admitted. I shall endeavor, notwithstanding, to enjoy her company as long as possible. Though I cannot possess her wholly myself, I will not tamely see her the property of another.

I am now going to call at General Richman's in hopes of an opportunity to profess my devotion to her. I know I am not a

welcome visitor to the family, but I am independent of their censure or esteem and mean to act accordingly.

Peter Sanford.

LETTER XIX

To Miss Lucy Freeman.

New Haven

I find the ideas of sobriety and domestic solitude I have been cultivating for three days past somewhat deranged by the interruption of a visitor, with whom I know you will not be pleased. It is no other than Major Sanford. I was walking alone in the garden yesterday, when he suddenly appeared to my view. "How happy am I," said he, seizing my hand, "in this opportunity of finding you alone—an opportunity, Miss Wharton, which I must improve in expatiating on a theme that fills my heart and solely animates my frame!"

I was startled at his impetuosity and displeased with his freedom. Withdrawing my hand, I told him that my retirement was sacred. He bowed submissively; begged pardon for his intrusion; alleged that he found nobody but the servants in the house who informed him I was alone in the garden—which intelligence was too pleasing for him to consult any forms of ceremony for the regulation of his conduct. He then went on rhapsodically to declare his passion and his suspicions that I was forming a connection with Mr. Boyer, which would effectually destroy all his hopes of future happiness. He painted the restraint, the confinement, the embarrassments to which a woman connected with a man of Mr. Boyer's profession must be subjected, however agreeable his person might be. He asked if my generous mind could submit to cares and perplexities like these; whether I could not find greater sources of enjoyment in a more elevated sphere of life, or share pleasures better suited to my genius and disposition even in a single state. I listened to him involuntarily. My heart did not approve his sentiments; but my ear was charmed with his rhetoric, and my fancy captivated by his address.

He invited my confidence by the most ardent professions of

friendship and labored to remove my suspicions by vows of sincerity. I was induced by his importunity gradually to disclose the state of affairs between Mr. Boyer and myself. He listened eagerly; wished not, he said, to influence me unduly; but if I were not otherwise engaged, might he presume to solicit a place in my friendship and esteem, be admitted to enjoy my society, to visit me as an acquaintance, and to attend my excursions and amusements as a brother, if not more? I replied that I was a pensioner of friendship at present; that friends were extremely refined in their notions of propriety; that I had no right to receive visitants independent of them. "I understand you, madam," said he. "You intimate that my company is not agreeable to them, but I know not why. Surely my rank in life is as elevated, and my knowledge of and acceptance in the world are as extensive, as General Richman's." "I hope," said I, "since we are engaged in the conversation that you will excuse my frankness if I tell you that the understanding and virtue of this worthy couple induce them, without any regard to rank, to bestow their esteem wherever it is merited. I cannot say that you are not a sharer. Your own heart can best determine whether upon their principles you are or not." He appeared mortified and chagrined; we had walked some distance without exchanging a word or a look. At last he rejoined, "I plead guilty to the charge, madam, which they have undoubtedly brought against me, of imprudence and folly in many particulars; yet of malignancy and vice I am innocent. Brought up in affluence, inured from my infancy to the gratification of every passion, the indulgence of every wish, it is not strange that a life of dissipation and gaiety should prove alluring to a youthful mind which had no care but to procure what is deemed enjoyment. In this pursuit I have, perhaps, deviated from the rigid rules of discretion and the harsher laws of morality. But let the veil of charity be drawn over my faults; let the eye of candor impartially examine my present behavior; let the kind and lenient hand of friendship assist in directing my future steps; and perhaps I may not prove unworthy of associating with the respectable inhabitants of this happy mansion, for such I am sure it must be while honored with Miss Wharton's presence. But, circumstanced as you and I are at present, I will not sue for your attention as a lover, but rest contented, if possible, with that share of kindness and regard which your benevolence may afford me as a friend." I

bowed in approbation of his resolution. He pressed my hand with ardor to his lips, and at that instant General Richman entered the garden. He approached us cheerfully, offered Major Sanford his hand with apparent cordiality, and told us pleasantly that he hoped he should not be considered an intruder. "By no means, sir," said Major Sanford; "it is I who have incurred that imputation. I called this afternoon to pay you my respects when, being informed that you and your lady were abroad, and that Miss Wharton was in the garden, I took the liberty to invade her retirement. She has graciously forgiven my crime, and I was just affixing the seal to my pardon as you entered."

We then returned into the house. Mrs. Richman received us politely. During tea the conversation turned on literary subjects, in which I cannot say that the Major bore a very distinguished part. After he was gone, Mrs. Richman said, "I hope you have been agreeably entertained, Miss Wharton." "I did not choose my company, madam," said I. "Nor," said she, "did you refuse it, I presume." "Would you not have me respect the rights of hospitality towards your guests when you are absent, madam?" "If you had acted from that motive, I own my obligations to you, my dear; but even that consideration can hardly reconcile me to the sacrifice of time which you have made to the amusement of a seducer." "I hope, madam, you do not think me an object of seduction." "I do not think you seducible, nor was Richardson's Clarissa until she made herself the victim by her own indiscretion. Pardon me, Eliza— this is a second Lovelace. I am alarmed by his artful intrusions. His insinuating attentions to you are characteristic of the man. Come, I presume you are not interested to keep his secrets if you know them; will you give me a little sketch of his conversation?" "Most willingly," said I, and accordingly related the whole. When I had concluded, she shook her head and replied, "Beware, my friend, of his arts. Your own heart is too sincere to suspect treachery and dissimulation in another; but suffer not your ear to be charmed by the siren voice of flattery, nor your eye to be caught by the phantom of gaiety and pleasure. Remember your engagements to Mr. Boyer. Let sincerity and virtue be your guides, and they will lead you to happiness and peace." She waited not for an answer but, immediately rising, begged leave to retire, alleging that she was fatigued. General Richman accompanied her; and I hastened to my apartment, where I have written thus far and shall send it

on for your comments. I begin to think of returning soon to
your circle. One inducement is that I may be free from the
intrusions of this man. Adieu.

Eliza Wharton.

LETTER XX

To Mrs. M. Wharton.

New Haven

From the conversation of the polite, the sedate, the engaging,
and the gay—from corresponding with the learned, the sentimen-
tal, and the refined—my heart and my pen turn with ardor and
alacrity to a tender and affectionate parent, the faithful guardian
and guide of my youth, the unchanging friend of my riper years.
The different dispositions of various associates sometimes per-
plex the mind which seeks direction; but in the disinterested
affection of the maternal breast we fear no dissonance of pas-
sion, no jarring interests, no disunion of love. In this seat of
felicity is every enjoyment which fancy can form, or friendship
with affluence bestow; but still my mind frequently returns to
the happy shades of my nativity. I wish there to impart my
pleasures and share the counsels of my best, my long-tried, and
experienced friend. At this time, my dear mamma, I am pe-
culiarly solicitous for your advice. I am again importuned to
listen to the voice of love, again called upon to accept the
addresses of a gentleman of merit and respectability. You will
know the character of the man when I tell you it is Mr. Boyer.
But his situation in life! I dare not enter it. My disposition is
not calculated for that sphere. There are duties arising from the
station which I fear I should not be able to fulfill, cares and
restraints to which I could not submit. *This* man is not disagree-
able to me; but if I must enter the connubial state, are there not
others who may be equally pleasing in their person and whose
profession may be more conformable to my taste? You, madam,
have passed through this scene of trial with honor and applause.
But, alas! can your volatile daughter ever acquire your wisdom—
ever possess your resolution, dignity, and prudence?

I hope soon to converse with you personally upon the subject

and to profit by your precepts and example. I anticipate the hour of my return to your bosom with impatience. My daily thoughts and nightly dreams restore me to the society of my beloved mamma; and until I enjoy it in reality, I subscribe myself your dutiful daughter,

Eliza Wharton.

LETTER XXI

To Miss Eliza Wharton.

Hartford

How welcome to me, my dear Eliza, are the tidings of your return! My widowed heart has mourned your absence and languished for the company of its now dearest connection. When stripped of one dependence, the mind naturally collects and rests itself in another. Your father's death deprived me for a while of every enjoyment. But a reviving sense of the duties which I owed to a rising family roused me from the lethargy of grief. In my cares I found an alleviation of my sorrows. The expanding virtues of my children soothed and exhilarated my drooping spirits, and my attention to their education and interest was amply rewarded by their proficiency and duty. In them every hope, every pleasure, now centers. They are the axis on which revolves the temporal felicity of their mother. Judge, then, my dear, how anxiously I must watch, how solicitously I must regard, every circumstance which relates to their welfare and prosperity! Exquisitely alive to these sensations, your letter awakens my hopes and my fears. As you are young and charming, a thousand dangers lurk unseen around you. I wish you to find a friend and protector worthy of being rewarded by your love and your society. Such a one I think Mr. Boyer will prove. I am therefore sorry, since there can be no other, that his profession should be an objection in your mind. You say that I have experienced the scenes of trial connected with that station. I have, indeed; and I will tell you the result of this experience. It is that I have found it replete with happiness. No class of society has domestic enjoyment more at command than clergymen. Their circumstances are generally a decent competency.

They are removed alike from the perplexing cares of want and from the distracting parade of wealth. They are respected by all ranks, and partakers of the best company. With regard to its being a dependent situation, what one is not so? Are we not all links in the great chain of society, some more, some less important, but each upheld by others, throughout the confederated whole? In whatever situation we are placed, our greater or less degree of happiness must be derived from ourselves. Happiness is in a great measure the result of our own dispositions and actions. Let us conduct ourselves uprightly and justly: with propriety and steadiness, not servilely cringing for favor nor arrogantly claiming more attention and respect than our due; let us bear with fortitude the providential and unavoidable evils of life, and we shall spend our days with respectability and contentment at least.

I will not expatiate on the topic of your letter until we have a personal interview, for which I am indeed impatient. Return, my daughter, as soon as politeness will allow, to your expecting friends--more especially to the fond embraces of your affectionate mother.

<div align="right">M. Wharton.</div>

LETTER XXII

To Miss Eliza Wharton

<div align="right">Hampshire</div>

Can time, can distance, can absence allay or extinguish the sentiments of refined affection, the ardor of true love? No, my dear Eliza. If I may judge by my own heart, I shall say they cannot. Amidst the parade which has attended me, the interesting scenes in which I have been engaged and the weighty cares which have occupied my attention, your idea has been the solace of my retired moments, the soother of every anxious thought. I recall with pleasure the conversation which we have shared. I dwell with rapture on the marks of favor which I have received from you. My first wish is the continuance and increase of these favors; my highest ambition is to deserve them. I look forward and anticipate with impatience the future enjoyment of your society, and hope we shall one day experience the reality of those beautiful lines of Thomson:

—an elegant sufficiency,
Content, retirement, rural quiet, friendship,
Books, ease, and alternate labor; useful life,
Progressive virtue, and approving Heaven;
These are the matchless joys of virtuous love.

Mr. Selby, my particular friend, will have the honor of delivering this letter. He will be able to give you any information, relative to our public transactions, which you may wish. May I solicit the favor of a line through him, in return? It will relieve, in some measure, the tediousness of this separation. I intend to pay my respects to you personally in about a fortnight; until then I subscribe myself your sincere and affectionate friend,

J. Boyer.

LETTER XXIII

To the Rev. J. Boyer.

New Haven

I have executed your commission and been amply rewarded for my trouble by the pleasures I enjoyed in the society of the agreeable family to which I was introduced, especially of the amiable and accomplished lady who is the object of your particular regard. I think she fully justifies your partiality to her. She appears to possess both the virtues and the graces. Her form is fine, and her countenance interests us at once in her favor. There is a mixture of dignity and ease which commands respect and conciliates affection. After these encomiums, will you permit me to say there is an air of gaiety in her appearance and deportment which savors a little of coquetry? I am persuaded, however, that she has too much good sense to practice its arts. She received your letter very graciously, asked leave to retire a few moments, and returned with a smile of complacency on her brow, which I construe favorably to you.

There was a Mr. Lawrence, with his lady and daughter, and a certain Major Sanford at the house. The latter, I believe, in the modern sense of the phrase, is *much of a gentleman*: that is, a man of show and fashion.

Miss Wharton asked me when I should leave town, and when I should return or have an opportunity of conveyance to Hampshire. I told her I should write by the next post and, if she had any commands, would be happy to execute them. She would send a line to her friend, she said, if I would take the trouble to enclose it in my letter. I readily consented and told her that I would call and receive her favor tomorrow morning. This chitchat was a little aside; but I could not but observe that the aforesaid Major Sanford had dropped his part in the conversation of the rest of the company and was attending to us, though he endeavored to conceal his attention by looking carelessly over a play which lay on the window by him. Yet he evidently watched every word and action of Miss Wharton, as if he were really interested in her movements.

It is said she has many admirers; and I conceive it very possible that this may be one of them, though, truly, I do not think that she would esteem such a conquest any great honor. I now joined in the general topic of conversation, which was politics; Mrs. Richman and Miss Wharton judiciously, yet modestly, bore a part while the other ladies amused themselves with Major Sanford, who was making his sage remarks on the play which he still kept in his hand. General Richman at length observed that we had formed into parties. Major Sanford upon this, laid aside his book. Miss Lawrence simpered and looked as if she was well pleased with being in a party with so fine a man, while her mother replied that she never meddled with politics. "Miss Wharton and I," said Mrs. Richman, "must beg leave to differ from you madam. We think ourselves interested in the welfare and prosperity of our country; and, consequently, we claim the right of inquiring into those affairs which may conduce to or interfere with the common weal. We shall not be called to the senate or the field to assert its privileges and defend its rights, but we shall feel for the honor and safety of our friends and connections who are thus employed. If the community flourish and enjoy health and freedom, shall we not share in the happy effects? If it be oppressed and disturbed, shall we not endure our proportion of the evil? Why, then, should the love of our country be a masculine passion only? Why should government, which involves the peace and order of the society of which we are a part, be wholly excluded from our observation?" Mrs. Lawrence made some slight reply and waived the subject. The gentlemen

applauded Mrs. Richman's sentiments as truly Roman and, what was more, they said, truly republican.

I rose to take leave, observing to Miss Wharton that I should call tomorrow, as agreed. Upon this, General Richman politely requested the favor of my company at dinner. I accepted his invitation and bade them good night. I shall do the same to you for the present, as I intend, tomorrow, to scribble the cover which is to enclose your Eliza's letter.

T. Selby.

LETTER XXIV

To the Rev. J. Boyer.

New Haven

I resume my pen, having just returned from General Richman's—not with an expectation, however, of your reading this until you have perused and reperused the enclosed. I can bear such neglect in this case, as I have been alike interested myself.

I went to General Richman's at twelve o'clock. About a mile from thence, upon turning a corner, I observed a gentleman and lady on horseback some way before me, riding at a very moderate pace and seemingly in close conversation. I kept at the same distance from them until I saw them stop at the general's gate. I then put on and, coming up with them just as they alighted, was surprised to find them no other than Major Sanford and Miss Wharton. They were both a little disconcerted at my salutation: I know not why. Miss Wharton invited him in; but he declined, being engaged to dine. General Richman received us at the door. As I handed Miss Wharton in, he observed, jocosely, that she had changed company. "Yes, sir," she replied, "more than once since I went out, as you doubtless observed." "I was not aware," said Mrs. Richman, "that Major Sanford was to be of your party today." "It was quite accidental, madam," said Miss Wharton. "Miss Lawrence and I had agreed, last evening, to take a little airing this forenoon. A young gentleman, a relation of hers, who is making them a visit, was to attend us."

"We had not ridden more than two miles when we were overtaken by Major Sanford, who very politely asked leave to join

our party. Miss Lawrence very readily consented and we had a very sociable ride. The fineness of the day induced me to protract the enjoyment of it abroad; but Miss Lawrence declined riding so far as I proposed, as she had engaged company to dine. We therefore parted till the evening, when we are to meet again." "What, another engagement!" said Mrs. Richman. "Only to the assembly, madam." "May I inquire after your gallant, my dear? But I have no right, perhaps, to be inquisitive," said Mrs. Richman. Miss Wharton made no reply, and the conversation took a general turn. Miss Wharton sustained her part with great propriety. Indeed, she discovers a fund of useful knowledge and extensive reading, which render her peculiarly entertaining; and the brilliancy of her wit, the fluency of her language, the vivacity and ease of her manners are inexpressibly engaging. I am going myself to the assembly this evening, though I did not mention it to General Richman. I therefore took my leave soon after dinner.

I have heard so much in praise of Miss Wharton's penmanship, in addition to her other endowments, that I am almost tempted to break the seal of her letter to you; but I forbear. Wishing you much happiness in the perusal of it, and more in the possession of its writer, I subscribe myself yours,

<div align="right">T. Selby.</div>

LETTER XXV

To the Rev. J. Boyer.

<div align="right">New Haven</div>

Sir: Your favor of the 4th instant came to hand yesterday. I received it with pleasure and embrace this early opportunity of contributing my part to a correspondence tending to promote a friendly and social intercourse. An epistolary communication between the sexes has been with some a subject of satire and censure, but unjustly in my opinion. With persons of refinement and information, it may be a source of entertainment and utility. The knowledge and masculine virtues of your sex may be softened and rendered more diffusive by the inquisitiveness, vivacity, and docility of ours, drawn forth and exercised by each other.

In regard to the *particular* subject of yours, I shall be silent. Ideas of that kind are better conveyed, on my part, by words than by the pen.

I congratulate you on your agreeable settlement and hope it will be productive of real and lasting happiness. I am convinced that felicity is not confined to any particular station or condition in life; yet, methinks, some are better calculated to afford it to me than others.

Your extract from a favorite poet is charmingly descriptive; but is it not difficult to ascertain what we can pronounce "an elegant sufficiency"? Perhaps you will answer, as some others have done, that we can attain it by circumscribing our wishes within the compass of our abilities. I am not very avaricious, yet I must own that I should like to enjoy it without so much trouble as that would cost me.

Excuse my seeming levity. You have flattered my cheerfulness by commending it and must, therefore, indulge me in the exercise of it. I cannot conveniently be at the pains of restraining its sallies when I write in confidence.

Is a sprightly disposition, in your view, indicative of a giddy mind or an innocent heart? Of the latter, I presume; for I know you are not a misanthrope.

We expect the pleasure of Mr. Selby's company to dinner. You are certainly under obligations to his friendship for the liberal encomiums he bestowed on you and your prospects yesterday. Mrs. Richman rallied me, after he was gone, on my listening ear. The general and she unite in requesting me to present their respects.

Wishing you health and happiness, I subscribe myself your friend,

<div style="text-align:right">Eliza Wharton.</div>

LETTER XXVI

To Miss Lucy Freeman.

<div style="text-align:right">New Haven</div>

I am perplexed and embarrassed, my friend, by the assiduous attentions of this Major Sanford. I shall write circumstantially and frankly to you, so that I may have the benefit of your

advice. He came here last Monday in company with Mr. Lawrence, his wife, and daughter, to make us a visit. While they were present, a Mr. Selby, a particular friend of Mr. Boyer, came in and delivered me a letter from him. I was really happy in the reception of this proof of his affection. His friend gave a very flattering account of his situation and prospects.

The watchful eye of Major Sanford traced every word and action respecting Mr. Boyer with an attention which seemed to border on anxiety. That, however, did not restrain, but rather accelerated, my vivacity and inquisitiveness on the subject; for I wished to know whether it would produce any real effect upon him or not.

After Mr. Selby's departure, he appeared pensive and thoughtful the remainder of the evening and evidently sought an opportunity of speaking to me aside, which I studiously avoided. Miss Lawrence and I formed an engagement to take an airing in the morning on horseback, attended by a relation of hers who is now with them. They called for me about ten, when we immediately set out upon our preconcerted excursion. We had not proceeded far before we were met by Major Sanford. He was extremely polite and, finding our destination was not particular, begged leave to join our party. This was granted; and we had an agreeable tour for several miles, the time being passed in easy and unstudied remarks upon obvious occurrences. Major Sanford could not, however, conceal his particular attention to me, which rather nettled Miss Lawrence. She grew somewhat serious and declined riding so far as we had intended, alleging that she expected company to dine.

Major Sanford, understanding that she was going to the assembly in the evening with Mr. Gordon, solicited me to accept a ticket and form a party with them. The entertainment was alluring, and I consented. When we had parted with Miss Lawrence, Major Sanford insisted on my riding a little farther, saying he must converse with me on a particular subject; and if I refused him this opportunity, he must visit me at my residence, let it offend whom it would. I yielded to his importunity, and we rode on. He then told me that his mind was in a state of suspense and agitation which was very painful to bear, and which I only could relieve; that my cheerful reception of Mr. Boyer's letter yesterday, and deportment respecting him, had awakened in his breast all the pangs of jealousy which the most

ardent love could feel; that my treatment of Mr. Boyer's friend convinced him that I was more interested in his affairs than I was willing to own; that he foresaw himself to be condemned to an eternal separation and the total loss of my favor and society, as soon as time and circumstances would allow.

His zeal, his pathos, alarmed me. I begged him to be calm. "To you," said I, "as a friend, I have intrusted my situation in relation to Mr. Boyer. You know that I am under no special obligation to him, and I do not intend to form any immediate connection." "Mr. Boyer must have different ideas, madam; and he has reason for them, if I may judge by appearances. When do you expect another visit from him?" "In about a fortnight." "And is my fate to be then decided, and so decided, as I fear it will be, through the influence of your friends, if not by your own inclination?" "My friends, sir, will not control me; they will only advise me to what they think most for my interest, and I hope that my conduct will not be unworthy of their approbation." "Pardon me, my dear Eliza," said he, "if I am impertinent; it is my regard for you which impels me to the presumption. Do you intend to give your hand to Mr. Boyer?" "I do not intend to give my hand to any man at present. I have but lately entered society and wish, for a while, to enjoy my freedom in the participation of pleasures suited to my age and sex." "These," said he, "you are aware, I suppose, when you form a connection with that man, you must renounce and content yourself with a confinement to the tedious round of domestic duties, the pedantic conversation of scholars, and the invidious criticisms of a whole town." "I have been accustomed," said I, "and am therefore attached, to men of letters; and as to the praise or censure of the populace, I hope always to enjoy that approbation of conscience which will render me superior to both. But you forget your promise not to talk in this style, and you have deviated far from the character of a friend and brother, with which you consented to rest satisfied." "Yes, but I find myself unequal to the task. I am not stoic enough tamely to make so great a sacrifice. I must plead for an interest in your favor until you banish me from your presence and tell me plainly that you hate me." We had by this time reached the gate and, as we dismounted, were unexpectedly accosted by Mr. Selby, who had come, agreeably to promise, to dine with us and receive my letter to Mr. Boyer.

Major Sanford took his leave as General Richman appeared at the door. The general and his lady rallied me on my change of company, but very prudently concealed their sentiments of Major Sanford while Mr. Selby was present. Nothing material occurred before and during dinner, soon after which Mr. Selby went away. I retired to dress for the assembly, and I had nearly completed the labor of the toilet when Mrs. Richman entered. "My friendship for you, my dear Eliza," said she, "interests me so much in your affairs that I cannot repress my curiosity to know who has the honor of your hand this evening." "If it be any honor," said I, "it will be conferred on Major Sanford." "I think it far too great to be thus bestowed," returned she. "It is perfectly astonishing to me that the virtuous part of my sex will countenance, caress, and encourage those men whose profession it is to blast their reputation, destroy their peace, and triumph in their infamy." "Is this, madam, the avowed design of Major Sanford?" "I know not what he avows, but his practice too plainly bespeaks his principles and views." "Does he now practice the arts you mention, or do you refer to past follies?" "I cannot answer for his present conduct; his past has established his character." "You, madam, are an advocate for charity; that, perhaps, if exercised in this instance, might lead you to think it possible for him to reform, to become a valuable member of society and, when connected with a lady of virtue and refinement, to be capable of making a good husband." "I cannot conceive that such a lady would be willing to risk her all upon the slender prospect of his reformation. I hope the one with whom I am conversing has no inclination to so hazardous an experiment." "Why, not much." "Not much! If you have any, why do you continue to encourage Mr. Boyer's addresses?" "I am not sufficiently acquainted with either, yet, to determine which to take. At present, I shall not confine myself in any way. In regard to these men, my fancy and my judgment are in scales; sometimes one preponderates, sometimes the other; which will finally prevail, time alone can reveal." "O my cousin, beware of the delusions of fancy! Reason must be our guide if we would expect durable happiness." At this instant a servant opened the door and told me that Major Sanford waited in the parlor. Being ready, I wished Mrs. Richman a good evening and went down. Neither General Richman nor his lady appeared. He

therefore handed me immediately into his phaeton, and we were soon in the assembly room.

I was surprised on my entrance to find Mr. Selby there, as he did not mention, at dinner, his intention of going. He attached himself to our party and, in the intervals of dancing, took every opportunity of conversing with me. These, however, were not many; for Major Sanford assiduously precluded the possibility of my being much engaged by anyone else. We passed the evening very agreeably; but the Major's importunity was rather troublesome as we returned home. He insisted upon my declaring whether Mr. Boyer really possessed my affections, and whether I intended to confer myself on him or not. "If," said he, "you answer me in the affirmative, I must despair; but if you have not absolutely decided against me, I will still hope that my persevering assiduity, my faithful love, may at last be rewarded." I told him that I was under no obligation to give him any account of my disposition towards another, that he must remember the terms of our present association to which he had subscribed. I therefore begged him to waive the subject now, if not forever. He asked my pardon, if he had been impertinent, but desired leave to renew his request that I would receive his visits, his friendly visits. I replied that I could not grant this, and that he must blame himself, not me, if he was an unwelcome guest at General Richman's. He lamented the prejudices which my friends had imbibed against him, but flattered himself that I was more liberal than to be influenced by them without any positive proof of demerit, as it was impossible that his conduct towards me should ever deviate from the strictest rules of honor and love.

What shall I say now, my friend? This man to an agreeable person has superadded graceful manners, an amiable temper, and a fortune sufficient to insure the enjoyments of all the pleasing varieties of social life. Perhaps a gay disposition and a lax education may have betrayed him into some scenes of dissipation. But is it not an adage generally received that "*a reformed rake makes the best husband*"? My fancy leads me for happiness to the festive haunts of fashionable life. I am at present, and know not but I ever shall be, too volatile for a confinement to domestic avocations and sedentary pleasures. I dare not, therefore, place myself in a situation where these must be indispensable.

Mr. Boyer's person and character are agreeable. I really esteem the man. My reason and judgments, as I have observed before, declare for a connection with him, as a state of tranquillity and rational happiness. But the idea of relinquishing those delightful amusements and flattering attentions which wealth and equipage bestow is painful. Why were not the virtues of the one and the graces and affluence of the other combined? I should then have been happy indeed. But, as the case now stands, I am loath to give up either—being doubtful which will conduce most to my felicity.

Pray write me impartially; let me know your real sentiments, for I rely greatly upon your opinion.

Eliza Wharton.

LETTER XXVIII

To the Rev. Mr. Boyer.

New Haven

I am quite a convert to Pope's assertion that

Every woman is at heart a rake.

How else can we account for the pleasure which they evidently receive from the society, the flattery, the caresses of men of that character? Even the most virtuous of them seem naturally prone to gaiety, to pleasure and, I had almost said, to dissipation. How else shall we account for the existence of this disposition in your favorite fair? It cannot be the result of her education. Such a one as she has received is calculated to give her a very different turn of mind. You must forgive me, my friend, for I am a little vexed and alarmed on your account. I went last evening to the assembly, as I told you in my last letter that I intended. I was purposely without a partner, that I might have the liberty to exercise my gallantry as circumstances should invite. Indeed I must own that my particular design was to observe Miss Wharton's movements, being rather inclined to jealousy in your behalf. She was handed into the assembly room by Major Sanford. The brilliance of their appearance, the levity of their manners, and the contrast of their characters, I found to

be a general subject of speculation. I endeavored to associate with Miss Wharton, but found it impossible to detach her a moment from the coxcomb who attended her. If she has any idea of a connection with you, why does she continue to associate with another, especially with one of so opposite a description? I am seriously afraid that there is more intimacy between them than there ought to be, considering the encouragement she has given you.

I hope you will not be offended by my freedom in this matter. It originates in a concern for your honor and future happiness. I am anxious lest you should be made the dupe of a coquette, and your peace of mind fall a sacrifice to an artful debauchee. Yet I must believe that Miss Wharton has, in reality, all that virtue and good sense of which she enjoys the reputation; but her present conduct is mysterious.

I have said enough (more than I ought, perhaps) to awaken your attention to circumstances which *may* lead to important events. If they appear of little or no consequence to you, you will at least ascribe the mention of them to motives of sincere regard in your friend and humble servant,

T. Selby.

LETTER XXVIII

To Mr. Charles Deighton.

New Haven

I go on finely with my amour. I have every encouragement that I could wish. Indeed my fair one does not verbally declare in my favor; but then, according to the vulgar proverb, that *"actions speak louder than words,"* I have no reason to complain—since she evidently approves my gallantry, is pleased with my company, and listens to my flattery. Her sagacious friends have undoubtedly given her a detail of my vices. If, therefore, my past conduct has been repugnant to her notions of propriety, why does she not act consistently and refuse at once to associate with a man whose character she cannot esteem? But no; that, Charles, is no part of the female plan; our entrapping a few of their sex only discovers the gaiety of our dispositions.

the insinuating graces of our manners, and the irresistible charms of our persons and address. These qualifications are very alluring to the sprightly fancy of the fair. They think to enjoy the pleasures which result from this source, while their vanity and ignorance prompt each one to imagine herself superior to delusion and to anticipate the honor of reclaiming the libertine and reforming the rake. I don't know, however, but this girl will really have that merit with me; for I am so much attached to her that I begin to suspect I should sooner become a convert to sobriety than lose her. I cannot find that I have made much impression on her heart as yet. Want of success in this point mortifies me extremely, as it is the first time I ever failed. Besides, I am apprehensive that she is prepossessed in favor of the other swain, the clerical lover, whom I have mentioned to you before. The chord, therefore, upon which I play the most is the dissimilarity of their dispositions and pleasures. I endeavor to detach her from him and disaffect her towards him—knowing that, if I can separate them entirely, I shall be more likely to succeed in my plan. Not that I have any thoughts of marrying her myself; that will not do at present. But I love her too well to see her connected with another for life. I must own myself a little revengeful, too, in this affair. I wish to punish her friends, as she calls them, for their malice towards me, for their cold and negligent treatment of me whenever I go to the house. I know that to frustrate their designs of a connection between Mr. Boyer and Eliza would be a grievous disappointment. I have not yet determined to seduce her, though, with all her pretensions to virtue, I do not think it impossible. And if I should, she can blame none but herself, since she knows my character and has no reason to wonder if I act consistently with it. If she will play with a lion, let her beware of his paw, I say. At present, I wish innocently to enjoy her society; it is a luxury which I never tasted before. She is the very soul of pleasure. The gayest circle is irradiated by her presence, and the highest entertainment receives its greatest charms from her smiles. Besides, I have purchased the seat of Captain Pribble, about a mile from her mother's; and can I think of suffering her to leave the neighborhood just as I enter it? I shall exert every nerve to prevent that and hope to meet with the usual success.

<div style="text-align: right">Peter Sanford.</div>

LETTER XXIX

To Miss Eliza Wharton.

Hartford

You desire me to write to you, my friend; but if you had not, I should by no means have refrained. I tremble at the precipice on which you stand and must echo and re-echo the seasonable admonition of the excellent Mrs. Richman, "Beware of the delusions of fancy." You are strangely infatuated by them! Let not the magic arts of that worthless Sanford lead you, like an *ignis fatuus,* from the path of rectitude and virtue.

I do not find, in all your conversations with him, that one word about marriage drops from his lips. This is mysterious. No, it is characteristic of the man. Suppose, however, that his views are honorable; yet what can you expect, what can you promise yourself, from such a connection? "A reformed rake," you say, "makes the best husband"—a trite, but a very erroneous maxim, as the fatal experience of thousands of our sex can testify. In the first place, I believe that rakes very seldom *do* reform while their fortunes and constitutions enable them to pursue their licentious pleasures. But even allowing this to happen, can a woman of refinement and delicacy enjoy the society of a man whose mind has been corrupted, whose taste has been vitiated, and who has contracted a depravity, both of sentiment and manners, which no degree of repentence can wholly efface? Besides, of true love they are absolutely incapable. Their passions have been much too hackneyed to admit so pure a flame. You cannot anticipate sincere and lasting respect from them. They have been so long accustomed to the company of those of our sex who deserve no esteem that the greatest dignity and purity of character can never excite it in their breasts. They are naturally prone to jealousy. Habituated to an intercourse with the baser part of the sex, they level the whole and seldom believe any to be incorruptible. They are always hard-hearted and cruel. How else could they triumph in the miseries which they frequently occasion? Their specious manners may render them agreeable companions abroad, but at home the evil propensities of their minds

will invariably predominate. They are steeled against the tender affections which render domestic life delightful—strangers to the kind, the endearing, sympathies of husband, father, and friend. The thousand nameless attentions which soften the rugged path of life are neglected and deemed unworthy of notice by persons who have been inured to scenes of dissipation and debauchery. And is a man of this description to be the partner, the companion, the bosom friend of my Eliza? Forbid it, Heaven! Let not the noble qualities so lavishly bestowed upon her be thus unworthily sacrificed!

You seem to be particularly charmed with the fortune of Major Sanford, with the gaiety of his appearance, with the splendor of his equipage, with the politeness of his manners, with what you call the graces of his person. These, alas! are superficial, ensnaring endowments. As to fortune, prudence, economy, and regularity are necessary to preserve it when possessed. Of these Major Sanford is certainly destitute—unless common fame (which more frequently tells the truth than some are willing to allow) does him great injustice. As to external parade, it will not satisfy the rational mind when it aspires to those substantial pleasures for which yours is formed. And as to the graces of person and manners, they are but a wretched substitute for those virtues which adorn and dignify human life. Can you—who have always been used to serenity and order in a family, to rational, refined, and improving conversation—relinquish them and launch into the whirlpool of frivolity, where the correct taste and the delicate sensibility which you possess must constantly be wounded by the frothy and illiberal sallies of licentious wit?

This, my dear, is but a faint picture of the situation to which you seem inclined. Reverse the scene, and you will perceive the alternative which is submitted to your option in a virtuous connection with Mr. Boyer. Remember that you are acting for life and that your happiness in this world, perhaps in the next, depends on your present choice.

I called last evening to see your mamma. She is fondly anticipating your return and rejoicing in the prospect of your agreeable and speedy settlement. I could not find it in my heart to distress her by intimating that you had other views. I wish her benevolent bosom nevermore to feel the pangs of disappointed hope.

I am busily engaged in preparing for my nuptials. The solemn words, "As long as ye both shall live," render me thoughtful and serious. I hope for your enlivening presence soon, which will prove a seasonable cordial to the spirits of your

Lucy Freeman.

LETTER XXX

To Miss Lucy Freeman.

New Haven

I believe your spirits need a cordial indeed, my dear Lucy, after drawing so dreadful a portrait of my swain. But I call him mine no longer. I renounce him entirely. My friends shall be gratified; and if their predictions are verified, I shall be happy in a union with a man of their choice. General Richman and lady have labored abundantly to prove that my ruin was inevitable if I did not immediately break all intercourse with Major Sanford. I promised a compliance with their wishes and have accomplished the task, though a hard one I found it. Last Thursday he was here and desired leave to spend an hour with me. I readily consented, assuring my friends it should be the last hour which I would ever spend in his company.

He told me that he was obliged to leave town for a few days; as I should probably see Mr. Boyer before his return, he could not depart in peace without once more endeavoring to interest me in his favor, to obtain some token of esteem, some glimpse of hope that I would not utterly reject him, to support him in his absence. I thanked him for the polite attention he had paid me since our acquaintance and told him that I should ever retain a grateful sense of his partiality to me, that he would ever share my best wishes, but that all connection of the kind to which he alluded must from that time forever cease.

He exerted all his eloquence to obtain a retraction of that sentence and ran with the greatest volubility through all the protestations, prayers, entreaties, professions, and assurances which love could feel or art contrive. I had resolution, however, to resist them and to command my own emotions on the occasion better than my natural sensibility gave me reason to expect.

Finding every effort vain, he rose precipitately and bade me adieu. I urged his tarrying to tea; but he declined, saying that he must retire to his chamber, being in his present state of mind unfit for any society, as he was banished from mine. I offered him my hand, which he pressed with ardor to his lips and, bowing in silence, left the room.

Thus terminated this affair—an affair which, perhaps, was only the effect of mere gallantry on his part, and of unmeaning pleasantry on mine. I am sorry to say that it has given my friends so much anxiety and concern. I am under obligations to them for their kind solicitude, however causeless it may have been.

As an agreeable companion, as a polite and finished gallant, Major Sanford is all that the most lively fancy could wish. And as you have always affirmed that I was a little inclined to coquetry, can you wonder at my exercising it upon so happy a subject? Besides, when I thought more seriously, his liberal fortune was extremely alluring to me, who, you know, have been hitherto confined to the rigid rules of prudence and economy, not to say necessity, in my finances.

Miss Lawrence called on me yesterday, as she was taking the air, and asked me whether Major Sanford took leave of me when he left town. "He was here last week," said I, "but I did not know that he was gone away." "O, yes," she replied, "he is gone to take possession of his seat which he has lately purchased of Captain Pribble. I am told it is superb; and it ought to be, if it has the honor of his residence." "Then you have a great opinion of Major Sanford," said I. "Certainly, and has not everybody else?" said she. "I am sure he is a very fine gentleman." Mrs. Richman smiled rather contemptuously, and I changed the subject. I believe that the innocent heart of this simple girl is a little taken in.

I have just received a letter from Mr. Boyer in the usual style. He expects the superlative happiness of kissing my hand next week. O, dear! I believe I must begin to fix my phiz. Let me run to the glass and try if I can make up one that will look *madamish*. Yes, I succeeded very well.

I congratulate you on your new neighbor; but I advise friend George to have the Gordian knot tied immediately, lest you should be ensnared by this bewitching squire.

I have been trying to seduce General Richman to accompany me to the assembly this evening, but I cannot prevail. Were Mrs.

Richman able to go with us, he would be very happy to wait on us together; but, to tell the truth, he had rather enjoy her company at home than any which is to be found abroad. I rallied him on his old-fashioned taste, but my heart approved and applauded his attachment. I despise the married man or woman who harbors an inclination to partake of separate pleasures.

I am told that a servant man inquires for me below—the messenger of some enamored swain, I suppose. I will step down and learn what message he brings.

Nothing extraordinary; it is only a card of compliments from a Mr. Emmons, a respectable merchant of this city, requesting the honor to wait on me to the assembly this evening—a welcome request which I made no hesitation to grant. If I must resign these favorite amusements, let me enjoy as large a share as possible until the time arrives. I must repair to the toilet and adorn for a new conquest the person of

<div align="right">Eliza Wharton.</div>

LETTER XXXI

To Miss Eliza Wharton.

<div align="right">Hartford</div>

I am very happy to find you are in so good spirits, Eliza, after parting with your favorite swain; for I perceive that he is really the favorite of your fancy, though your heart cannot esteem him; and, independent of that, no sensations can be durable.

I can tell you some news of this strange man. He has arrived and taken possession of his seat. Having given general invitations, he has been called upon and welcomed by most of the neighboring gentry. Yesterday he made an elegant entertainment. Friend George (as you call him) and I were of the number who had cards. Twenty-one couples went, I am told. We did not go. I consider my time too valuable to be spent in cultivating acquaintance with a person from whom neither pleasure nor improvement is to be expected. His profuseness may bribe the unthinking multitude to show him respect; but he must know that, though

Places and honors have been bought for gold,
Esteem and love were never to be sold.

I look upon the vicious habits and abandoned character of Major Sanford to have more pernicious effects on society than the perpetrations of the robber and the assassin. These, when detected, are rigidly punished by the laws of the land. If their lives be spared, they are shunned by society and treated with every mark of disapprobation and contempt. But, to the disgrace of humanity and virtue, the assassin of honor, the wretch who breaks the peace of families, who robs virgin innocence of its charms, who triumphs over the ill-placed confidence of the inexperienced, unsuspecting, and too credulous fair, is received and caressed, not only by his own sex, to which he is a reproach, but even by ours, who have every conceivable reason to despise and avoid him. Influenced by these principles, I am neither ashamed nor afraid openly to avow my sentiments of this man and my reasons for treating him with the most pointed neglect.

I write warmly on the subject, for it is a subject in which I think the honor and happiness of my sex concerned. I wish they would more generally espouse their own cause. It would conduce to the public weal and to their personal respectability. I rejoice heartily that you have had resolution to resist his allurements, to detect and repel his artifices. Resolution in such a case is absolutely necessary; for,

In spite of all the virtue we can boast,
The woman that deliberates is lost.

As I was riding out yesterday I met your mamma. She wondered that I was not one of the party at our new neighbor's. "The reason, madam," said I, "is, that I do not like the character of the man." "I know nothing of him," said she; "he is quite a stranger to me, only that he called at my house last week to pay me his respects, as he said, for the sake of my late husband, whose memory he revered; and that I was the mother of Miss Eliza Wharton, with whom he had the honor of some little acquaintance. His manners are engaging, and I am sorry to hear that his morals are corrupt."

This, my dear, is a very extraordinary visit. I fear that he has not yet laid aside his arts. Be still on your guard; this is the advice of your sincere and faithful friend,

Lucy Freeman.

LETTER XXXII

To Mr. Charles Deighton.

Hartford

I am really banished and rejected—desired nevermore to think of the girl I love with a view of indulging that love or of rendering it acceptable to its object. You will perhaps dispute the propriety of the term and tell me it is not love—it is only gallantry and a desire to exercise it with her as a favorite nymph. I neither know nor care by what appellation you distinguish it, but it truly gives me pain. I have not felt one sensation of genuine pleasure since I heard my sentence; yet I acquiesced in it and submissively took my leave, though I doubt not but I shall retaliate the indignity one time or other.

I have taken possession of my new purchase—an elegant and delightful residence. It is rendered more so by being in the vicinity of my charmer's native abode. This circumstance will conduce much to my enjoyment, if I can succeed in my plan of separating her from Mr. Boyer. I know that my situation and mode of life are far more pleasing to her than his, and I shall therefore trust to my appearance and address for a re-establishment in her favor. I intend, if possible, to ingratiate myself with her particular friends. For this purpose I called last week at her mother's to pay my respects to her (so I told the good woman) as an object of my particular regard, and as the parent of a young lady whom I had the honor to know and admire. She received me very civilly, thanked me for my attention, and invited me to call whenever I had opportunity—which was the very thing I wanted. I intend, likewise, to court popularity. I don't know but I must accept, by and by, some lucrative office in the civil department; yet I cannot bear the idea of confinement to business. It appears to me quite inconsistent with the character of a gentleman; I am sure it is with that of a man of pleasure. But something I must do; for I tell you, in confidence, that I was obliged to mortgage this place because I had not the wherewithal to pay for it. But I shall manage matters very well, I have no doubt, and keep up the appearance of affluence till I find some lady in a strait for a husband whose fortune will

enable me to extricate myself from these embarrassments. Do come and see me, Charles; for, notwithstanding all my gaiety and parade, I have some turns of the hypo, some qualms of conscience, you will call them; but I meddle not with such obsolete words. And so good-by to you, says

<div align="right">Peter Sanford.</div>

LETTER XXXIII

To Miss Lucy Freeman.

<div align="right">New Haven</div>

My dear friend: I believe I must begin to assume airs of gravity, and they will not be quite so foreign to my feelings now as at some other times. You shall know the reason. I have been associated for three days with sentiment and sobriety in the person of Mr. Boyer. I don't know but this man will seduce me into matrimony. He is very eloquent upon the subject; and his manners are so solemn that I am strongly tempted—yet I dare not—to laugh. Really, Lucy, there is something extremely engaging and soothing, too, in virtuous and refined conversation. It is a source of enjoyment which cannot be realized by the dissolute and unreflecting. But then this particular theme of his is not a favorite one to me: I mean as connected with its consequences—care and confinement. However, I have compounded the matter with him and conditioned that he shall expatiate on the subject—call it by what name he pleases, *platonic* or *conjugal*—provided he will let me take my own time for the consummation. I have consented that he shall escort me next week to see my mamma and my Lucy. O, how the idea of returning to that revered mansion, to those beloved friends, exhilarates my spirits!

General Richman's politeness to me has induced him to invite a large party of those gentlemen and ladies who have been particularly attentive to me during my residence here to dine and take tea tomorrow. After that, I expect to be engaged in making farewell visits till I leave the place. I shall, therefore, forego the pleasure of telling you any occurrences subsequent to this date until you see and converse with your sincere friend,

<div align="right">Eliza Wharton.</div>

LETTER XXXIV

To Mrs. Richman.

Hartford

Dear madam: The day after I left your hospitable dwelling brought me safe to that of my honored mamma—to the seat of maternal and filial affection; of social ease and domestic peace; of every species of happiness which can result from religion and virtue and from refinement in morals and manners.

I found my brother and his wife, with Lucy Freeman and Mr. Sumner, waiting to receive and bid me welcome. I flew with ecstasy to the bosom of my mamma, who received me with her accustomed affection, testified by the expressive tears of tenderness which stole silently down her widowed cheek. She was unable to speak. I was equally so. We therefore indulged a moment the pleasing emotions of sympathizing sensibility. When disengaged from her fond embrace, I was saluted by the others in turn; and, having recovered myself, I presented Mr. Boyer to each of the company, and each of the company to him. He was cordially received by all, but more especially by my mamma.

The next day I was called upon and welcomed by several of my neighboring acquaintance, among whom I was not a little surprised to see Major Sanford. He came in company with Mr. Stoddard and lady, whom he overtook, as he told me, near by; and, as they informed him that the design of their visit was to welcome me home, he readily accepted their invitation to partake of the pleasure which everyone must receive on my return. I bowed slightly at his compliment, taking no visible notice of any peculiarity of expression either in his words or looks.

His politeness to Mr. Boyer appeared to be the result of habit; Mr. Boyer's to him was forced by respect to the company to which he had gained admission. I dare say that each felt a conscious superiority—the one on the score of merit, the other on that for fortune. Which ought to outweigh the judicious mind will easily decide. The scale, as I once observed to you, will turn as fancy or reason preponderates. I believe the esteem which I now have for Mr. Boyer will keep me steady—except, perhaps, some little eccentricities now and then, just by way of variety. I

am going tomorrow morning to spend a few days with Lucy
Freeman, to assist in the preparation for, and the solemnization
of, her nuptials. Mr. Boyer in the mean time will tarry among
his friends in town. My mamma is excessively partial to him,
though I am not yet jealous that she means to rival me. I am
not certain, however, but it might be happy for him if she
should; for I suspect, notwithstanding the disparity of her age,
that she is better calculated to make him a good wife than I am
or ever shall be.

But to be sober. Please, madam, to make my compliments
acceptable to those of your neighbors, whose politeness and at-
tention to me while at your house have laid me under particular
obligations of gratitude and respect. My best regards attend Gen-
eral Richman. Pray tell him that, though I never expect to be so
good a wife as he is blessed with, I intend after a while (when I
have sowed all my wild oats) to make a tolerable one.

I am anxious to hear of a wished-for event and of your safe-
ty. All who know you feel interested in your health and happi-
ness, but none more warmly than your obliged and affectionate

Eliza Wharton.

LETTER XXXV

To Miss Eliza Wharton.

New Haven

I write a line at Mrs. Richman's request, just to inform you,
Eliza, that yesterday that lovely and beloved woman presented me
with a daughter. This event awakens new sensations in my mind
and calls into exercise a kind of affection which had before lain
dormant. I feel already the tenderness of a parent, while imagina-
tion fondly traces the mother's likeness in the infant form. Mrs.
Richman expects to receive your congratulations in a letter by the
next post. She bids me tell you, moreover, that she hopes soon to
receive an invitation and be able to attend to the consummation
you talk of. Give Mrs. Richman's and my particular regards to
your excellent mother and to the worthy Mr. Boyer. With senti-
ments of esteem and friendship, I am

S. Richman.

LETTER XXXVI

To Mrs. Richman.

Hartford

From the scenes of festive mirth, from the conviviality of rejoicing friends, and from the dissipating amusements of the gay world, I retire with alacrity to hail my beloved friend on the important charge which she has received; on the accession to her family and, may I not say, on the addition to her care, since that care will be more than counterbalanced by the pleasure it confers. Hail, happy babe! ushered into the world by the best of mothers; entitled by birthright to virtue and honor; defended by parental love from the weakness of infancy and childhood, by guardian wisdom from the perils of youth, and by affluent independence from the griping hand of poverty in more advanced life! May these animating prospects be realized by your little daughter, and may you long enjoy the rich reward of seeing her all that you wish.

Yesterday, my dear friend, Lucy Freeman, gave her hand to the amiable and accomplished Mr. George Sumner. A large circle of congratulating friends were present. Her dress was such as wealth and elegance required. Her deportment was every thing that modesty and propriety could suggest. They are, indeed, a charming couple. The consonance of their dispositions, the similarity of their tastes, and the equality of their ages are a sure pledge of happiness. Every eye beamed with pleasure on the occasion, and every tongue echoed the wishes of benevolence. Mine only was silent. Though not less interested in the felicity of my friend than the rest, yet the idea of a separation, perhaps of an alienation of affection, by means of her entire devotion to another, cast an involuntary gloom over my mind. Mr. Boyer took my hand after the ceremony was past. "Permit me, Miss Wharton," said he, "to lead you to your lovely friend; her happiness must be heightened by your participation of it." "O, no," said I, "I am too selfish for that. She has conferred upon another that affection which I wished to engross. My love was too fervent to admit a rival." "Retaliate, then," said he, "this fancied wrong by doing likewise." I observed that this was not a

proper time to discuss that subject and, resuming my seat, endeavored to put on the appearance of my accustomed vivacity. I need not relate the remaining particulars of the evening's entertainment. Mr. Boyer returned with my mamma, and I remained at Mrs. Freeman's.

We are to have a ball here this evening. Mr. Boyer has been with us and tried to monopolize my company; but in vain. I am too much engaged by the exhilarating scenes around for attending to a subject which affords no variety. I shall not close this till tomorrow.

I am rather fatigued with the amusements of last night, which were protracted to a late hour. Mr. Boyer was present; and I was pleased to see him not averse to the entertainment, though his profession prevented him from taking an active part. As all the neighboring gentry were invited, Mr. Freeman would by no means omit Major Sanford, whom his daughter earnestly solicited. It happened (unfortunately, shall I say?) that I drew him for a partner. Yet I must own that I felt very little reluctance to my lot. He is an excellent dancer and well calculated for the companion in the hours of mirth and gayety. I regretted Mr. Boyer's being present, however, because my enjoyment seemed to give him pain. I hope he is not inclined to the passion of jealousy. If he is, I fear it will be somewhat exercised.

Lucy Freeman, now Mrs. Sumner, removes next week to Boston. I have agreed to accompany her and spend a month or two in her family. This will give variety to the journey of life. Be so kind as to direct your next letter to me there.

Kiss the dear little babe for me. Give love, compliments, etc., as respectively due; and believe me, with every sentiment of respect, your affectionate

<div align="right">Eliza Wharton.</div>

LETTER XXXVII

To Mr. Charles Deighton.

<div align="right">Hartford</div>

Dear Charles: My hopes begin to revive. I am again permitted to associate with my Eliza—invited to the same entertainment.

She does not refuse to join with me in the mazy dance and partake the scenes of festive mirth. Nay, more; she allows me to press her hand to my lips and listens to the sighing accents of love. Love her I certainly do. Would to Heaven I could marry her! Would to Heaven I had preserved my fortune, or she had one to supply its place! I am distracted at the idea of losing her forever. I am sometimes tempted to solicit her hand in serious earnest; but if I should, poverty and want must be the consequence. Her disappointment in the expectation of affluence and splendor, which I believe her ruling passion, would afford a perpetual source of discontent and mutual wretchedness.

She is going to Boston with her friend, Mrs. Sumner. I must follow her. I must break the connection which is rapidly forming between her and Mr. Boyer and enjoy her society a while longer, if no more.

I have had a little intimation from New Haven that Miss Lawrence is partial to me and might easily be obtained, with a handsome property into the bargain. I am neither pleased with nor averse to the girl; but she has money, and that may supply the place of love by enabling me to pursue independent pleasures. This she must expect, if she marries a man of my cast. She, doubtless, knows my character; and if she is so vain of her charms or influence as to think of reforming or confining me, she must bear the consequences.

However, I can keep my head up at present without recourse to the noose of matrimony, and I shall therefore defer any particular attention to her until necessity requires it.

<div align="right">Peter Sanford.</div>

LETTER XXXVIII

To Mrs. M. Wharton.

<div align="right">Boston</div>

You commanded me, my dear mamma, to write to you. That command I cheerfully obey, in testimony of my ready submission and respect. No other avocation could arrest my time, which is now completely occupied in scenes of amusement.

Mrs. Sumner is agreeably settled and situated. She appears to

be possessed of every blessing which can render life desirable. Almost every day since our arrival has been engrossed by visitants. Our evenings we have devoted to company abroad—and that more generally than we should otherwise have done, as my stay is limited to so short a period. The museum, the theaters, the circus, and the assemblies have been frequented.

Mrs. Sumner has made me several presents; notwithstanding, the articles requisite to a fashionable appearance have involved me in considerable expense. I fear that you will think me extravagant when you are told how much.

Mr. Boyer tarried in town about a week, having business. He appeared a little concerned at my taste for dissipation, as he once termed it. He even took the liberty to converse seriously on the subject.

I was displeased with his freedom and reminded him that I had the disposal of my own time as yet and that, while I escaped the censure of my own heart, I hoped that no one else would presume to arraign it. He apologized and gave up his argument.

I was much surprised, the first time I went to the play, to see Major Sanford in the very next box. He immediately joined our party; and wherever I have been since, I have been almost sure to meet him.

Mr. Boyer has taken his departure and I do not expect to see him again till I return home.

O mamma, I am embarrassed about this man. His worth I acknowledge; nay, I esteem him very highly. But can there be happiness with such a disparity of dispositions?

I shall soon return to the bosom of domestic tranquillity, to the arms of maternal tenderness, where I can deliberate and advise at leisure about this important matter.

<div align="right">Eliza Wharton.</div>

LETTER XXXIX

To Mr. Selby.

Hampshire

I believe that I owe you an apology for my long silence. But my time has been much engrossed of late, and my mind much more so. When it will be otherwise I cannot foresee. I fear, my friend, that there is some foundation for your suspicions respecting my beloved Eliza. What pity it is that so fair a form, so accomplished a mind, should be tarnished in the smallest degree by the follies of coquetry! If this is the fact, which I am loath to believe, all my regard for her shall never make me the dupe of it.

When I arrived at her residence at New Haven, where I told you in my last letter I was soon to go, she gave me a most cordial reception. Her whole behavior to me was correspondent with those sentiments of esteem and affection which she modestly avowed. She permitted me to accompany her to Hartford, to restore her to her mother, and to declare my wish to receive her again from her hand. Thus far all was harmony and happiness. As all my wishes were consistent with virtue and honor, she readily indulged them. She took apparent pleasure in my company, encouraged my hopes of a future union, and listened to the tender accents of love.

But the scenes of gaiety which invited her attention reversed her conduct. The delightful hours of mutual confidence, of sentimental converse, and of the interchange of refined affection were no more. Instead of these, parties were formed unpleasing to my taste; and every opportunity was embraced to join in diversions in which she knew I could not consistently take a share. I, however, acquiesced in her pleasure though I sometimes thought myself neglected, and even hinted it to her mother. The old lady apologized for her daughter, by alleging that she had been absent for a long time; that her acquaintances were rejoiced at her return and welcomed her by striving to promote her amusement.

One of her most intimate friends was married during my stay, and she appeared deeply interested in the event. She spent

several days in assisting her previous to the celebration. I resided
in the mean time at her mamma's, visiting her at her friend's,
where Major Sanford among others was received as a guest. Mrs.
Sumner acquainted me that she had prevailed on Miss Wharton
to go and spend a few weeks with her at Boston, whither she
was removing, and urged my accompanying them. I endeavored
to excuse myself, as I had been absent from my people a con-
siderable time; and my return was now expected. But their
importunity was so great, and Eliza's declaration that it would
be very agreeable to her so tempting, that I consented. Here I
took lodgings and spent about a week, taking every opportunity
to converse with Eliza and striving to discover her real disposi-
tion towards me. I mentioned the inconvenience of visiting her
so often as I wished and suggested my desire to enter, as soon as
might be, into a family relation. I painted in the most alluring
colors the pleasures resulting from domestic tranquillity, mutual
confidence, and conjugal affection; and I insisted on her de-
claring frankly whether she designed to share this happiness with
me and when it should commence. She owned that she intended
to give me her hand; but when she should be ready, she could
not yet determine. She pretended a promise from me to wait
her time, to consent that she should share the pleasures of the
fashionable world as long as she chose, etc.

I then attempted to convince her of her mistaken ideas of
pleasure; that the scenes of dissipation, of which she was so
passionately fond, afforded no true enjoyment; that the adula-
tion of the coxcomb could not give durability to her charms or
secure the approbation of the wise and good; that the fasionable
amusements of brilliant assemblies and crowded theaters could
not furnish the mind with

> That which nothing earthly gives or can destroy—
> The soul's calm sunshine and the heartfelt joy.

These friendly suggestions, I found, were considered the
theme of a priest, and my desire to detach her from such empty
pursuits the selfishness of a lover. She was even offended at my
freedom and warmly affirmed that no one had a right to arraign
her conduct. I mentioned Major Sanford, who was then in town
and who (though she went to places of public resort with Mr.
and Mrs. Sumner) always met and gallanted her home. She ral-
lied me upon my jealousy, as she termed it, wished that I would

attend her myself, so that she should need no other gallant. I answered that I had rather resign that honor to another, but wished for her sake that he might be a gentleman whose character would not disgrace the company with which he associated. She appeared mortified and chagrined in the extreme. However, she studiously suppressed her emotions and even soothed me with the blandishments of female softness. We parted amicably. She promised to return soon and prepare for a compliance with my wishes. I cannot refuse to believe her. I cannot cease to love her. My heart is in her possession. She has a perfect command of my passions. Persuasion dwells on her tongue. With all the boasted fortitude and resolution of our sex, we are but mere machines. Let love once pervade our breasts, and its object may mold us into any form that pleases her fancy, or even caprice.

I have just received a letter from Eliza, informing me of her return to Hartford. Tomorrow I shall set out on a visit to the dear girl; for, my friend, notwithstanding all her foibles, she is very dear to me. Before you hear from me again, I expect that the happy day will be fixed—the day which shall unite in the most sacred bands this lovely maid and your faithful friend,

J. Boyer.

LETTER XL

To Mr. Selby.

Hampshire

I have returned; and the day, indeed, is fixed—but how different from my fond expectations! It is not the day of union, but the day of final separation; the day which divides me from my charmer; the day which breaks asunder the bands of love; the day on which my reason assumes its empire and triumphs over the arts of a finished coquette. Congratulate me, my friend, that I have thus overcome my feelings and repelled the infatuating wiles of a deceitful girl. I would not be understood to impeach Miss Wharton's virtue; I mean her chastity. Virtue, in the common acceptation of the term as applied to the sex, is confined to that particular, you know. But in my view, this is of little importance where all other virtues are wanting.

When I arrived at Mrs. Wharton's and inquired for Eliza. I was told that she had ridden out but was soon expected home. An hour after, a phaeton stopped at the door, from which my fair one alighted, and was handed into the house by Major Sanford, who immediately took leave. I met her and offered my hand, which she received with apparent tenderness.

When the family had retired after supper and left us to talk on our particular affairs, I found the same indecision, the same loathness to bring our courtship to a period, as formerly. Her previous excuses were renewed, and her wishes to have a union still longer delayed were zealously urged. She could not bear the idea of confinement to the cares of a married life at present and begged me to defer all solicitation on that subject to some future day. I found my temper rise and told her plainly that I was not thus to be trifled with; that, if her regard for me was sincere, if she really intended to form a connection with me, she could not thus protract the time, try my patience, and prefer every other pleasure to the rational interchange of affection and to the calm delights of domestic life. But in vain did I argue against her false notions of happiness; in vain did I represent the dangerous system of conduct which she now pursued and urge her to accept, before it was too late, the hand and heart which were devoted to her service. That, she said, she purposed ere long to do, and hoped amply to reward my faithful love; but she could not fix the time this evening. She must consider a little further and likewise consult her mother. "Is it not Major Sanford whom you wish to consult, madam?" said I. She blushed and gave me no answer. "Tell me, Eliza," I continued, "tell me frankly, if he has not supplanted me in your affections —if he is not the cause of my being thus evasively, thus cruelly, treated. "Major Sanford, sir," replied she, "has done you no harm. He is a particular friend of mine, a polite gentleman, and an agreeable neighbor, and therefore I treat him with civility; but he is not so much interested in my concerns as to alter my disposition towards any other person." "Why," said I, "do you talk of friendship with a man of his character? Between his society and mine there is a great contrast. Such opposite pursuits and inclinations cannot be equally pleasing to the same taste. It is, therefore, necessary that you renounce the one to enjoy the other; I will give you time to decide which. I am going to a friend's house to spend the night and will call on you

tomorrow, if agreeable, and converse with you further upon the matter." She bowed assent, and I retired.

The next afternoon I went, as agreed, and found her mamma and her alone in the parlor. She was very pensive and appeared to have been in tears. The sight affected me. The idea of having treated her harshly the evening before disarmed me of my resolution to insist on her decision that day. I invited her to ride with me and visit a friend, to which she readily consented. We spent our time agreeably. I forbore to press her on the subject of our future union, but strove rather to soothe her mind and inspire her with sentiments of tenderness towards me. I conducted her home and returned early in the evening to my friend's. He met me at the door and jocosely told me that he expected that I should now rob them of their agreeable neighbor. "But," added he, "we have been apprehensive that you would be rivaled if you delayed your visit much longer." "I did not suspect a rival," said I. "Who can the happy man be?" "I can say nothing from personal observation," said he; "but fame, of late, has talked loudly of Major Sanford and Miss Wharton. Be not alarmed," continued he, seeing me look grave; "I presume no harm is intended; the Major is a man of gallantry, and Miss Wharton is a gay lady; but I dare say that your connection will be happy, *if it be formed.*" I noticed a particular emphasis on the word *if*; and, as we were alone, I followed him with questions till the whole affair was developed. I informed him of my embarrassment, and he gave me to understand that Eliza's conduct had, for some time past, been a subject of speculation in the town; that, formerly, her character was highly esteemed; but that her intimacy with a man of Sanford's known libertinism, more especially as she was supposed to be engaged to another, had rendered her very censurable; that they were often together; that wherever she went he was sure to follow, as if by appointment; that they walked, talked, sang, and danced together in all companies; that some supposed he would marry her; others that he only meditated adding her name to the black catalogue of deluded wretches whom he had already ruined.

I rose and walked the room in great agitation. He apologized for his freedom; was sorry if he had wounded my feelings; but said that friendship alone had induced him frankly to declare the truth, that I might guard against duplicity and deceit. I thanked him for his kind intentions and assured him that I

should not quit the town until I had determined this affair in one way or another.

I retired to bed, but sleep was a stranger to my eyes. With the dawn I rose; and after breakfast I walked to Mrs. Wharton's. She informed me that Eliza was in her chamber writing to a friend and would be down in a few minutes. I entered into conversation with the old lady on the subject of her daughter's conduct, hinted my suspicions of the cause, and declared my resolution of knowing my destiny immediately. She endeavored to extenuate and excuse her as much as possible, but frankly owned that her behavior was mysterious; that no pains had been wanting, on her part, to alter and rectify it; that she had remonstrated, expostulated, advised, and entreated as often as occasion required. She hoped that my resolution would have a good effect, as she knew that her daughter esteemed me very highly.

In this manner we conversed until the clock struck twelve; and Eliza, not appearing, I desired her mamma to send up word that I waited to see her. The maid returned with an answer that she was indisposed and had lain down. Mrs. Wharton observed that she had not slept for several nights and complained of the headache in the morning. The girl added that she would wait on Mr. Boyer in the evening. Upon this information I rose and abruptly took my leave. I went to dine with a friend, to whom I had engaged myself the day before; but my mind was too much agitated to enjoy either the company or the dinner. I excused myself from tarrying to tea and returned to Miss Wharton's. On inquiry, I was told that Eliza had gone to walk in the garden, but desired that no person might intrude on her retirement. The singularity of the request awakened my curiosity and determined me to follow her. I sought her in vain in different parts of the garden until, going towards an arbor almost concealed from sight by surrounding shrubbery, I discovered her sitting in close conversation with Major Sanford! My blood chilled in my veins, and I stood petrified with astonishment at the disclosure of such baseness and deceit. They both rose in visible confusion. I dared not trust myself to accost them. My passions were raised, and I feared that I might say or do something unbecoming my character. I therefore gave them a look of indignation and contempt and retreated to the house. I traversed the parlor hastily, overwhelmed with chagrin and resentment. Mrs. Wharton inquired the cause. I attempted to tell her, but my tongue refused utter-

ance. While in this situation, Eliza entered the room. She was not less discomposed than myself. She sat down at the window and wept. Her mamma wept likewise. At length she recovered herself, in a degree, and desired me to sit down. I answered, No, and continued walking. "Will you," said she, "permit me to vindicate my conduct and explain my motives?" "Your conduct," said I, "cannot be vindicated; your motives need no explanation; they are too apparent. How, Miss Wharton, have I merited this treatment from you? But I can bear it no longer. Your indifference to me proceeds from an attachment to another, and, forgive me if I add. to one who is the disgrace of his own sex and the destroyer of yours. I have been too long the dupe of your dissimulation and coquetry; too long has my peace of mind been sacrificed to the arts of a woman whose conduct has proved her unworthy of my regard—insensible to love, gratitude, and honor.

"To you, madam," said I, turning to her mother, "I acknowledge my obligations for your friendship, politeness, and attention. I once hoped for the privilege of rocking for you the cradle of declining age. I am deprived of that privilege, but I pray that you may never want a child whose love and duty shall prove a source of consolation and comfort.

"Farewell. If we never meet again in this life, I hope and trust we shall in a better—where the parent's eye shall cease to weep for the disobedience of a child and the lover's heart to bleed for the infidelity of his mistress."

I turned to Eliza and attempted to speak; but her extreme emotion softened me, and I could not command my voice. I took her hand and, bowing in token of an adieu, went precipitately out of the house. The residence of my friend, with whom I lodged, was at no great distance; and thither I repaired. As I met him in the entry, I rushed by him and betook myself to my chamber. The fever of resentment and the tumult of passion began now to give place to the softer emotions of the soul. I found myself perfectly unmanned. I gave free scope to the sensibility of my heart, and the effeminate relief of tears materially lightened the load which oppressed me.

After this arduous struggle I went to bed and slept more calmly than for several nights before. The next morning I wrote a farewell letter to Eliza (a copy of which I shall enclose to you) and, ordering my horse to be brought, left town immediately.

My resentment of her behavior has much assisted me in erasing her image from my breast. In this exertion I have suceeded beyond my most sanguine expectations. The more I reflect on her temper and disposition, the more my gratitude is enlivened towards the wise Disposer of all events for enabling me to break asunder the snares of the deluder. I am convinced that the gaiety and extravagance of her taste, the frivolous levity of her manners, disqualify her for the station in which I wished to have placed her. These considerations, together with that resignation to an overruling Providence which the religion I profess and teach requires me to cultivate, induce me cheerfully to adopt the following lines of an ingenious poet:

> Since all the downward tracts of time
> God's watchful eye surveys,
> O, who so wise to choose our lot,
> Or regulate our ways?
>
> Since none can doubt his equal love,
> Unmeasurably kind,
> To his unerring, gracious will
> Be every wish resigned.
>
> Good when he gives, supremely good;
> Not less when he denies;
> Even crosses from his soverign hand
> Are blessings in disguise.

<div align="right">J. Boyer.</div>

To Miss Eliza Wharton.

[Enclosed in the foregoing.]

<div align="right">Hartford.</div>

Madam: Fearing that my resolution may not be proof against the eloquence of those charms which has so long commanded me, I take this method of bidding you a final adieu. I write not as a lover—that connection between us is forever dissolved—but I address you as a friend; as a friend to your happiness, to your reputation, to your temporal and eternal welfare. I will not rehearse the innumerable instances of your imprudence and misconduct which have fallen under my observation. Your own

heart must be your monitor. Suffice it for me to warn you against the dangerous tendency of so dissipated a life, and to tell you that I have traced (I believe aright) the cause of your dissimulation and indifference to me. They are an aversion to the sober, rational, frugal mode of living to which my profession leads; a fondness for the parade, the gaiety, not to say the licentiousness, of a station calculated to gratify such a disposition; and a prepossession for Major Sanford, infused into your giddy mind by the frippery, flattery, and artifice of that worthless and abandoned man. Hence you preferred a connection with him, if it could be accomplished; but a doubt whether it could, together with the advice of your friends who have kindly espoused my cause, has restrained you from the avowal of your real sentiments and led you to continue your civilities to me. What the result of your coquetry would have been had I waited for it, I cannot say; nor have I now any desire or interest to know. I tear from my breast the idea which I have long cherished of future union and happiness with you in the conjugal state. I bid a last farewell to these fond hopes and leave you forever.

For your own sake, however, let me conjure you to review your conduct and, before you have advanced beyond the possibility of returning to recitude and honor, to restrain your steps from the dangerous path in which you now tread.

Fly Major Sanford. That man is a deceiver. Trust not his professions. They are certainly insincere, or he would not affect concealment; he would not induce you to a clandestine intercourse. Many have been the victims to his treachery. O Eliza, add not to the number. Banish him from your society if you wish to preserve your virtue unsullied, your character unsuspicious. It already begins to depreciate. Snatch it from the unvenomed tongue of slander before it receives an incurable wound.

Many faults have been visible to me, over which my affection once drew a veil. That veil is now removed; and acting the part of a disinterested friend, I shall mention some few of them with freedom. There is a levity in your manners which is inconsistent with the solidity and decorum becoming a lady who has arrived to years of discretion. There is also an unwarrantable extravagance betrayed in your dress. Prudence and economy are such necessary, at least such decent, virtues that they claim the atten-

tion of every female, whatever be her station or her property. To these virtues you are apparently inattentive. Too large a portion of your time is devoted to the adorning of your person.

Think not that I write thus plainly from resentment. No, it is from benevolence. I mention your foibles, not that I reproach you with them but that you may consider their nature and effects and renounce them.

I wish you to regard this letter as the legacy of a friend, and to improve it accordingly. I shall leave town before you receive it. O, how different are my sensations at going from what they were when I came! But I forbear description. Think not, Eliza, that I leave you with indifference. The conquest is great, the trial more than I can calmly support; yet the consciousness of duty affords consolation—a duty I conceive it to be which I owe to myself and to the people of my charge, who are interested in my future connection.

I wish not for an answer; my resolution is unalterably fixed. But should you hereafter be convinced of the justice of my conduct and become a convert to my advice, I shall be happy to hear it.

That you may have wisdom to keep you from falling and conduct you safely through this state of trial to the regions of immortal bliss is the fervent prayer of your sincere friend and humble servant,

<div align="right">J. Boyer.</div>

LETTER XLI

To Mrs. Lucy Sumner.

<div align="right">Hartford</div>

The retirement of my native home is not so gloomy, since my return from Boston, as I expected, from the contrast between them. Indeed, the customs and amusements of this place are materially altered since the residence of Major Sanford among us. The dull, old-fashioned sobriety which formerly prevailed is nearly banished; and cheerfulness, vivacity, and enjoyment are substituted in its stead. Pleasure is now diffused through all ranks of the people, especially the rich; and surely it ought to

be cultivated, since the wisest of men informs us that a merry heart "doth good like a medicine." As human life hath many diseases which require medicines, are we not right in selecting the most agreeable and palatable? Major Sanford's example has had great influence upon our society in general; and though some of our old ones think him rather licentious, yet, for aught I can see, he is as strict an observer of decorum as the best of them. True, he seldom goes to church; but what of that? The Deity is not confined to temples made with hands. He may worship him as devoutly elsewhere, if he chooses; and who has a right to say he does not?

His return from Boston was but a day or two after mine. He paid me an early visit and, indeed, has been very attentive ever since. My mamma is somewhat precise in her notions of propriety and, of course, blames me for associating so freely with him. She says that my engagements to Mr. Boyer ought to render me more sedate and more indifferent to the gallantry of mere pleasure *hunters*, to use her phrase. But I think otherwise. If I am to become a recluse, let me at least enjoy those amusements which are suited to my taste a short time first. Why should I refuse the polite attentions of this gentleman? They smooth the rugged path of life and wonderfully accelerate the lagging wheels of time.

Indeed, Lucy, he has an admirable talent for contributing to vary and increase amusement. We have few hours unimproved. Some new plan of pleasure and sociability is constantly courting our adoption. He lives in all the magnificence of a prince; and why should I, who can doubtless share that magnificence if I please, forego the advantages and indulgences it offers, merely to gratify those friends who pretend to be better judges of my happiness than I am myself? I have not yet told my mamma that he entertains me with the lover's theme or, at least, that I listen to it. Yet I must own to you, from whom I have never concealed an action or idea, that his situation in life charms my imagination; that the apparent fervor and sincerity of his passion affect my heart. Yet there is something extremely problematical in his conduct. He is very urgent with me to dissolve my connection with Mr. Boyer and engage not to marry him without his consent or knowledge, to say no more. He warmly applauds my wish still longer to enjoy the freedom and independence of a single state, and professedly adopts it for his own. While he

would disconnect me from another, he mysteriously conceals his own intentions and views. In conversation with him yesterday, I plainly told him that his conduct was unaccountable; that, if his professions and designs were honorable, he could not neglect to mention them to my mamma; that I should no longer consent to carry on a clandestine intercourse with him; that I hourly expected Mr. Boyer, whom I esteemed and who was the favorite of my friends; and that, unless he acted openly in this affair before his arrival, I should give my hand to him.

He appeared thunderstruck at this declaration. All his words and actions were indicative of the most violent emotions of mind. He entreated me to recall the sentence; for I knew not, he said, his motives for secrecy; yet he solemnly swore that they were honorable. I replied in the words of the poet—

> Trust not a man; they are by nature cruel,
> False, deceitful, treacherous, and inconstant.
> When a man talks of love, with caution hear him;
> But if he swear, he'll certainly deceive you.

He begged that he might know by what means he had provoked my suspicions; by what means he had forfeited my confidence. His importunity vanquished my fortitude; and before we parted, I again promised to make him acquainted, from time to time, with the progress of my connection with Mr. Boyer.

Now, my dear friend, I want your advice more than ever. I am inadvertently embarrassed by this man; and how to extricate myself I know not. I am sensible that the power is in my hands; but the disposition (shall I confess it?) is wanting.

> I know the right, and I approve it too;
> I know the wrong, and yet the wrong pursue.

I have just received a card from Major Sanford, inviting me to ride this afternoon. At first I thought of returning a negative answer; but, recollecting that Mr. Boyer must soon be here, I concluded it best to embrace this opportunity of talking further with him. I must now prepare to go, but I shall not close this letter; for I intend writing in continuation, as events occur, till this important business is decided.

Tuesday evening—The little tour which I mentioned to you this afternoon was not productive of a final determination. The same plea was repeated over and over again without closing the

cause. On my return I found Mr. Boyer waiting to receive me. My heart beat an involuntary welcome. I received him very cordially, though with a kind of pleasure mixed with apprehension. I must own that his conversation and manners are much better calculated to bear the scrutinizing eye of a refined understanding and taste than Major Sanford's. But whether the fancy ought not to be consulted about our settlement in life is with me a question.

When we parted last I had promised Mr. Boyer to inform his positively, at this visit, when my hand should be given. He therefore came, as he told me in the course of our conversation, with the resolution of claiming the fulfillment of this promise.

I begged absolution, told him that I could not possibly satisfy his claim, and sought still to evade and put off the important decision. He grew warm and affirmed that I treated him ungenerously and made needless delays. He even accused me of indifference towards him and of partiality to another. Major Sanford, he believed, was the man who robbed him of the affection which he had supposed his due. He warned me against any intercourse with him and insisted that I must renounce the society of the one or the other immediately.

He would leave me, he said, this evening and call tomorrow to know the result of my determination. It was late before he bade me good night, since which I have written these particulars. It is now time to lay aside my pen and deliberate what course to take.

Wednesday evening—Last night I closed not my eyes. I rose this morning with the sun and went into the garden till breakfast. My mamma doubtless saw the disorder of my mind but kindly avoided any inquiry about it. She was affectionately attentive to me but said nothing of my particular concerns. I mentioned not my embarrassment to her. She had declared herself in favor of Mr. Boyer; therefore, I had no expectation that she would advise impartially. I retired to my chamber and remained in a kind of revery for more than an hour, when I was roused by the rattling of a carriage at the door. I hastened to the window and saw Major Sanford just driving away. The idea of his having been to converse with my mamma gave me new sensations. A thousand perplexities occurred to my mind relative to the part most proper for me to act in this critical situation. All these might have been avoided, had I gone down and in-

quired into the matter; but this I delayed till dinner. My mamma then informed me that Major Sanford had been with her and inquired for me, but that she thought it unnecessary to call me as she presumed I had no particular business with him. I knew the motives by which she was actuated and was vexed at her evasions. I told her plainly that she would never carry her point in this way; that I thought myself capable of conducting my own affair and wished her not to interfere, except by her advice, which I should always listen to and comply with when I could possibly make it consistent with my inclination and interest. She wept at my undutiful anger (of which I have severely repented since) and affectionately replied that my happiness was the object of her wishes and prayers; conformably, she felt constrained freely to speak her mind though it incurred my displeasure. She then went through again with all the comparative circumstances and merits of the two candidates for my favor, which have perpetually rung in my ears for months. I shed tears at the idea of my embarrassment, and in this condition Mr Boyer found us. He appeared to be affected by my visible disorder and, without inquiring the cause, endeavored to dissipate it. This was kindly done. He conversed upon indifferent subjects and invited me to ride and take tea with your mamma, to which I readily consented. We found her at home and passed the time agreeably, excepting the alloy of your absence. Mr. Boyer touched lightly on the subject of our last evening's debate, but expatiated largely on the pleasing power of love and hoped that we should one day both realize and exemplify it in perfection. When we returned he observed that it was late; he took his leave, telling me that he should call tomorrow and begged that I would then relieve his suspense. As I was retiring to bed, the maid gave me a hint that Major Sanford's servant had been here and left a letter. I turned instantly back to my mamma and, telling her my information, demanded the letter. She hesitated, but I insisted on having it; and seeing me resolute, she reluctantly gave it into my hand. It contained the following words:

"Am I forsaken? Am I abandoned? O my adorable Eliza, have you sacrificed me to my rival? Have you condemned me to perpetual banishment without a hearing?

"I came this day to plead my cause at your feet, but I was cruelly denied the privilege of seeing you. My mind is all an-

archy and confusion. My soul is harrowed up with jealousy. I will be revenged on those who separate us. if that distracting event take place. But it is from your lips only that I can hear my sentence. You must witness its effects. To what lengths my despair may carry me I know not. You are the arbitress of my fate.

"Let me conjure you to meet me in your garden tomorrow at any hour you shall appoint. My servant will call for an answer in the morning. Deny me not an interview, but have pity on your faithful

Sanford."

I wrote for answer that I would meet him tomorrow, at five o'clock in the afternoon.

I have now before me another night for consideration, and I shall pass it in that employment. I purpose not to see Mr. Boyer until I have conversed with Major Sanford.

Thursday morning—The morning dawns and ushers in the day —a day, perhaps, big with the fate of your friend. What that fate may be is wrapped in the womb of futurity—that futurity which a kind Providence has wisely concealed from the penetration of mortals.

After mature consideration, after revolving and re-revolving every circumstance on both sides of the question, I have nearly determined, in compliance with the advice of my friends and the dictates of my own judgment, to give Mr. Boyer the preference and with him to tread the future round of life.

As to the despair of Major Sanford, it does not much alarm me. Such violent passions are seldom so deeply rooted as to produce lasting effects. I must, however, keep my word and meet him according to promise.

Mr. Boyer is below. My mamma has just sent me word that he wished to see me. My reply was that I had lain down, which was a fact.

One o'clock—My mamma, alarmed by my indisposition, has visited my apartment. I soon convinced her that it was but trifling, owing principally to the want of sleep, and that an airing in the garden, which I intended towards night, would restore me.

Ten o'clock at night—The day is past; and such a day it has been as I hope nevermore to see. At the hour appointed, I went, tolerably composed and resolute, into the garden. I had taken

several turns and retired into the little arbor, where you and I have spent so many happy hours, before Major Sanford entered. When he appeared, a consciousness of the impropriety of this clandestine intercourse suffused my cheek and gave a coldness to my manners. He immediately penetrated the cause and observed that my very countenance told him he was no longer a welcome guest to me. I asked him if he ought so to be, since his motives for seeking admission were unworthy of being communicated to my friends. That, he said, was not the case—but that prudence in the present instance required a temporary concealment.

He then undertook to exculpate himself from blame—assuring me that, as soon as I should discountenance the expectations of Mr. Boyer and discontinue the reception of his address, his intentions should be made known. He was enlarging upon this topic when we heard a footstep approaching us and, looking up, saw Mr. Boyer within a few paces of the arbor. Confusion seized us both. We rose involuntarily from our seats but were mute as statues. He spoke not a word, but casting a look of indignant accusation at me—a glance which penetrated my very soul—turned on his heel and walked hastily back to the house.

I stood a few moments considering what course to take, though shame and regret had almost taken from me the power of thought.

Major Sanford took my hand. I withdrew it from him. "I *must* leave you," said I. "Where will you go?" said he. "I will go and try to retrieve my character. It has suffered greatly by this fatal interview."

He threw himself at my feet and exclaimed, "Leave me not, Eliza; I conjure you not to leave me." "Let me go now," I rejoined, "or I bid you farewell forever." I flew precipitately by him and went into the parlor where I found Mr. Boyer and my mamma, the one traversing the room in the greatest agitation and the other in a flood of tears. Their appearance affected me, and I wept like an infant. When I had a little recovered myself, I begged him to sit down. He answered, No. I then told him that, however unjustifiable my conduct might appear, perhaps I might explain it to his satisfaction, if he would hear me; that my motives were innocent, though they doubtless wore the aspect of criminality in his view. He sternly replied that no palliation could avail; that my motives were sufficiently notorious. He accused me of treating him ill, of rendering him the dupe of

coquetting artifice, of having an intrigue with Major Sanford; he declared his determination to leave me forever, unworthy of his regard and incapable of love, gratitude, or honor. There was too much reason in support of his accusations for me to gainsay them, had his impetuosity suffered me to attempt it.

But, in truth, I had no inclination to self-defense. My natural vivacity had forsaken me, and I listened without interrupting him to the fluency of reproachful language which his resentment inspired. He took a very solemn and affectionate leave of my mamma, thanking her for her politeness and wishing her much future felicity. He attempted to address me, I suppose somewhat in the same way; but his sensibility somewhat overcame him, and he only took my hand and, bowing in silence, departed.

The want of rest for two long nights together, the exercise of mind, and conflict of passions which now tortured my breast, were too much for me to support.

When I saw that he was gone, that he had actually forsaken me, I fainted. My mamma, with the assistance of the maid, soon restored me.

When I opened my eyes and beheld this amiable and tender parent watching and attending me with the most anxious concern, without one reproachful word, without one accusing look, my reflections upon the part I had acted in defeating her benevolent wishes were exquisitely afflictive. But we mutually forbore to mention the occasion of my illness, and I complied with her advice to take some refreshment and retire to my chamber. I am so much fatigued by the exertions of the day that rest is absolutely necessary, and I lay aside my pen to seek it.

Friday morning—When I shall again receive the balmy influence of sleep, I know not. It has absolutely forsaken me at present. I have had a most restless night. Every awakening idea presented itself to my imagination; whether I had sustained a real loss in Mr. Boyer's departure, reflections on my own misconduct, the censure of my friends, and the ill-natured remarks of my enemies excited the most painful anxiety in my mind.

I am going down; but how shall I see my mamma? To her I will confess my faults, in her maternal breast repose my cares, and by her friendly advice regulate my conduct. Had I done this before, I might have escaped this trouble and saved both her and myself many distressing emotions.

Friday evening—I have had a long conversation with my

mamma, which has greatly relieved my mind. She has soothed me with the most endearing tenderness.

Mr. Atkins, with whom Mr. Boyer lodged while in town, called here this afternoon. I did not see him; but he told my mamma that Mr. Boyer had returned home and left a letter for me, which he had promised to convey with his own hand. By this I am convinced that the die is absolutely cast with respect to him, and that no attempts on my part to bring about a reconciliation would be either prudent or successful. He has penetrated the cause of my proceedings, and such is his resentment that I am inclined not much to regret his avoiding another interview.

My excuses would be deemed utterly insufficient, and truth would not befriend and justify me.

As I know you are impatient to hear from me, I will now dispatch this long letter without any other addition than that I am your sincere friend,

<div align="right">Eliza Wharton.</div>

LETTER XLII

To Mr. Charles Deighton.

<div align="right">Hartford</div>

Well, Charles, the show is over, as we Yankees say, and the girl is my own—that is, if I will have her. I shall take my own time for that, however. I have carried my point and am amply revenged on the whole posse of those dear friends of hers. She was entangled by a promise (not to marry this priest without my knowledge), which her conscience would not let her break. Thank God, I have no conscience. If I had, I believe it would make wretched work with me. I suppose she intended to have one or the other of us, but she preferred me. I have escaped the noose this time, and I'll be fairly hanged if I ever get so near it again; for, indeed, Charles, I was seriously alarmed. I watched all their motions, and the appearance of harmony between them awakened all my activity and zeal. So great was my infatuation that I verily believe I should have asked her in marriage and risked the consequences, rather than have lost her.

I went to the house while Mr. Boyer was in town; but her mamma refused to call her, or to acquaint her that I was there. I then wrote a despairing letter and obtained a conference with her in the garden. This was a fortunate event for me. True, Eliza was very haughty and resolutely insisted on an immediate declaration or rejection; and I cannot say what would have been the result if Mr. Boyer had not surprised us together. He gave us a pretty harsh look and retired without speaking a word.

I endeavored to detain Eliza but in vain. She left me on my knees, which are always ready to bend on such occasions.

This finished the matter, it seems. I rose and went into a neighbor's to observe what happened, and in about half an hour I saw Mr. Boyer come out and go to his lodgings. "This," said I to myself, "is a good omen." I went home and was informed next day that he had mounted his horse and departed.

I heard nothing more of her until yesterday, when I determined to know how she stood affected towards me. I therefore paid her a visit, her mamma being luckily abroad.

She received me very placidly and told me, on inquiry, that Mr. Boyer's resentment at her meeting me in the garden was so great that he had bade her a final adieu. I congratulated myself on having no rival; I hoped that her favor would now be unbiased, and in due time that I should reap the reward of my fidelity. She begged me not to mention the subject, said she had been perplexed by our competition, and wished not to hear anything further about it at present. I bowed in obedience to her commands and changed the discourse.

I informed her that I was about to take a tour to the southward; I would be absent several months and trusted that on my return her embarrassments would be over.

I left her with regret. After all, Charles, she is the *summum bonum* of my life. I must have her in some way or other. Nobody else shall, I am resolved.

I am making preparations for my journey, which, between you and me, is occasioned by the prospect of making a speculation by which I hope to mend my affairs. The voyage will at least lessen my expenses and screen me from the importunity of creditors till I can look about me.

Peter Sanford.

LETTER XLIII

To Miss Eliza Wharton.

New Haven

Through the medium of my friends at Hartford, I have been informed of the progress of your affairs as they have transpired. The detail which my sister gave me of your separation from Mr. Boyer was painful, as I had long contemplated a happy union between you; but still more disagreeable sensations possessed my breast when I was told that you had suffered your lively spirits to be depressed and resigned yourself to solitude and dejection.

Why, my dear friend, should you allow this event thus to affect you? Heaven, I doubt not, has happiness still in store for you—perhaps greater than you could have enjoyed in that connection. If the conviction of any misconduct on your part gives you pain, dissipate it by the reflection that unerring rectitude is not the lot of mortals; that few are found who have not deviated, in a greater or less degree, from the maxims of prudence. Our greatest mistakes may teach lessons which will be useful through life.

But I will not moralize. Come and see us, and we will talk over the matter once and then dismiss it forever. Do prevail on your mamma to part with you a month or two at least. I wish you to witness how well I manage my nursery business. You will be charmed with little Harriet. I am already enough of the mother to think her a miniature of beauty and perfection.

How natural and how easy the transition from one stage of life to another! Not long since, I was a gay, volatile girl, seeking satisfaction in fasionable circles and amusements; but now I am thoroughly domesticated. All my happiness is centered within the limits of my own walls, and I grudge every moment that calls me from the pleasing scenes of domestic life. Not that I am so selfish as to exclude my friends from my affection or society. I feel interested in their concerns and enjoy their company. I must own, however, that conjugal and parental love are the mainsprings of my life. The conduct of some mothers, in depriving their helpless offspring of the care and kindness which none but a mother can feel, is to me unaccountable. There are

many nameless attentions which nothing short of maternal tenderness and solicitude can pay and for which the endearing smiles and progressive improvements of the lovely babe are an ample reward.

How delightful to trace from day to day the expansion of reason and the dawnings of intelligence! O, how I anticipate the time when these faculties shall be displayed by the organs of speech; when the lisping accent shall heighten our present pleasure; when the young idea is capable of direction "how to shoot"! General Richman is not less interested by these enjoyments than myself. All the father beams in his eye; all the husband reigns in his heart and pervades his every action.

Miss Lawrence is soon to be married to Mr. Layton. I believe he is a mere fortune hunter. Indeed, she has little to recommend her to any other. Nature has not been very bountiful either to her body or mind. Her parents have been shamefully deficient in her education, but have secured to her what they think the chief good—not considering that happiness is by no means the invariable attendant of wealth.

I hope this incoherent scrawl will amuse, while it induces you speedily to favor us with another visit.

My best wishes attend your honored mamma, while I subscribe myself

A. Richman.

LETTER XLIV

To Mrs. Lucy Sumner.

Hartford

I am extremely depressed, my dear Lucy. The agitating scenes through which I have lately passed have broken my spirits and rendered me unfit for society. Major Sanford has visited me and taken his leave. He is gone to the southward on a tour of two or three months. I declined any further conversation with him on the subject of love. At present I wish not to hear it mentioned by any one.

I have received a very friendly and consolatory letter from Mrs. Richman. She invites me to spend a few months with her

which, with my mamma's consent, I shall do. I hope the change of situation and company will dissipate the gloom which hangs over my mind.

It is a common observation that we know not the value of a blessing but by deprivation. This is strictly verified in my case. I was insensible of my regard for Mr. Boyer until this fatal separation took place. His merit and worth now appear in the brightest colors. I am convinced of that excellence which I once slighted, and the shade of departed happiness haunts me perpetually. I am sometimes tempted to write to him and confess my faults; to tell him the situation of my mind; to offer him my hand; but he has precluded all hopes of success by the severity of his letter to me. At any rate, I shall do nothing of the kind until my return from New Haven.

I am the more willing to leave home as my affairs are made a town talk. My mamma persuades me to disregard it; but how can I rise superior to "the world's dread laugh, which scarce the firm philosopher can scorn"?

Pray remember me to Mr. Sumner. You are happy, my friend, in the love and esteem of a worthy man, but more happy still in deserving them. Adieu.

<div align="right">Eliza Wharton.</div>

LETTER XLV

To Mrs. Lucy Sumner.

<div align="right">Hartford</div>

I have returned to the once smiling seat of maternal affection, but I find not repose and happiness even here.

In the society of my amiable friends at New Haven, I enjoyed everything that friendship could bestow; but rest to a disturbed mind was not in their power.

I was on various parties of pleasure and passed through different scenes of amustment, but with me they have lost their charms. I relished them not as formerly.

Mrs. Richman advises me to write to Mr. Boyer, and I have concluded to act accordingly. If it answers no other purpose, it will be a relief to my mind. If he ever felt for me the tenderness

and regard which he professed, I think they cannot be entirely obliterated. If they still remain, perhaps I may rekindle the gentle flame; and we may both be happy. I may at least recall his esteem, and that will be a satisfaction to my conscious mind.

I wonder what has become of Major Sanford. Has he, too, forsaken me? Is it possible for him wilfully to neglect me? I will not entertain so injurious a suspicion. Yet, if it were the case, it would not affect me like Mr. Boyer's disaffection; for I frankly own that my fancy, and a taste for gaiety of life, induced me to cherish the idea of a connection with Major Sanford; yet Mr. Boyer's real merit has imprinted those sentiments of esteem and love in my heart which time can never efface.

Instead of two or three months, more than twelve months have elapsed; and I have not received a line from Major Sanford in all that time, which I fully expected, though he made no mention of writing; nor have I heard a syllable about him, except a report circulated by his servants that he is on the point of marrying, which I do not believe. No, it is impossible. I am persuaded that his passion for me was sincere, however deceitful he may have been with others. But I will not bestow an anxious thought upon him. My design relative to Mr. Boyer demands my whole attention.

My hopes and fears alternately prevail, and my resolution is extremely fluctuating. How it finally terminates you shall hear in my next. Pray write to me soon. I stand in need of the consoling power of friendship. Nothing can beguile my pensive hours and exhilarate my drooping spirits like your letters.

Let me know how you are to be entertained this winter at the theater. That, you know, is a favorite amusement of mine. You see I can step out of myself a little. Afford an assisting hand, and perhaps I may again be fit for society.

<div align="right">Eliza Wharton.</div>

LETTER XLVI

To the Rev. J. Boyer.

Hartford

It is partly in compliance with your desire in your last letter to me—in which you tell me "that, when I am convinced of the justice of your conduct and become a convert to your advice, you shall be happy to hear it"—and partly from a wish to inform you that such is in truth my present state of mind that I now write to you.

I cannot but hope that this letter, coming from the hand which you once sought, will not be unacceptable.

Pope very justly observes that "every year is a critic on the last." The truth of this observation is fully exemplified in my years. How severely this condemns the follies of the preceding, my own heart alone can testify.

I shall not offer any palliation or apology for my misconduct. You told me it admitted none. I frankly confess it; and if the most humble acknowledgment of my offenses, with an assurance that they have cost me the deepest repentance, can in any degree atone for them, I now make that atonement. Casting off the veil of dissimulation, I shall write with frankness, believing you possessed of more honor than to make ungenerous use of the confidence reposed in you.

To say that I ever esteemed you may, perhaps, appear paradoxical when compared with certain circumstances which occurred during our acquaintance; but to assert that I loved you may be deemed still more so. Yet these are real facts—facts of which I was then sensible and by which I am now more than ever affected.

I think you formerly remarked that absence served but to heighten real love. This I find by experience. Need I blush to declare these sentiments, when occasion like this calls for the avowal? I will go even further and offer you that heart which you once prized, that hand which you once solicited. The sentiments of affection which you then cultivated, though suppressed, I flatter myself are not wholly obliterated. Suffer me, then, to rekindle the latent flame, to revive that friendship and

tenderness which I have so foolishly neglected. The endeavor of my future life shall be to reward your benevolence, and perhaps we may yet be happy together.

But let not this offer of myself constrain you. Let not pity influence your conduct. I would have your return, if that pleasing event takes place, a voluntary act. Receive, or consent not to confer, happiness.

I thought it a duty which I owed to you, and to myself, to make this expiation, this sacrifice of female reserve for the wrongs I have done you. As such I wish you to accept it; and if your affections are entirely alienated or otherwise engaged, if you cannot again command the respect and love which I would recall, do not despise me for the concessions I have made. Think as favorably of my past faults and of my present disposition as charity will allow. Continue, if possible, to be my friend, though you cease to be my lover.

Should this letter find you in the full possession of happiness, let not the idea of your once-loved Eliza thus intruding itself again upon your thoughts interrupt your enjoyments. May some distinguished female, as deserving as fair, partake with you of that bliss which I have forfeited.

Whatever may be my destiny, my best wishes shall ever attend you, and a pleasing remembrance of your honorable attentions preside, until death, in the breast of

Eliza Wharton.

LETTER XLVII

To Miss Eliza Wharton.

Hampshire

As I was sitting last evening in my study, a letter was handed me by a servant; I no sooner cast my eye on it than I recognized, with surprise, the hand and seal of my once-loved, but to me long-lost, Eliza. I opened it hastily and with still greater surprise read the contents.

You write with frankness; I shall answer in the same manner.

On reviewing our former intercourse, be assured that I have not an accusing thought in my heart. The regard which I felt for

you was tender and animated, but it was not of that passionate kind which ends in death or despair. It was governed by reason and had a nobler object in view than mere sensual gratification. It was excited by the appearance of excellent qualities. Your conduct, at length, convinced me it was misplaced; that you possessed not in reality those charms which I had fondly ascribed to you. They were inconsistent, I conceived, with that artifice and dissimulation of which you strove to render me the dupe. But, thank Heaven, the snare was broken. My eyes were open to discover your folly; and my heart, engaged as it was, exerted resolution and strength to burst asunder the chain by which you held me enslaved and to assert the rights of an injured man.

The parting scene you remember. I reluctantly bade you adieu. I tore myself from you, determined to eradicate your idea from my breast. Long and severe was the struggle; at last I vanquished, as I thought, every tender passion of my soul (for they all centered in you) and resigned myself to my God and my duty, devoting those affections to friendship which had been disappointed in love. But they are again called into exercise. The virtuous, the amiable, the accomplished Maria Selby possesses my entire confidence and esteem; and I trust I am not deceived when I think her highly deserving of both. With her I expect soon to be united in the most sacred and endearing of human relations, with her to pass my future days in serenity and peace.

Your letter, therefore, came too late, were there no other obstacle to the renewal of our connection. I hope at the close of life, when we take a retrospect of the past, that neither of us shall have reason to regret our separation.

Permit me to add, that for your own sake and for the sake of your ever-valued friends, I sincerely rejoice that your mind has regained its native strength and beauty; that you have emerged from the shade of fanciful vanity. For although, to adopt your own phrase, I cease to style myself your lover, among the number of your friends I am happy to be reckoned. As such let me conjure you by all that is dear and desirable, both in this life and another, to adhere with undeviating exactness to the paths of rectitude and innocence and to improve the noble talents which Heaven has liberally bestowed upon you in rendering yourself amiable and useful to your friends. Thus will you secure your own happiness, while you promote the happiness of all around you.

I shall ever cherish sentiments of kindness towards you, and with gratitude remember your condescension in the testimony of regard which you have given me in your last letter.

I hope soon to hear that your heart and hand are bestowed on some worthy man who deserves the happiness you are formed to communicate. Whatever we may have called errors will, on my part, be forever buried in oblivion; and for your own peace of mind I entreat you to forget that any idea of a connection between us ever existed.

I shall always rejoice at the news of your welfare, and my ardent prayers will daily arise for your temporal and eternal felicity.

<div style="text-align: right">J. Boyer.</div>

LETTER XLVIII

To Mrs. Lucy Sumner.

<div style="text-align: right">Hartford</div>

Health, placid serenity, and every domestic pleasure are the lot of my friend; and I, who once possessed the means of each and the capacity of tasting them, have been tossed upon the waves of folly until I am shipwrecked on the shoals of despair.

O my friend, I am undone. I am slighted, rejected, by the man who once sought my hand, by the man who still retains my heart. And what adds an insupportable poignancy to the reflection is self-condemnation. From this inward torture where shall I flee? Where shall I seek that happiness which I have madly trifled away?

The enclosed letters* will show you whence this tumult of soul arises. But I blame not Mr. Boyer. He has acted nobly. I approve his conduct, though it operates my ruin.

He is worthy of his intended bride, and she is—what I am not—worthy of him. Peace and joy be their portion both here and hereafter. But what are now my prospects? What are to be the future enjoyments of my life?

O that I had not written to Mr. Boyer! By confessing my faults and by avowing my partiality to him, I have given him the

*See the two preceding letters. [Mrs. Foster's note]

power of triumphing in my distress; of returning to my tortured heart all the pangs of slighted love. And what have I now to console me? My bloom is decreasing; my health is sensibly impaired. Those talents, with the possession of which I have been flattered, will be of little avail when unsupported by respectability of character. My mamma, who knows too well the distraction of my mind, endeavors to soothe and compose me on Christian principles; but they have not their desired effect. I dare not converse freely with her on the subject of my present uneasiness lest I should distress her. I am therefore obliged to conceal my disquietude and appear as cheerful as possible in her company, though my heart is ready to burst with grief. O that you were near me, as formerly, to share and alleviate my cares! To have some friend in whom I could repose confidence and with whom I could freely converse and advise on this occasion would be an unspeakable comfort. Such a one, next to yourself, I think Julia Granby to be. With your leave and consent, I should esteem it a special favor if she would come and spend a few months with me. My mamma joins in this request. I would write to her on the subject, but I cannot compose myself at present. Will you prefer my petition for me?

If I have not forfeited your friendship, my dear Mrs. Sumner, write to me and pour its healing balm into the wounded mind of your

<div style="text-align: right">Eliza Wharton.</div>

LETTER XLIX

To Miss Eliza Wharton.

<div style="text-align: right">Boston</div>

Your truly romantic letter came safe to hand. Indeed, my dear, it would make a very pretty figure in a novel. A bleeding heart, slighted love, and all the *et ceteras* of romance enter into the composition.

Excuse this raillery, and I will now write more seriously. You refer yourself to my friendship for consolation. It shall be exerted for the purpose. But I must act the part of a skilful surgeon and probe the wound which I undertake to heal.

Where, O Eliza Wharton, where is that fund of sense and sentiment which once animated your engaging form? Where are that strength of mind, that independence of soul, that alacrity and sprightliness of deportment, which formerly raised you superior to every adverse occurrence? Why have you resigned these valuable endowments and suffered yourself to become the sport of contending passions?

You have now emerged from that mist of fanciful folly which in a measure obscured the brilliance of your youthful days.

True, you figured among the first-rate coquettes while your friends, who knew your accomplishments, lamented the misapplication of them; but now they rejoice at the returning empire of reason.

True, you have erred—misled by the gaiety of your disposition and that volatility and inconsideration which were incident to your years; but you have seen and nobly confessed your errors. Why do you talk of slighted love? True, Mr. Boyer, supposing you disregarded him, transferred his affections to another object; but have you not your admirers still among men of real merit? Are you not esteemed and caressed by numbers who know you capable of shining in a distinguished sphere of life? Turn then, my friend, from the gloomy prospect which your disturbed imagination has brought into view. Let reason and religion erect their throne in your breast; obey their dictates and be happy. Past experience will point out the quicksands which you are to avoid in your future course.

Date then from this a new era of life, and may every moment be attended with felicity. Follow Mr. Boyer's advice and forget all former connections.

Julia accepts your invitation. Nothing short of your request could induce me to part with her. She is a good girl, and her society will amuse and instruct you.

<div style="text-align: right">Lucy Sumner.</div>

LETTER L

To Mrs. Lucy Sumner.

Hartford

My Julia Granby has arrived. She is all that I once was—easy, sprightly, *debonnaire*. Already has she done much towards relieving my mind. She endeavors to divert and lead my thoughts into a different channel from that to which they are now prone. Yesterday we had each an invitation to a ball. She labored hard to prevail on me to go, but I obstinately refused. I cannot yet mix with gay and cheerful circles. I therefore alleged that I was indisposed and persuaded her to go without me.

The events of my life have always been unaccountably wayward. In many instances I have been ready to suppose that some evil genius presided over my actions, which has directed them contrary to the sober dictates of my own judgment. I am sometimes tempted to adopt the sentiment expressed in the following lines of the poet:

> To you, great gods, I make my last appeal;
> O, clear my conscience, or my crimes reveal!
> If wandering through the paths of life I've run,
> And backward trod the steps I sought to shun,
> Impute my errors to your own decree;
> My feet were guilty, but my heart was free.

I suppose you will tell me that the fate I accuse through the poet is only the result of my own imprudence. Well, be it what it may—either the impulse of my own passions or some higher efficiency—sure I am that I pay dear for its operation.

I have heard it remarked that experience is the preceptor of fools, but that the wise need not its instruction. I believe I must be content to rank accordingly and endeavor to reap advantage from its tuition.

Julia urges me to revisit the scenes of amusements and pleasure, in which, she tells me, she is actuated by selfish motives. She wishes it for her own sake. She likes neither to be secluded from them nor to go alone. I am sometimes half inclined to seek in festive mirth a refuge from thought and reflection. I would

escape, if possible, from the idea of Mr. Boyer. This I have never been able to accomplish since he dropped a tear upon my hand and left me. I marked the spot with my eye, and twenty times in a day do I view it and fondly imagine it still there. How could I give him pain! I hope his happy Maria never will. I hope she will reward that merit which I have slighted. But I forbear. This theme carries away my pen if I but touch upon it. And no wonder, for it is the sole exercise of my thoughts. Yet I will endeavor to divert them. Send me some new books—not such, however, as will require much attention. Let them be plays and novels or anything else that will amuse or extort a smile. Julia and I have been rambling in the garden. She insisted upon my going with her into the arbor, where I was surprised with Major Sanford. What a crowd of painful ideas rushed upon my imagination! I believe she repented of her rashness. But no more of this. I must lay aside my pen, for I can write nothing else.

<div align="right">Eliza Wharton.</div>

LETTER LI

To Mrs. Lucy Sumner.

<div align="right">Hartford</div>

You commanded me to write you respecting Miss Wharton, and I obey. But I cannot describe to you the surprising change which she has undergone. Her vivacity has certainly forsaken her; and she has actually become what she once dreaded above all things, a recluse. She flies from company as eagerly as she formerly sought it; her mamma is exceedingly distressed by the settled melancholy which appears in her darling child. Neither of us think it best to mention the subject to her. We endeavor to find means to amuse her, and we flatter ourselves that the prospect of success rather increases. It would add greatly to my happiness to contribute in any degree to restore her to herself, to her friends, and to society.

We are all invited to dine abroad tomorrow; and to oblige me, she has consented to go.

Pray, madam, write to her often. Your letters may do much for her. She is still feelingly alive to the power of friendship,

and none can exercise it upon her to greater acceptance or with more advantage than yourself.

Major Sanford's house is undergoing a complete repair. The report is that he is soon to be married. Miss Wharton has heard, but she does not believe it. I hope for her sake it will prove true; for, at any rate, he is about returning; and from her mamma's account of his past conduct towards Eliza, were he to return unconnected, he would probably renew his attentions; and though they might end in marriage, her happiness would not be secured. She has too nice a sense of love and honor to compound with his licentious principles. A man who has been dissolute before marriage will very seldom be faithful afterwards.

I went into Eliza's chamber the other day and found her with a miniature picture in her hand. "You pretend to be a physiognomist, Julia," said she. "What can you trace in that countenance?" I guessed whose it was; and looking wistfully at it, I replied, "I believe the original is an artful, designing man. He looks to me like a Chesterfieldian. Pray who is he?" "Major Sanford," said she; "and I am afraid you have hit his character exactly. Sure I am that the appearance of those traits in it has made my heart ache." She wept as she spoke it.

Poor girl, I wish he may never give you greater cause to weep! She is strongly blind to the vices and imperfections of this man. Though naturally penetrating, he has somehow or other cast a deceptive mist over her imagination with respect to himself. She professes neither to love nor esteem him and owns that his ungenerous artifice misled her in her treatment of Mr. Boyer. Yet she has forgiven him and thinks him a pleasing companion.

How prone to error is the human mind! how much lighter than the breath of zephyrs the operations of fancy! Strange, then, it should ever preponderate over the weightier powers of the understanding.

But I will not moralize. My business here is to dissipate, not to collect, ideas; and I must regulate myself accordingly.

I am endeavoring to prepare Eliza, by degrees, to accompany me to Boston the ensuing winter, but I think it doubtful whether I shall succeed. I shall, however, return myself.

Julia Granby.

LETTER LII

To Miss Eliza Wharton.

Boston

I received yours of the 24th ult.; and I thank you for it, though it did not afford me those lively sensations of pleasure which I usually feel at the perusal of your letters. It inspired me both with concern and chagrin—with concern lest your dejection of mind should affect your health; with chagrin at your apparent indulgence of melancholy. Indeed, my friend, your own happiness and honor require you to dissipate the cloud which hangs over your imagination.

Rise then above it, and prove yourself superior to the adverse occurrences which have befallen you. It is by surmounting difficulties, not by sinking under them, that we discover our fortitude. True courage consists not in flying from the storms of life, but in braving and steering through them with prudence. Avoid solitude. It is the bane of a disordered mind, though of great utility to a healthy one. Your once favorite amusements court your attention. Refuse not their solicitations. I have contributed my mite by sending you a few books, such as you requested. They are of the lighter kind of reading, yet perfectly chaste and, if I mistake not, well adapted to your taste.

You wish to hear from our theater. I believe it will be well supplied with performers this winter. Come and see whether they can afford you any entertainment. Last evening I attended a tragedy, but never will I attend another. I have not yet been able to erase the gloom which it impressed upon my mind. It was Romeo and Juliet. Distressing enough to sensibility this! Are there not real woes (if not in our own families, at least among our own friends and neighbors) sufficient to exercise our sympathy and pity, without introducing fictitious ones into our very diversions? How can that be a diversion which racks the soul with grief, even though that grief be imaginary? The introduction of a funeral solemnity upon the stage is shocking indeed!

Death is too serious a matter to be sported with. An opening grave cannot be a source of amusement to any considerate mind. The closing scene of life can be no pastime when realized. It

must therefore awaken painful sensations in the representation.

The circus is a place of fashionable resort of late, but not agreeable to me. I think it inconsistent with the delicacy of a lady even to witness the indecorums which are practiced there, especially when the performers of equestrian feats are of our own sex. To see a woman depart so far from the female character as to assume the masculine habit and attitude, and appear entirely indifferent even to the externals of modesty, is truly disgusting; and it ought not to be countenanced by our attendance, much less by our approbation. But, setting aside the circumstance, I cannot conceive it to be a pleasure to sit a whole evening trembling with apprehension lest the poor wight of a horseman, or juggler, or whatever he is to be called, should break his neck in contributing to our entertainment.

With Mr. Bowen's museum I think you were much pleased. He has made a number of judicious additions to it since you were here. It is a source of rational and refined amusement. Here the eye is gratified, the imagination charmed, and the understanding improved. It will bear frequent reviews without palling on the taste. It always affords something new; and, for one, I am never a weary spectator. Our other public and private places of resort are much as you left them.

I am happy in my present situation; but when the summer returns, I intend to visit my native home. Again, my Eliza, will we ramble together in those retired shades which friendship has rendered so delightful to us. Adieu, my friend, till then. Be cheerful, and you will yet be happy.

<div style="text-align: right">Lucy Sumner.</div>

LETTER LIII

To Mrs. Lucy Sumner.

<div style="text-align: right">Hartford</div>

Gracious Heaven! What have I heard? Major Sanford is married! Yes, the ungrateful, the deceitful wretch is married. He has forsworn; he has perjured and given himself to another. That, you will say, is nothing strange. It is characteristic of the man. It may be so, but I could not be convinced of his perfidy till now.

Perhaps it is all for the best. Perhaps, had he remained unconnected, he might still have deceived me; but now I defy his arts.

They tell me he has married a woman of fortune. I suppose he thinks, as I once did, that wealth can insure happiness. I wish he may enjoy it.

This event would not affect me at all were it not for the depression of spirits which I feel in consequence of a previous disappointment, since which everything of the kind agitates and overcomes me. I will not see him. If I do, I shall betray my weakness and flatter his vanity, as he will doubtless think he has the power of mortifying me by his connection with another.

Before this news discomposed me, I had attained to a good degree of cheerfulness. Your kind letter, seconded by Julia's exertions, had assisted me in regulating my sensibility. I have been frequently into company and find my relish for it gradually returning.

I intend to accept the pleasure, to which you invite me, of spending a little time with you this winter. Julia and I will come together. Varying the scene may contribute effectually to dissipate the gloom of my imagination. I would fly to almost any resort rather than to my own mind. What a dreadful thing it is to be afraid of one's own reflections, which ought to be a constant source of enjoyment! But I will not moralize. I am sufficiently melancholy without any additional cause to increase it.

Eliza Wharton.

LETTER LIV

To Mr. Charles Deighton.

Hartford

Who do you think is writing to you? Why, it is your old friend, metamorphosed into a *married man!* You stare and can hardly credit the assertion. I cannot realize it myself; yet I assure you, Charles, it is absolutely true. Necessity, dire necessity, forced me into this dernier resort. I told you some time ago it would come to this.

I stood aloof as long as possible, but in vain did I attempt to shun the noose. I must either fly to this resource or give up all

my show, equipage, and pleasure and degenerate into a downright, plodding money catcher for a subsistence. I chose the first, and who would not? Yet I feel some remorse at taking the girl to wife from no better motives. She is really too good for such an imposition. But she must blame herself if she suffers hereafter, for she was visibly captivated by my external appearance and wanted but very little solicitation to confer herself and fortune on so charming a fellow. Her parents opposed her inclination for a while, because I was a stranger and rather too gay for their taste. But she had not been used to contradiction and could not bear it and therefore they ventured not to cross her. So I bore off the prize; and a prize she really is—five thousand pounds in possession, and more in reversion if I do not forfeit it. This will compensate for some of my past mistakes and set matters right for the present. I think it doing much better than to have taken the little Lawrence girl I told you of with half the sum. Besides, my Nancy is a handsomer and more agreeable person; but that is of little consequence to me, you know. "Beauty soon grows familiar to the lover." Were I a lover, it would be of no great avail. A lover I am, yet not of my wife. The dart which I received from Miss Wharton sticks fast in my heart; and, I assure you, I could hardly persuade myself even to appear unfaithful to her. O Eliza! accuse me not of infidelity; your image is my constant companion. A thousand times have I cursed the unpropitious stars which withheld from her a fortune, which would have enabled me to marry her; and with her even wedlock would have been supportable.

I am told that she is still single. Her sober lover never returned. Had he loved as I did, and do, he could not have been so precipitate. But these stoic souls are good for nothing that I know of, but

> Fixed, like a plant, to one peculiar spot,
> To draw nutrition, propagate, and rot.

I want to see Eliza, and I must see her; yet I dread an interview. I shall frankly confess my motives for marrying and the reasons of my conduct before I went away. I shall own that my circumstances would not allow me to possess her, yet that I could not resign her to another.

When I make up the matter with her, I shall solicit her friendship for my wife. By this means I may enjoy her society, at

least, which will alleviate the confinement of a married state. To my spouse I must be as civil as possible. I really wish she had less merit that I might have a plausible excuse for neglecting her. Tomorrow I shall go to Mrs. Wharton's. I am very much taken up with complimental visits at present. What deference is always paid to equipage! They may talk of their virtue, their learning, and what not; but, without either of them, I shall bear off the palm of respect from those who have them, unadorned with gold and its shining appendages.

Everything hereabouts recalls Eliza to my mind, I impatiently anticipate the hour which will convey me to her presence.

<div align="right">Peter Sanford.</div>

LETTER LV

To Mrs. Lucy Sumner.

<div align="right">Hartford</div>

A new scene has opened upon us today, my dear Mrs. Sumner—a visit from Major Sanford. My mamma, Miss Granby, and I were sitting together in the chamber. Miss Granby was entertaining us by reading aloud in Millot's *Elements of History*, when a servent rapped at the door and handed in the following billet:

"Will Miss Wharton condescend to converse a few moments with her once-favored Sanford? He is but too sensible that he has forfeited all claim to the privilege. He therefore presumes not to request it on the score of merit, nor of former acquaintance, but solicits it from her benevolence and pity."

I read and showed it to my mamma and Julia. "What," said I, "shall I do? I wish not to see him. His artifice has destroyed my peace of mind, and his presence may open the wounds which time is closing." "Act," said my mamma, "agreeably to the dictates of your own judgment." "I see no harm in conversing with him," said Julia. "Perhaps it may remove some disagreeable thoughts which now oppress and give you pain. And as he is no longer a candidate for your affections," added she with a smile, "it will be less hazardous than formerly. He will not have the insolence to speak, nor you the folly to hear, the language of love."

He was accordingly invited in. When I rose to go down, I hestitated, and even trembled. "I fear," said I to myself, "it will be too much for me: yet why should it? Conscious innocence will support me. This he has not." When I entered the room he stepped forward to meet me. Confusion and shame were visibly depicted in his countenance. He approached me hastily and, without uttering a word, took my hand. I withdrew it. "O Miss Wharton," said he, "despise me not. I am convinced that I deserve your displeasure and disdain; but my own heart has avenged your cause." "To your own heart, then," said I, "I will leave you. But why do you again seek an interview with one whom you have endeavored to mislead—with one whom you have treated with unmerited neglect?" "Justice to myself required my appearing before you, that, by confessing my faults and obtaining your forgiveness, I might soften the reproaches of my own mind." "Will you be seated, sir?" said I. "Will you," rejoined he, "condescend to sit with me, Eliza?" "I will, sir," answered I. "The rights of hospitality, I shall not infringe. In my own house, therefore, I shall treat you with civility." "Indeed," said he, "you are very severe; but I have provoked all the coldness and reserve which you can inflict.

"I am a married man, Eliza." "So I understand," said I; "and I hope you will never treat your wife with that dissimulation and falsehood which you have exercised towards me." "Would to Heaven," exclaimed he, "that you were my wife. I should not then fail in my love or duty as a husband; yet she is an amiable girl; and, had I a heart to give her, I might still be happy; but that, alas! I can never recall." "Why, then," said I, "did you marry her? You were, doubtless, master of your own actions." "No," said he, "I was not. The embarrassed state of my affairs precluded the possibility of acting as I wished. Loving you most ardently, I was anxious to prevent your union with another, until I could so far improve my circumstances as to secure you from poverty and want in a connection with me. My regard was too sincere to permit me to deceive you by a marriage which might have proved unhappy for us both. My pride forbade my telling you the motives of my delay, and I left you to see if I could place myself in a situation worthy of your acceptance. This I could not effect and, therefore, have run the risk of my future happiness by marrying a lady of affluence. This secures to me the externals of enjoyment, but my heart, I fear, will never

participate it; yet it affords me some degree of satisfaction that I have not involved you in distress. The only alleviation of which my banishment from you is capable is your forgiveness. In compassion, then, refuse it not. I cannot injure you. To me it will be worth millions." He wept. Yes, Lucy, this libertine, this man of pleasure and gallantry, wept. I really pitied him from my heart. "I forgive you," said I, "and wish you happy—yet on this condition only, that you never again pollute my ears with the recital of your infamous passion. Yes, infamous I call it; for what softer appellation can be given to such professions from a married man? Harbor not an idea of me, in future, inconsistent with the love and fidelity which you owe your wife; much less presume to mention it, if you wish not to be detested by me and forever banished from my presence." He expressed gratitude for his absolution, even upon these terms, and hoped his future conduct would entitle him to my friendship and esteem. "That," I replied, "time only can determine."

One favor more he begged leave to solicit, which was that I would be a neighbor to his wife. "She was a stranger," he said, "and would deem my society a particular privilege." This, I told him I could not grant at present, whatever I might do hereafter. He did not urge it any further, but inquired about my mamma and expressed a wish to see her. I rang the bell and ordered her and Miss Granby to be called. When they came he was very polite to them both; and, after usual compliments, he told my mamma that he was happy in having obtained my forgiveness, to which he was anxious to have her seal affixed. "My daughter," said she, "is the injured party; and if she be satisfied, I shall not complain." He thanked her for her condescension, informed her that he was married, and requested her to visit his wife. We then conversed upon different subjects for a short time, and he took his leave. A sigh escaped him as he departed, and a gloom was visible in his countenance which I never observed before.

I must acknowledge that this interview has given me satisfaction. I have often told you that if I married Major Sanford, it would be from a predilection for his situation in life. How wretched must have been my lot, had I discovered too late, that he was by no means possessed of the independence which I fondly anticipated! I knew not my own heart when I contemplated a connection with him. Little did I think that my regard for Mr. Boyer was so deeply rooted as I now find it. I foolishly

imagined that I could turn my affections into what channel I pleased. What then must have been my feelings when I found myself deprived both of inward peace and outward enjoyment! I begin now to emerge from the darkness in which I have been long benighted. I hope the tragic comedy in which I have acted so conspicuous a part will come to a happy end.

Julia and I talk now and then of a journey to Boston. As yet, I have not resolution to act with much decision upon the subject; but, wherever I am and whatever may be my fate, I shall always be yours in truth,

<div align="right">Eliza Wharton.</div>

LETTER LVI

To Mrs. Lucy Sumner.

<div align="right">Hartford</div>

I begin to hope we shall come to rights here by and by. Major Sanford has returned, has made us a visit; and a treaty of peace and amity (but not of commerce) is ratified. Eliza appears to be rapidly returning to her former cheerfulness—if not gaiety. I hope she will not diverge too far from her present sedateness and solidity, yet I am not without apprehensions of danger on that score. One extreme commonly succeeds another. She tells me that she assiduously cultivates her natural vivacity; that she finds her taste for company and amusements increasing; that she dreads being alone because past scenes arise to view which vex and discompose her.

These are indications of a mind not perfectly right. I flatter myself, however, that the time is not far distant when her passions will vibrate with regularity.

I need not repeat to you anything relative to Major Sanford's conciliatory visit. Eliza has given you a particular and, I believe, a faithful detail. I was called down to see this wonderful man and disliked him exceedingly. I am astonished that Eliza's penetrating eye has not long since read his vices in his very countenance. I am told by a friend, who has visited them, that he has an agreeable wife; and I wish she may find him a husband of the same description; but I very much doubt the accomplishment of

my wish, for I have no charity for these reformed rakes.

We were walking abroad the other afternoon and met Major Sanford and lady. Eliza did not see them until they were very near us. She started, turned pale, and then colored like crimson. I cannot but think a little envy rankled in her heart. Major Sanford very politely accosted us and congratulated Mrs. Sanford on this opportunity of introducing her to a particular friend, presenting Eliza. She received her with an easy dignity and bade her welcome to this part of the country. Mrs. Sanford answered her modestly, hoped for the pleasure of a further acquaintance, and urged us, as we were not far from their house, to return with them to tea. We declined and wishing each other good evening, parted. Major Sanford's eyes were riveted on Eliza the whole time we were together, and he seemed loath to remove them when we separated. I suspect there is some truth in his tale of love. I shall therefore discourage Eliza from associating with him under any pretext whatever. She appeared more pensive and thoughtful than common as we returned home and said little the rest of the evening, but next morning she was as chatty as ever.

She is warm in the praises of Mrs. Sanford, thinks her an accomplished woman, and wonders that the Major could suggest an idea of marrying her for her money. She intends, she says, to visit her soon and wishes me to accompany her. This, for her own sake, I shall defer as long as possible.

<div align="right">Julia Granby.</div>

LETTER LVII

To Mrs. Lucy Sumner.

<div align="right">Hartford</div>

By Julia's advice we have neglected the repeated invitations of Major Sanford to visit and commence neighborhood with them until yesterday, when we received a polite billet requesting the honor of our company to dine. My mamma declined going, but she said she had no objection to our compliance with the message if we thought it proper. Julia and I accordingly went. We found a large company assembled in a spacious hall, splendidly

furnished and decorated. They were all very polite and attentive to me, but none more so than Major Sanford and his lady who jointly strove to dissipate the pensiveness of my mind which I found it impossible to conceal. When we were summoned to dinner, the major, being near me, offered his hand and, leading me into the dining room, seated me at a table furnished with all the variety which could please the eye or regale the taste of the most luxurious epicure. The conversation turned on various subjects—literary, political, amd miscellaneous. In the evening we had a ball. Major Sanford gave the hand of his wife to a Mr. Grey, alleging that he was a stranger and therefore entitled to particular attention and then solicited mine himself. I was on the point of refusing him; but recollecting that it might have the appearance of a continued resentment contrary to my declaration of forgiving what was past, I complied. He was all kindness and assiduity—the more so, I imagined, with a view to make amends for his former ingratitude and neglect. Tenderness is now peculiarly soothing to my wounded heart. He took an opportunity of conversing with his wife and me together, hoped she would be honored with my friendship and acquaintance, and begged for her sake that I would not be a stranger at his house. His Nancy, he said, was far removed from her maternal friends; but I could supply their place if I would generously undertake the task. She joined in expressing the same sentiments and wishes. "Alas! sir," said I, "Eliza Wharton is not now what she once was. I labor under a depression of spirits which must render my company rather painful than pleasing to my friends." The idea of what I had been, contrasted with what I then was, touched my sensibility; and I could not restrain the too officious tear from stealing down my cheek. He took me by the hand and said, "You distress me, Miss Wharton; indeed you distress me. Happiness must and shall attend you. Cursed be the wretch who could would a heart like yours."

Julia Granby now joined us. An inquisitive concern was visible in her countenance.

I related this conversation to her after we returned home, but she approved it not.

She thought Major Sanford too particularly attentive to me, considering what had previously happened. She said it would be noticed by others, and the world would make unfavorable remarks upon any appearance of intimacy between us. "I care not

for that," said I; "it is an ill-natured, misjudging world, and I am not obliged to sacrifice my friends to its opinion. Were Major Sanford a single man, I should avoid his society; but since he is married, since his wife is young, beautiful, and lovely, he can have no temptation to injure me. I therefore see no evil which can arise from the cultivation of friendship with her at least. I relish company so little that I may surely be indulged in selecting that which is most agreeable to my taste, to prevent my becoming quite a misanthrope."

I thank you, my dear Mrs. Sumner, for your kind letter. It was a seasonable cordial to my mind, and I will endeavor to profit by your advice. Your remarks on the public entertainments are amusing and, as far as I am a judge, perfectly just. I think it a pity they have not female managers for the theater. I believe it would be under much better regulations than at present.

With cordial respects to Mr. Sumner, I subscribe myself, yours in sincerity,

<div align="right">Eliza Wharton.</div>

LETTER LVIII

To Mr. Charles Deighton.

<div align="right">Hartford</div>

Rejoice with me, my friend, that I have made my peace with the mistress of my heart. No devotee could have been more sincere in his penitence than I was in mine. Indeed, Charles, I never knew I had so much sensibility before. Why, I was as much a woman as the very weakest of the sex.

But I dealt very plainly and sincerely with her, to be sure; and this atones for any past offenses, and procures absolution for many others yet to be committed.

The dear girl was not inexorable; she was as placable and condescending as I could expect, considering the nature of the crime, which was apparently slighting her person and charms by marrying another. This, you know, is one of the nicest points with the ladies. Attack their honor—that is, their chastity—and they construe it to be the effect of excessive love, which hurries

you a little beyond the bounds of prudence. But touch their vanity by preferring another, and they will seldom pardon you. You will say I am very severe upon the sex; and have I not reason to be so, since I have found so many frail ones among them? This, however, is departing from my subject.

Eliza is extremely altered. Her pale, dejected countenance, with the sedateness of her manners, so different from the lively glow of health, cheerfulness, and activity which formerly animated her appearance and deportment, struck me very disagreeably.

With all my gallantry and fluency in love matters, I was unable to acquit myself tolerably, or to address her with any degree of ease and confidence. She was very calm, and spoke with great indifference about my marriage, etc., which mortified me exceedingly. Yet I cannot consent to believe that her present depression of spirits arises solely from Mr. Boyer's infidelity. I flatter myself that I am of sufficient consequence to her to have contributed in a degree.

When I inquired after her health, she told me she had been indisposed but was now much better. This indisposition, I am informed, was purely mental; and I am happy to observe her recovering from it. I frequently visit her, sometimes with and sometimes without my wife, of whom, through my mediation, she has become a favorite. I have married and according to the general opinion reformed. Yet I suspect my reformation, like most others of the kind, will prove unstable as "the baselsss fabric of a vision" unless I banish myself entirely from her society. But that I can never do; for she is still lovely in my eyes, and I cannot control my passions.

When absent from her I am lost to everything but her idea. My wife begins to rally me on my fondness for Miss Wharton. She asked me the other day if she had a fortune. "No," said I; "if she had I should have married her." This wounded her sensibility. I repented of my sincerity and made my peace for that time. Yet I find myself growing extremely irritable, and she must take heed how she provokes me; for I do not love her, and I think the name of wife becomes more and more distasteful to me every day.

In my mind, Eliza has no competitor. But I must keep up appearances though I endeavor to regain her love. I imagine that the enjoyment of her society as a neighbor and friend may

content me for the present and render my condition supportable.

Farewell, Charles. I hope you will never be embarrassed with a wife, nor lack some favorite nymph to supply the place of one.

Peter Sanford.

LETTER LIX

To Mrs. Lucy Sumner.

Hartford

I intended this week to have journeyed to Boston with Julia Granby, but my resolution fails me. I find it painful even to think of mixing again with the gay multitude. I believe the melancholy reflections by which I am oppressed will be more effectually, if not more easily, surmounted by tarrying where they are rendered familiar than by going from them awhile and then returning.

Julia will therefore go without me. I envy her no enjoyment there, except your company.

The substitution of friendship, in the place of love, for Major Sanford, I find productive of agreeable sensations. With him, he assures me, it is a far more calm and rational pleasure. *He* treats me with the affection and tenderness of a brother, and his *wife*, who exceeds him in professions of regard, with all the consoling softness and attention of a sister. Indeed, their politeness has greatly contributed to revive the cheerfulness of my natural disposition. I believe the Major's former partiality to me as a lover is entirely obliterated; and for my part, I feel as little restraint in his company and his lady's as in that of any other in the neighborhood.

I very much regret the departure of Julia and hope you will permit her to return to me again as soon as possible. She is a valuable friend. Her mind is well cultivated, and she has treasured up a fund of knowledge and information which renders her company both agreeable and useful in every situation of life. We lately spent the afternoon and evening at Mr. Smith's. They had a considerable number of visitants, and among the rest Major

Sanford. His wife was expected but did not come, being indisposed.

I believe, my friend, you must excuse me if my letters are shorter than formerly. Writing is not so agreeable to me as it used to be. I love my friends as well as ever, but I think they must be weary of the gloom and dullness which pervade my present correspondence. When my pen shall have regained its original fluency and alertness, I will resume and prolong the pleasing task.

I am, my dear Lucy, yours most affectionately,

Eliza Wharton.

LETTER LX

Mrs. Lucy Sumner.

Hartford

Agreeably to your desire every art has been tried, every allurement held out, every argument used, and every plan adopted which Mrs. Wharton and I could devise to induce Eliza to accompany me to Boston; but they were all in vain. Sometimes she has been almost persuaded to a compliance with our united request, but soon she has resolutely determined against it. I have observed her sentiments to be suddenly changed after being in company with Major Sanford. This alarms us exceedingly. Indeed, the Major seems to have insinuated himself into her good opinion more than ever. She is flattered into the belief that his attention to her is purely the result of friendship and benevolence.

I have not so favorable an opinion of the man as to suppose him capable of either. He has become very familiar here. He calls in almost every day. Sometimes he but just inquires after our health, and sometimes he makes long visits. The latter is his invariable practice when he finds Eliza alone. Mrs. Wharton always avoids seeing him if she can. She dreads, she says, his approaching the house.

I entered the parlor the other day, somewhat suddenly, and found him sitting very near Eliza in a low conversation. They both rose in apparent confusion, and he soon retired.

When he was gone, "I suspect," said I, "that the Major was whispering a tale of love, Eliza." "Do you imagine," said she, "that I would listen to such a theme from a married man?" "I hope not," said I, "but his conduct towards you indicates a revival of his former sentiments, at least." "I was not aware of that," said she. "As yet I have observed nothing in his behavior to me inconsistent with the purest friendship."

We drank tea not long since at Mr. Smith's. Late in the afternoon Major Sanford made his appearance to apologize, as he said, for Mrs. Sanford, who was indisposed and could not enjoy the pleasure of the visit she had contemplated. He was very gay the whole evening; and when the company separated, he was the first to present his arm to Eliza, who accepted it without hesitation. A Mr. Newhall attended me, and we endeavored to keep them company; but they evidently chose to walk by themselves. Mr. Newhall observed that if Major Sanford were not married he should suspect he still intended a union with Miss Wharton. I replied that their former intercourse, having terminated in friendship, rendered them more familiar with each other than with the generality of their acquaintance.

When we reached the house, Mr. Newhall chose not to go in and took his leave. I waited at the door for Eliza and Major Sanford. At some little distance, I saw him press her hand to his lips. It vexed me exceedingly; and no sooner had they come up, then I sullenly bade them good night and walked directly in. Eliza soon followed me. I sat down by the fire in a thoughtful posture. She did the same. In this situation we both remained for some time without speaking a word. At length she said, "You seem not to have enjoyed your walk, Miss Granby: did you not like your gallant?" "Yes," said I, "very well; but I am mortified that you were not better provided for." "I make no complaint," rejoined she; "I was very well entertained." "That is what displeases me," said I; "I mean your visible fondness for the society of such a man. Were you averse to it, as you ought to be, there would be no danger. But he has an alluring tongue and a treacherous heart. How can you be pleased and entertained by his conversation? To me it appears totally repugnant to that refinement and delicacy for which you have always been esteemed.

"His assiduity and obtrusion ought to alarm you. You well know what his character has been. Marriage has not changed his

disposition. It is only a cloak which conceals it. Trust him not, then, my dear Eliza; if you do, depend upon it you will find his professions of friendship to be mere hypocrisy and deceit. I fear that he is acting over again the same unworthy arts which formerly misled you. Beware of his wiles. Your friends are anxious for you. They tremble at your professed regard and apparent intimacy with that unprincipled man."

"My friends," said she, "are very jealous of me lately. I know not how I have forfeited their confidence or incurred their suspicion."

"By encouraging that attention," I warmly replied, "and receiving those caresses from a married man which are due from him to none but his wife. He is a villain if he deceived her into marriage by insincere professions of love. If he had then an affection for her and has already discarded it, he is equally guilty. Can *you* expect sincerity from the man who withholds it from an amiable and deserving wife? No, Eliza; it is not love which induces him to entertain you with the subject. It is a baser passion; and if you disdain not his artifice, if you listen to his flattery, you will, I fear, fall a victim to his evil machinations. If he conducted himself like a man of honor, he would merit your esteem; but his behavior is quite the reverse: yet, vile as he is, he would not dare to lisp his insolent hopes of your regard if you punished his presumption with the indignation it deserves; if you spurned from your presence the ungrateful wretch who would requite your condescension by triumphing in your ruin."

She now burst into tears and begged me to drop the subject. Her mind, she said, was racked by her own reflections. She could bear but little. Kindness deceived and censure distressed her.

I assured her of my good intentions; as I saw her danger, I thought it a duty of the friendship and affection I bore her solemnly to warn her against it before we parted. We talked over the matter more calmly until she professed herself resolved in future to avoid his company and reject his insinuations.

The next day, as I walked out, I met Major Sanford. He accosted me very civilly. I barely bade him good morning and passed on.

I made it in my way to call at his house and bid Mrs. Sanford adieu, not expecting another opportunity equally favorable.

When I entered the parlor, she was playing a melancholy air on the harpsichord. She rose and gave me a polite and graceful reception. I told her that, as I was soon to leave the town, I called to take my leave of her—a compliment which her attention to me required. "Are you going to leave us then, Miss Granby?" said she. "I shall regret your departure exceedingly. I have so few friends in this part of the country that it will give me sensible pain to part with one I so highly value."

I told her, in the course of conversation, that I expected the pleasure of seeing her yesterday at Mr. Smith's and was very sorry for the indisposition which prevented her favoring us with her company. "Indeed," said she, "I did not know I was expected there. Were you there, pray?" "Yes," said I, "and Major Sanford excused your not coming on the account I have mentioned." "Well," said she, "this is the first word that I ever heard about it; he told me that business led him abroad. Did he gallant any lady?" "O," said I, "he was with us all together. We had no particular gallants."

Seeing her curiosity excited, I heartily repented saying anything of the matter and waived the subject. Little did I suspect him to have been guilty of so base an artifice. It was evidently contrived to facilitate an interview with Eliza.

When I returned, I related this affair to Mrs. Wharton and her daughter. The old lady and I expatiated largely on the vileness of this conduct and endeavored to expose it to Eliza's view in its true colors. She pretended not to justify it, yet she looked as if she wished it in her power.

I am now preparing for my journey to Boston, which I must, however, defer another week for the sake of a more agreeable passage in the stage. I regret leaving Eliza. I tremble at her danger. She has not the resolution to resist temptation which she once possessed. Her mind is surprisingly weakened. She appears sensible of this, yet adds to it by yielding to her own imbecility. You will receive a letter from her with this, though I had much difficulty to persuade her to write. She has unfortunately become very averse to this, her once favorite amusement.

As I shall soon have the pleasure of conversing with you personally, I conclude without any other addition to this scrawl than the name of your obliged

Julia Granby.

LETTER LXI

To Miss Eliza Wharton.

Boston

I have received your letters and must own to you that the perusal of them give me pain. Pardon my suspicions, Eliza; they are excited by real friendship. Julia, you say, approves not Major Sanford's particular attention to you. Neither do I. If you recollect and examine his conversation in his conciliatory visit, you will find it replete with sentiments for the avowal of which he ought to be banished from all virtuous society.

Does he not insidiously declare that you are the only object of his affections, that his union with another was formed from interested views; that, although his wife is acknowledged to be amiable and excellent, still he has not a heart to bestow and expects not happiness with her? Does this discover even the appearance of amendment? Has he not by false pretensions misled a virtuous woman and induced her to form a connection with him? She was a stranger to his manner of life and doubtless allured, as you had been, by flattery, deceit, and external appearance, to trust his honor, little thinking him wholly devoid of that sacred tie. What is the reward of her confidence? Insensibility to her charms, neglect of her person, and professed attachment to another!

Is he a man, my dear Eliza, whose friendship you wish to cultivate? Can that heavenly passion reside in a breast which is the seat of treachery, duplicity, and ingratitude? You are too sensible of its purity and worth to suppose it possible. The confessions of his own mouth condemn him. They convince me that he is still the abandoned libertine, and that marriage is but the cloak of his intrigues. His officious attentions to you are alarming to your friends. Your own mind weakened and peculiarly susceptible of tender impressions, beware how you receive them from him. Listen not a moment to his flattering professions; it is an insult upon your understanding for him to offer them; it is derogatory to virtue for you to hear them.

Slight not the opinion of the world. We are dependent beings; and while the smallest traces of virtuous sensibility remain, we

must feel the force of that dependence in a greater or less de-
gree. No female, whose mind is uncorrupted, can be indifferent
to reputation. It is an inestimable jewel, the loss of which can
never be repaired. While retained, it affords conscious peace to our
own minds and insures the esteem and respect of all around us.

Blessed with the company of so disinterested and faithful a
friend as Julia Granby, some deference is certainly due to her
opinion and advice. To an enlarged understanding, a cultivated
taste, and an extensive knowledge of the world, she unites the
most liberal sentiments with a benevolence and candor of dis-
position which render her equally deserving of your confidence
and affection.

I cannot relinquish my claim to a visit from you this winter.
Marriage has not alienated nor weakened my regard for my
friends. Come, then, to your faithful Lucy. Have you sorrows? I
will soothe and alleviate them. Have you cares? I will dispel
them. Have you pleasures? I will heighten them. Come, then, let
me fold you to my expecting heart. My happiness will be partly
suspended until your society renders it complete. Adieu.

<div align="right">Lucy Sumner.</div>

LETTER LXII

To Miss Julia Granby.

<div align="right">Hartford</div>

I hope Mrs. Sumner and you will excuse my writing but one
letter in answer to the number I have received from you both.
Writing is an employment which suits me not at present. It was
pleasing to me formerly; therefore, by recalling the idea of cir-
cumstances and events which frequently occupied my pen in
happier days, it now gives me pain. Yet I have just written a
long consolatory letter to Mrs. Richman. She has buried her
babe—her little Harriet, of whom she was dotingly fond.

It was a custom with some of the ancients, we are told, to
weep at the birth of their children. Often should we be impelled
to a compliance with this custom, could we foresee the future
incidents of their lives. I think, at least, that the uncertainty of
their conduct and condition in more advanced age may reconcile

us to their removal to a happier state before they are capable of tasting the bitterness of woe.

> Happy the babe who, privileged by fate
> To shorter labors and a lighter weight,
> Received but yesterday the gift of breath,
> Ordered tomorrow to return to death.

Our domestic affairs are much as when you left us. Nothing remarkable has occurred in the neighborhood worth communicating. The company and amusements of the town are as usual, I suppose. I frequent neither of them. Having incurred so much censure by the indulgence of a gay disposition, I am now trying what a recluse and solitary mode of life will produce. You will call me splenetic. I own it. I am pleased with nobody, still less with myself. I look around for happiness and find it not. The world is to me a desert. If I indulge myself in temporary enjoyment, the consciousness or apprehension of doing amiss destroys my peace of mind. And when I have recourse to books, if I read those of serious descriptions, they remind me of an awful futurity for which I am unprepared; if history, it discloses facts in which I have no interest; if novels, they exhibit scenes of pleasure which I have no prospect of realizing.

My mamma is solicitously attentive to my happiness; and though she fails of promoting it, yet I endeavor to save her the pangs of disappointment by appearing what she wishes.

I anticipate, and yet I dread your return; a paradox is this, which time alone can solve.

Continue writing to me, and entreat Mrs. Sumner in my name to do likewise. Your benevolence must be your reward.

<div style="text-align: right">Eliza Wharton.</div>

LETTER LXIII

To Miss Eliza Wharton.

<div style="text-align: right">Boston</div>

A paradox, indeed, is the greater part of your letter to us, my dear Eliza. We had fondly flattered ourselves that the melancholy of your mind was exterminated. I hope no new cause has

revived it. Little did I intend when I left you to have been absent so long; but Mrs. Sumner's disappointment, in her plan of spending the summer at Hartford, induced me in compliance with her request to prolong my residence here. But for your sake she now consents to my leaving her, in hopes I may be so happy as to contribute to your amusement.

I am both pleased and instructed by the conduct of this amiable woman. As I always endeavored to imitate her discreet and modest behavior in a single state, so likewise shall I take her for a pattern should I ever enter a married life. She is most happily united. I was once present when a person was recommended to her for a husband. She objected that he was a rake. "True," said the other, "he has been, but he has reformed." "That will never do for me," rejoined she; "I wish my future companion to need no reformation"—a sentiment worthy the attention of our whole sex; if such were in the general adoption, I am persuaded, it would have a happy influence upon the manners of the other.

Mr. Sumner, also, to all the graces and accomplishments of the gentleman, adds the still more important and essential properties of virtue, integrity, and honor.

I hope neither you nor I, Eliza, shall ever be tried by a man of debauched principles. Such characters I conceive to be totally unfit for the society of women who have any claim to virtue and delicacy.

I intend to be with you in about a month. If agreeable to you, we will visit and spend a few weeks with the afflicted Mrs. Richman. I sincerely sympathize with her under her bereavement. I know her fondness for you will render your company very consoling to her, and I flatter myself that I should not be an unwelcome guest.

Make my respects to your mamma, and believe me ever yours,

Julia Granby.

LETTER LXIV

To Mrs. Lucy Sumner.

Hartford

I have arrived in safety to the mansion of our once happy and social friends. But I cannot describe to you how changed, how greatly changed, this amiable family appears since I left it. Mrs. Wharton met me at the door and, tenderly embracing, bade me a cordial welcome. "You are come, Julia," said she, "I hope, to revive and comfort us. We have been very solitary during your absence." "I am happy, madam," said I, "to return; and my endeavors to restore cheerfulness and content shall not be wanting. But where is Eliza?" By this time we had reached the back parlor, whither Mrs. Wharton led me; and, the door being open, I saw Eliza reclined on a settee in a very thoughtful posture. When I advanced to meet her, she never moved but sat "like Patience on a monument, smiling at Grief."

I stopped involuntarily, and involuntarily raising my eyes to heaven, exclaimed, "Is that Eliza Wharton?" She burst into tears and attempted to rise, but sank again into her seat. Seeing her thus affected, I sat down by her; and, throwing my arm about her neck, I said, "Why these tears? Why this distress, my dear friend? Let not the return of your Julia give you pain; she comes to soothe you with the consolations of friendship." "It is not pain," said she, clasping me to her breast; "it is pleasure too exquisite for my weak nerves to bear. See you not, Julia, how I am altered? Should you have known me for the sprightly girl who was always welcome at the haunts of hilarity and mirth?" "Indeed," said I, "you appear indisposed; but I will be your physician. Company and change of air will, I doubt not, restore you." "Will these cure disorders of the mind, Julia?" "They will have a powerful tendency to remove them, if rightly applied; and I profess considerable skill in that art. Come," continued I, "we will try these medicines in the morning. Let us rise early and step into the chaise and, after riding a few miles, call and breakfast with Mrs. Freeman. I have some commissions from her daughter. We shall be agreeably entertained there, you know."

Being summoned to supper, I took her by the hand and

walked into another room, where we found her brother and his wife, with her mamma, waiting for us. We were all very chatty, even Eliza resumed in a degree her former sociability. A settled gloom, notwithstanding, brooded on her countenance; and a deep sigh often escaped her in spite of her evident endeavors to suppress it. She went to bed before us, when her mamma informed me that her health had been declining for some months; that she never complained but studiously concealed every symptom of indisposition. Whether it were any real disorder of body or whether it arose from her depression of spirits, she could not tell, but she supposed they operated together, and mutually heightened each other.

I inquired after Major Sanford: whether he and Eliza had associated together during my absence. Sometimes, she said, they seemed on good terms; and he frequently called to see her; at others they had very little, if any, correspondence at all. She told me that Eliza never went abroad and was very loath to see company at home; that her chief amusement consisted in solitary walks; that the dreadful idea of her meeting Major Sanford in these walks had now and then intruded upon her imagination; that she had not the least evidence of the fact, however, and indeed was afraid to make an inquiries into the matter, lest her own suspicions should be discovered; that the Major's character was worse than ever; that he was much abroad and frequently entertained large parties of worthless bacchanalians at his house; that common report said he treated his wife with indifference, neglect, and ill nature. There were many other circumstances which it is not material to relate.

Adieu, my dear friend, for the present. When occasion requires, you shall hear again from your affectionate

Julia Granby.

LETTER LXV

To Mr. Charles Deighton.

Hartford

Good news, Charles, good news! I have arrived to the utmost bounds of my wishes—the full possession of my adorable Eliza. I have heard a quotation from a certain book, but what book it was I have forgotten if I ever knew. No matter for that—the quotation is that "stolen waters are sweet, and bread eaten in secret is pleasant." If it has reference to the pleasures which I have enjoyed with Eliza, I like it hugely—as Tristram Shandy's father said of Yorick's sermon; and I think it is fully verified.

I had a long and tedious seige. Every method which love could suggest, or art invent, was adopted. I was sometimes ready to despair under an idea that her resolution was unconquerable, her virtue impregnable. Indeed, I should have given over the pursuit long ago, but for the hopes of success I entertained from her parleying with me and, in reliance upon her own strength, endeavoring to combat and counteract my designs. Whenever this has been the case, Charles, I have never yet been defeated in my plan. If a lady will consent to enter the lists against the antagonist of her honor, she may be sure of losing the prize. Besides, were her delicacy genuine, she would banish the man at once who presumed to doubt, which he certainly does who attempts to vanquish it. But far be it from me to criticize the pretensions of the sex. If I gain the rich reward of my dissimulation and gallantry, that, you know, is all I want.

To return, then, to the point. An unlucky, but not a miraculous, accident has taken place which must soon expose our amour. What can be done? At the first discovery, absolute distraction seized the soul of Eliza, which has since terminated in a fixed melancholy. Her health, too, is much impaired. She thinks herself rapidly declining, and I tremble when I see her emaciated form.

My wife has been reduced very low of late. She brought me a boy a few weeks past, a dead one though.

These circumstances give me neither pain nor pleasure. I am too much engrossed by my divinity to take an interest in any-

thing else. True, I have lately suffered myself to be somewhat engaged here and there by a few jovial lads who assist me in dispelling the anxious thought which my perplexed situation excites. I must, however, seek some means to relieve Eliza's distress. My finances are low; but the last fraction shall be expended in her service, if she need it.

Julia Granby is expected at Mrs. Wharton's every hour. I fear that her inquisitorial eye will soon detect our intrigue and obstruct its continuation. Now, there's a girl, Charles, I should never attempt to seduce; yet she is a most alluring object, I assure you. But the dignity of her manners forbids all assaults upon her virtue. Why, the very expression of her eye blasts in the bud every thought derogatory to her honor and tells you plainly that the first insinuation of the kind would be punished with eternal banishment and displeasure. Of her there is no danger. But I can write no more.

<div style="text-align: right">Peter Sanford.</div>

LETTER LXVI

To Mrs. Lucy Sumner.

<div style="text-align: right">Hartford</div>

O my friend, I have a tale to unfold—a tale which will rend every nerve of sympathizing pity, which will rack the breast of sensibility and unspeakably distress your benevolent heart. Eliza —O, the ruined, lost Eliza!

I want words to express the emotions of indignation and grief which oppress me. But I will endeavor to compose myself and relate the circumstances as they came to my knowledge.

After my last letter Eliza remained much in the same gloomy situation as I found her. She refused to go, agreeably to her promise, to visit your mamma and under one pretext or another has constantly declined accompanying me anywhere else since my arrival.

Until last Thursday night she slept in the same bed with me, when she excused herself by saying she was restless and should disturb my repose. I yielded to her humor of taking a different apartment, little suspecting the real cause. She frequently walked

out and, though I sometimes followed, I very seldom found her.
Two or three times, when I happened to be awake, I heard her
go down stairs; and, on inquiry in the morning, she told me that
she was very thirsty and went down for water. I observed a
degree of hesitancy in her answers for which I could not ac-
count. But last night the dreadful mystery was developed. A
little before day, I heard the front door open with great caution.
I sprang from my bed and, running to the window, saw by the
light of the moon a man going from the house. Soon after, I
perceived a footstep upon the stairs, which carefully approached,
and entered Eliza's chamber.

Judge of my astonishment, my surprise, my feelings upon this
occasion. I doubted not but Major Sanford was the person I had
seen; and the discovery of Eliza's guilt in this infamous intrigue
almost deprived me of thought and recollection. My blood
thrilled with horror at this sacrifice of virtue. After a while I
recovered myself and put on my clothes. But what to do I knew
not—whether to go directly to her chamber and let her know
that she was detected, or to wait another opportunity.

I resolved on the first. The day had now dawned. I tapped at
her door, and she bade me come in. She was sitting in an easy
chair by the side of her bed. As I entered she withdrew her
handkerchief from her face and, looking earnestly at me, said,
"What procures me the favor of a visit at this early hour, Miss
Granby?" "I was disturbed," said I, "and wished not to return
to my bed. But what breaks your rest and calls you up so
unseasonably, Eliza?" "Remorse and despair," answered she,
weeping. "After what I have witnessed, this morning," rejoined
I, "I cannot wonder at it. Was it not Major Sanford whom I saw
go from the house some time ago?" She was silent, but tears
flowed abundantly. "It is too late," continued I, "to deny or
evade. Answer my question sincerely; for, believe me, Eliza, it is
not malice, but concern for you, which prompts it." "I will
answer you, Julia," said she. "You have discovered a secret
which harrows up my very soul—a secret which I wished you to
know but could not exert resolution to reveal. Yes, it was Major
Sanford—the man who has robbed me of my peace, who has
triumphed in my destruction, and who will cause my sun to set
at noon."

"I shudder," said I, "at your confession! Wretched, deluded
girl! Is this a return for your parent's love and assiduous care;

for your friends' solicitude and premonitory advice? You are ruined, you say! You have sacrificed your virtue to an abandoned, despicable profligate! And you live to acknowledge and bear your infamy!" "I do," said she; "but not long shall I support this burden. See you not, Julia, my decaying frame, my faded cheek, my tottering limbs? Soon shall I be insensible to censure and reproach. Soon shall I be sequestered in that mansion 'where the wicked cease from troubling, and where the weary are at rest.'" "Rest!" said I; "can you expect to find rest, either in this world or another, with such a weight of guilt on your head?" She exclaimed with great emotion, "Add not to the upbraidings of a wounded spirit. Have pity upon me, O my friend; have pity upon me. Could you know what I suffer, you would think me sufficiently punished." "I wish you no other punishment," said I, "than what may effect your repentance and reformation. But your mother, Eliza! She cannot long be ignorant of your fall, and I tremble to think of her distress. It will break her widowed heart. How has she loved, how has she doted upon you! Dreadful is the requital which you have made." "My mother," rejoined she, "O, name her not! The very sound is distraction to me. O my Julia, if your heart be not shut against mercy and compassion towards me, aid me through this trying scene. Let my situation call forth your pity and induce you, undeserving as I am, to exert it in my behalf."

During this time I had walked the chamber. My spirits had been raised above their natural key and were exhausted. I sat down and thought I would faint, but a copious flood of tears gave me relief. Eliza was extremely affected. The appearance of calamity which she exhibited would have softened the most obdurate anger. Indeed, I feared some immediate and fatal effect. I therefore seated myself beside her; and assuming an air of kindness, I said, "Compose yourself, Eliza; I repeat what I told you before—it is the purest friendship which thus interests me in your concerns. This, under the direction of charity, induces me again to offer you my hand. Yet you have erred against knowledge and reason, against warning and counsel. You have forfeited the favor of your friends, and reluctant will be their forgiveness." "I plead guilty," said she, "to all your charges. From the general voice I expect no clemency. If I can make my peace with my mother, it is all I seek or wish on this side the grave. In your benevolence I confide for this. In you I hope to find an

intercessor. By the remembrance of our former affection and happiness, I conjure you to refuse me not. At present, I entreat you to conceal from her this distressing tale. A short reprieve is all I ask." "Why," said I, "should you defer it? When the painful task if over, you may find relief in her lenient kindness." "After she knows my condition, I cannot see her," resumed she, "until I am assured of her forgiveness. I have not strength to support the appearance of her anger and grief. I will write to her what I cannot speak. You must bear the melancholy message and plead for me, so that her displeasure may not follow me to the grave whither I am rapidly hastening." "Be assured," replied I, "that I will keep your secret as long as prudence requires. But I must leave you now; your mamma will wonder at our being thus closeted together. When opportunity presents, we will converse further on the subject. In the meantime keep yourself as composed as possible, if you would avoid suspicion." She raised her clasped hands; and with a piteous look, she threw her handkerchief over her face and reclined in her chair without speaking a word. I returned to my chamber and endeavored to dissipate every idea which might tend to disorder my countenance and break the silence I wished to observe relative to what had happened.

When I went down, Mrs. Wharton desired me to step up and inform Eliza that breakfast was ready. She told me she could not yet compose herself sufficiently to see her mamma and begged me to excuse her absence as I thought proper. I accordingly returned for answer to Mrs. Wharton that Eliza had rested but indifferently, and being somewhat indisposed, she would not come down but wished me to bring her a bowl of chocolate when we had breakfasted. I was obliged studiously to suppress even my thoughts concerning her, lest the emotions they excited might be observed. Mrs. Wharton conversed much of her daughter and expressed great concern about her health and state of mind. Her return to this state of dejection, after having recovered her spirits and cheerfulness in a great degree, was owing, she feared, to some cause unknown to her; and she entreated me to extract the secret, if possible. I assured her of my best endeavors and doubted not, I told her, that I should be able in a few days to effect what she wished.

Eliza came down and walked in the garden before dinner; she commanded herself much better than I expected. She said that a little ride might, she imagined, be of service to her and asked me

if I would accompany her a few miles in the afternoon. Her mamma was much pleased with the proposition, and the chaise was accordingly ordered.

I observed to Eliza, as we rode, that—with her natural and acquired abilities, with her advantages of education, with her opportunities of knowing the world and of tracing the virtues and vices of mankind to their origin—I was surprised at her becoming the prey of an insidious libertine with whose character she was well acquainted and whose principles, she was fully apprised, would prompt him to deceive and betray her. "Your surprise is very natural," said she. "The same will doubtless be felt and expressed by everyone to whom my sad story is related. But the cause may be found in that unrestrained levity of disposition, that fondness of dissipation and coquetry, which alienated the affections of Mr. Boyer from me. This event fatally depressed and enfeebled my mind. I embraced with avidity the consoling power of friendship, ensnaringly offered by my seducer; I vainly inferred, from his marriage with a virtuous woman, that he had seen the error of his ways and forsaken his licentious practices, as he affirmed. I, fool that I was, believed it.

"It is needless for me to rehearse the perfidious arts by which he insinuated himself into my affections and gained my confidence. Suffice it to say, he effected his purpose. But not long did I continue in the delusive dream of sensual gratification. I soon awoke to a most poignant sense of his baseness and of my own crime and misery. I would have fled him; I would have renounced him forever and, by a life of sincere humility and repentance, endeavored to make my peace with Heaven and to obliterate, by the recitude of my future conduct, the guilt I had incurred; but I found it too late. My circumstances called for attention; and I had no one to participate my cares, to witness my distress, and to alleviate my sorrows but him. I could not therefore prevail on myself wholly to renounce his society. At times I have admitted his visits, always meeting him in the garden, or grove adjoining; of late, the weather and my ill health induced me to comply with his solicitations and receive him into the parlor.

"Not long, however, shall I be subject to these embarrassments. Grief has undermined my constitution. My health has fallen a sacrifice to a disordered mind. But I regret not its departure. I have not a single wish to live. Nothing which the world affords can restore my former serenity and happiness.

"The little innocent I bear will quickly disclose its mother's shame. God Almighty grant it may not live as a monument of my guilt, and a partaker of the infamy and sorrow which is all I have to bequeath it. Should it be continued in life, it will never know the tenderness of a parent; and, perhaps, want and disgrace may be its wretched portion. The greatest consolation I can have will be to carry it with me to a state of eternal rest, which, vile as I am, I hope to obtain, through the infinite mercy of Heaven as revealed in the gospel of Christ. I must see Major Sanford again. It is necessary to converse further with him in order to carry my plan of operation into execution."

"What is this plan of operation, Eliza?" said I. "I am on the rack of anxiety for your safety." "Be patient," continued she, "and you shall soon be informed. Tomorrow I shall write my dreadful story to my mother. She will be acquainted with my future intentions; and you shall know, at the same time, the destination of your lost friend." "I hope," said I, "that you have formed no resolution against your own life." "God forbid," rejoined she. "My breath is in his hands; let him do what seemeth good in his sight! Keep my secret one day longer, and I will never more impose so painful a silence upon you."

By this time we had reached home. She drank tea with composure and soon retired to rest. Mrs. Wharton eagerly inquired whether I had found out the cause of Eliza's melancholy. "I have urged her," said I, "on the subject, but she alleges that she has particular reasons for present concealment. She has, notwithstanding, promised to let me know the day after tomorrow." "O," said she, "I shall not rest until the period arrives." "Dear, good woman," said I to myself, "I fear you will never rest afterwards."

This is our present situation. Think what a scene rises to the view of your Julia. She must share the distress of others, though her own feelings on this unhappy occasion are too keen to admit a moment's serenity. My greatest relief is in writing to you, which I shall do again by the next post. In the meantime, I must beg leave to subscribe myself sincerely yours

<div align="right">Julia Granby.</div>

LETTER LXVII

To Mrs. Lucy Sumner.

Hartford

All is now lost, lost indeed! She is gone! Yes, my dear friend, our beloved Eliza is gone! Never more shall we behold this once amiable companion, this once innocent and happy girl. She has forsaken and, as she says, bid an everlasting adieu to her home, her afflicted parent, and her friends. But I will take up my melancholy story where I left it in my last letter.

She went, as she told me she expected to do, into the garden and met her detestable paramour. In about an hour she returned and went directly to her chamber. At one o'clock I went up and found her writing and weeping. I begged her to compose herself and go down to dinner. No, she said, she should not eat; and she was not fit to appear before any body. I remonstrated against her immoderate grief, represented the injury she must sustain by the indulgence of it, and conjured her to suppress the violence of its emotions.

She entreated me to excuse her to her mamma; she said that she was writing to her and found it a task too painful to be performed with any degree of composure; that she was almost ready to sink under the weight of her affliction; but that she hoped and prayed for support both in this and another trying scene which awaited her. In compliance with her desire, I now left her and told her mamma that she was very busy writing, wished not to be interrupted at present, but would take some refreshment an hour or two hence. I visited her again about four o'clock when she appeared more calm and tranquil.

"It is finished," said she, as I entered her apartment; "it is finished." "What," said I, "is finished?" "No matter," replied she; "you will know all tomorrow, Julia." She complained of excessive fatigue and expressed an inclination to lie down; I assisted her and then retired. Some time after, her mamma went up and found her still on the bed. She rose, however, and accompanied her downstairs. I met her at the door of the parlor and, taking her by the hand, inquired how she did. "O Julia, miserably indeed," said she. "How severely does my mother's

kindness reproach me! How insupportably it increases my self-condemnation!" She wept; she rung her hands and walked the room in the greatest agony. Mrs. Wharton was exceedingly distressed by her appearance. "Tell me, Eliza," said she, "tell me the cause of your trouble. O, kill me not by your mysterious concealment. My dear child, let me by sharing alleviate your affliction." "Ask me not, madam," said she; "O my mother, I conjure you not to insist on my divulging tonight the fatal secret which engrosses and distracts my mind; tomorrow I will hide nothing from you." "I will press you no further," rejoined her mamma. "Choose your own time, my dear; but remember that I must participate in your grief, though I know not the cause."

Supper was brought in, and we endeavored to prevail on Eliza to eat in vain. She sat down in compliance with our united importunities; but neither of us tasted food. It was removed untouched. For a while, Mrs. Wharton and I gazed in silent anguish upon the spectacle of woe before us. At length Eliza rose to retire. "Julia," said she, "you will call at my chamber as you pass to your own?" I assented. She then approached her mamma, fell upon her knees before her, and, clasping her hand, said in broken accents, "O madam, can you forgive a wretch who has forfeited your love, your kindness, and your compassion?" "Surely, Eliza," said she, "you are not that being! No, it is impossible! But however great your transgression, be assured of my forgiveness, my compassion, and my continued love." Saying this, she threw her arms about her daughter's neck and affectionately kissed her. Eliza struggled from her embrace and, looking at her with wild despair, exclaimed, "This is too much! O, this unmerited goodness is more than I can bear!" She then rushed precipitately out of the room and left us overwhelmed in sympathy and astonishment.

When Mrs. Wharton had recovered herself a little, she observed that Eliza's brain was evidently disordered. "Nothing else," continued she, "could impel her to act in this extraordinary manner." At first she was resolved to follow her; but I dissuaded her from it, alleging that, as she had desired me to come into her chamber, I thought it better for me to go alone. She acquiesced, said she should not think of going to bed, but would, however, retire to her chamber and seek consolation there. I bade her good night and went up to Eliza, who took me

by the hand and led me to the toilet upon which she laid the two enclosed letters, the one to her mamma and the other to me. "These," said she, "contain what I had not resolution to express. Promise me, Julia, that they shall not be opened till tomorrow morning." "I will," said I. "I have thought and wept," continued she, "until I have almost exhausted my strength and my reason. I would now obtain a little respite, that I may prepare my mind for the account I am one day to give at a higher tribunal than that of earthly friends. For this purpose, what I have written and what I shall yet say to you must close the account between you and me." "I have certainly no balance against you," said I. "In my breast you are fully acquitted. Your penitential tears have obliterated your guilt and blotted our your errors with Julia. Henceforth, be they all forgotten. Live and be happy." "Talk not," said she, "of life; it would be a vain hope, though I cherished it myself.

> That I must die, it is my only comfort;
> Death is the privilege of human nature,
> And life without it were not worth the taking.
> Thither the poor, the prisoner, and the mourner
> Fly for relief, and lay their burdens down.

You have forgiven me, Julia; my mother has assured me of her forgiveness; and what have I more to wish? My heart is much lightened by these kind assurances; they will be a great support to me in the dreadful hour which awaits me." "What mean you, Eliza?" said I. "I fear some dreadful purpose labors in your mind." "O, no," she replied; "you may be assured your fear is groundless. I know not what I say; my brain is on fire; I am all confusion. Leave me, Julia; when I have had a little rest, I shall be composed. These letters have almost distracted me; but they are written, and I am comparatively easy." "I will not leave you. Eliza," said I, "unless you will go directly to bed and endeavor to rest." "I will," said she, "and the sooner the better." I tenderly embraced her and retired, though not to bed. About an hour after, I returned to her chamber and, opening the door very softly, found her apparently asleep. I acquainted Mrs. Wharton with her situation, which was a great consolation to us both, and then suggested that we both go to bed. Having suffered much in my mind, and being much fatigued, I soon fell asleep; but the rattling of a carriage, which appeared to stop a little

distance from the house, awoke me. I listened a moment and heard the door turn slowly on its hinges. I sprang from my bed and reached the window just in time to see a female handed into a chaise by a man who hastily followed her and drove furiously away. I at once concluded they could be no other than Eliza and Major Sanford. Under this impression I made no delay but ran immediately to her chamber. A candle was burning on the table, but Eliza was not there. I thought it best to acquaint her mamma with the melancholy discovery and, stepping to her apartment for the purpose, found her rising. She had heard me walk and was anxious to know the cause. "What is the matter, Julia?" said she; "what is the matter?" "Dear Madam," said I, "arm yourself with fortitude." "What new occurrence demands it?" rejoined she. "Eliza has left us," "Left us! What mean you?" "She has just gone; I saw her handed into a chaise which instantly disappeared."

At this intelligence she gave a shriek and fell back on her bed. I alarmed the family, and by their assistance we soon recovered her. She desired me to inform her of every particular relative to her elopement, which I did, and then delivered her the letter which Eliza had left for her. "I suspect," said she, as she took it; "I have long suspected what I had dared not believe. The anguish of my mind has been known only to myself and my God." I could not answer her and therefore withdrew. When I had read Eliza's letter to me and wept over the sad fall, and, as I fear, the total loss of this once amiable and accomplished girl, I returned to Mrs. Wharton. She was sitting in her easy chair and still held the fatal letter in her hand. When I entered, she fixed her streaming eyes upon me and exclaimed, "O Julia, this is more than the bitterness of death." "True, madam," said I, "your affliction must be great; yet that all-gracious Being who controls every event is able and I trust disposed to support you." "To him," replied she, "I desire humbly to resign myself, but I think I could have borne almost any other calamity with greater resignation and composure than this. With how much comparative ease could I have followed her to the grave at any period since her birth! O, my child, my child! dear, very dear, hast thou been to my fond heart. Little did I think it possible for you to prepare so dreadful a cup of sorrow for your widowed mother. But where," continued she, "where can the poor fugitive have fled? Where can she find that protection and

tenderness, which, notwithstanding her great apostasy, I should never have withheld? From whom can she receive those kind attentions which her situation demands?"

The agitation of her mind had exhausted her strength, and I prevailed on her to refresh and endeavor to compose herself to rest, assuring her of my utmost exertions to find out Eliza's retreat and restore her to a mother's arms.

I am obliged to suppress my own emotions and to bend all my thoughts towards the alleviation of Mrs. Wharton's anxiety and grief.

Major Sanford is from home, as I expected; and I am determined, if he return, to see him myself and extort from him the place of Eliza's concealment. Her flight in her present state of health is inexpressibly distressing to her mother; and unless we find her soon, I dread the effects.

I shall not close this until I have seen or heard from the vile miscreant who has involved a worthy family in wretchedness.

Friday morning—Two days have elapsed without affording us much relief. Last evening I was told that Major Sanford was at home. I immediately wrote him a billet, entreating and conjuring him to let me know where the hapless Eliza had fled. He returned me the following answer:

"Miss Granby need be under no apprehensions respecting the situation of our beloved Eliza. She is well provided for, conveniently accommodated, and has everything to make her happy which love and affluence can give.

"Major Sanford has solemnly sworn not to discover her retreat. She wishes to avoid the accusations of her friends until she is better able to bear them.

"Her mother may rest assured of immediate information should any danger threaten her amiable daughter, and also of having seasonable notice of her safety."

Although little dependence can be placed upon this man, yet these assurances have in a great degree calmed our minds. We are, however, contriving means to explore the refuge of the wanderer and hope, by tracing his steps, to accomplish our purpose. This we have engaged a friend to do.

I know, my dear Mrs. Sumner, the kind interest you will take in this disastrous affair. I tremble to think what the event may be. To relieve your suspense, however, I shall write you every circumstance as it occurs; but at present, I shall only enclose

Eliza's letters to her mamma and me and subscribe myself your sincere and obliged friend,

Julia Granby.

LETTER LXVIII

To Mrs. M. Wharton.

Tuesday

My honored and dear mamma, in what words, in what language, shall I address you? What shall I say on a subject which deprives me of the power of expression? Would to God I had been totally deprived of that power before so fatal a subject required its exertion. Repentance comes too late, when it cannot prevent the evil lamented: for your kindness, your more than maternal affection towards me from my infancy to the present moment, a long life of filial duty and unerring rectitude could hardly compensate. How greatly deficient in gratitude must I appear, then, while I confess that precept and example, counsel and advice, instruction and admonition, have been all lost upon me!

Your kind endeavors to promote my happiness have been repaid by the inexcusable folly of sacrificing it. The various emotions of shame and remorse, penitence and regret, which torture and distract my guilty breast, exceed description. Yes, madam, your Eliza has fallen, fallen indeed. She has become the victim of her own indiscretion, and of the intrigue and artifice of a designing libertine who is the husband of another. She is polluted and no more worthy of her parentage. She flies from you, not to conceal her guilt (that she humbly and penitently owns), but to avoid what she has never experienced and feels herself unable to support—a mother's frown—and to escape the heartrending sight of a parent's grief occasioned by the crimes of her guilty child.

I have become a reproach and disgrace to my friends. The consciousness of having forfeited their favor and incurred their disapprobation and resentment induces me to conceal from them the place of my retirement; but lest your benevolence should render you anxious for my comfort in my present situation, I take the liberty to assure you that I am amply provided for.

I have no claim even upon your pity; but from my long experience of your tenderness, I presume to hope it will be extended to me. O my mother, if you knew what the state of my mind is, and has been for months past, you would surely compassionate my case. Could tears efface the stain which I have brought upon my family, it would long since have been washed away; but, alas! tears are in vain; and vain is my bitter repentance; it cannot obliterate my crime nor restore me to innocence and peace. In this life I have no ideas of happiness. These I have wholly resigned. The only hope which affords me any solace is that of your forgiveness. If the deepest contrition can make an atonement—if the severest pains, both of body and mind, can restore me to your charity—you will not be inexorable. O, let my sufferings be deemed a sufficient punishment and add not the insupportable weight of a parent's wrath. At present I cannot see you. The effect of my crime is too obvious to be longer concealed, to elude the invidious eye of curiosity. This night, therefore, I leave your hospitable mansion. This night I become a wretched wanderer from my paternal roof. O that the grave were this night to be my lodging! Then should I lie down and be at rest. Trusting in the mercy of God, through the mediation of his Son, I think I could meet my heavenly Father with more composure and confidence than my earthly parent.

Let not the faults and misfortunes of your daughter oppress your mind. Rather let the conviction of having faithfully discharged your duty to your lost child support and console you in this trying scene.

Since I wrote the above, you have kindly granted me your forgiveness though you knew not how great, how aggravated was my offence. You forgive me, you say. O, the harmonious. the transporting sound! It nas revived my droopong spirits and will enable me to encounter with resolution the trails before me.

Farewell, my dear mamma! Pity and pray for your ruined child; and be assured that affection and gratitude will be the last sentiments which expire in the best of your repenting daughter,

Eliza Wharton

LETTER LXIX

To my dear friend, Miss Julia Granby.

Tuesday

By that endearing title you permit me still to address you, and such you have always proved yourself by a participation of my distresses as well as by the consoling voice of pity and forgiveness. What destiny Providence designs for me I know not, but I have my forebodings that this is the last time I shall ever accost you. Nor does this apprehension arise merely from a disturbed imagination. I have reason to think myself in a confirmed consumption, which commonly proves fatal to persons in my situation. I have carefully concealed every complaint of the kind from my mamma for fear of distressing her; yet I have never been insensible of their probable issue and have bidden a sincere welcome to them, as the harbingers of my speedy release from a life of guilt and woe.

I am going from you, Julia. This night separates us, perhaps forever. I have not resolution to encounter the tears of my friends and therefore seek shelter among strangers, where none knows or is interested in my melancholy story. The place of my seclusion I studiously conceal, yet I shall take measures that you may be apprised of my fate.

Should it please God to spare and restore me to health, I shall return and endeavor, by a life of penitence and rectitude, to expiate my past offences. But should I be called from this scene of action and leave behind me a helpless babe, the innocent sufferer of its mother's shame, O Julia, let your friendship for me extend to the little stranger. Intercede with my mother to take it under her protection and transfer to it all her affection for me; to train it up in the ways of piety and virtue that it may compensate her for the afflictions which I have occasioned.

One thing more I have to request. Plead for me with my two best friends, Mrs. Richman and Mrs. Sumner. I ask you not to palliate my faults—that cannot be done—but to obtain, if possible, their forgiveness. I cannot write all my full mind suggests on this subject. You know the purport and can better express it for me.

And now, my dear Julia, I recommend myself again to your benevolence, to your charity, and (may I add) to your affection, and entreat that the fatal consequences of my folly now fallen upon my devoted head may suffice for my punishment. Let me conjure you to bury my crimes in the grave with me and to preserve the remembrance of my former virtues which engaged your love and confidence; more especially I express that ardent esteem for you, which will glow till the last expiring breath of your despairing

<div align="right">Eliza Wharton.</div>

LETTER LXX

To Mr. Charles Deighton.

<div align="right">Hartford</div>

I have at last accomplished the removal of my darling girl from a place where she thought every eye accused and every heart condemned her.

She has become quite romantic in her notions. She would not permit me to accompany her, lest it should be reported that we had eloped together. I provided amply for her future exigencies and conveyed her by night to the distance of ten or twelve miles, where we met the stage in which I had previously secured her a seat. The agony of her grief at being thus obliged to leave her mother's house baffles all description.

It very sensibly affected me, I know. I was almost a penitent. I am sure I acted like one, whether I were sincere or not. She chose to go where she was totally unknown. She would leave the stage, she said, before it reached Boston and take passage in a more private carriage to Salem, or its vicinity, where she would fix her abode and chalk the initials of my name over the door, as a signal to me of her residence.

She is exceedingly depressed and says she neither expects nor wishes to survive her lying in. Insanity, for aught I know, must be my lot if she should die. But I will not harbor the idea. I hope, one time or other, to have the power to make her amends, even by marriage. My wife may be provoked, I imagine, to sue for a divorce. If she should, she would find no difficulty

in obtaining it, and then I would take Eliza in her stead—though I confess that the idea of being thus connected with a woman whom I have been enabled to dishonor would be rather hard to surmount. It would hurt even my delicacy, little as you may think me to possess, to have a wife whom I know to be seducible. And on this account I cannot be positive that even Eliza would retain my love.

My Nancy and I have lived a pretty uncomfortable life of late. She has been very suspicious of my amour with Eliza, and now and then she expressed her jealous sentiments a little more warmly than my patience would bear. But the news of Eliza's circumstances and retirement, being publicly talked of, have reached her ears and rendered her quite outrageous. She tells me she will no longer brook my indifference and infidelity; she intends soon to return to her father's house and extricate herself from me entirely. My general reply to all this is that she knew my character before we married and could reasonably expect nothing less than what has happened. I shall not oppose her leaving me, as it may conduce to the execution of the plan I have hinted above.

Tomorrow I shall set out to visit my disconsolate fair one. From my very soul I pity her and wish I could have preserved her virtue consistently with the indulgence of my passion. To her I lay not the principal blame, as in like cases I do the sex in general. My finesse was too well planned for detection, and my snares too deeply laid for anyone to escape who had the least warmth in her constitution or affection in her heart. I shall, therefore, be the less whimsical about a future connection and the more solicitous to make her reparation, should it ever be in my power.

Her friends are all in arms about her. I dare say I have the imprecations of the whole fraternity. They may thank themselves in part, for I always swore revenge for their dislike and coldness towards me. Had they been politic, they would have conducted themselves more like the aborigines of the country, who are said to worship the devil out of fear.

I am afraid I shall be obliged to remove my quarters, for Eliza was so great a favorite in town that I am looked upon with an evil eye. I pleaded with her before we parted last to forgive my seducing her, alleged my ardent love, and my inability to possess her in any other way. "How," said she, "can that be love which

destroys its object? But granting what you say, you have frus-
trated your own purpose. You have deprived yourself of my
society, which might have been innocently enjoyed. You have
cut me off from life in the midst of my days. You have ren-
dered me the reproach of my friends, the disgrace of my family
and a dishonor to virtue and my sex. But I forgive you," added
she. "Yes, Sanford, I forgive you and sincerely pray for your
repentance and reformation. I hope to be the last wretched fe-
male sacrificed by you to the arts of falsehood and seduction.
May my unhappy story serve as a beacon to warn the American
fair of the dangerous tendency and destructive consequences of
associating with men of your character, of destroying their time
and risking their reputation by the practice of coquetry and its
attendant follies. But for these I might have been honorably
connected and capable, at this moment, of diffusing and receiv-
ing happiness. But for your arts I might have remained a blessing
to society as well as the delight and comfort of my friends. You
being a married man unspeakably aggravates both your guilt and
mine. This circumstance annexes indelible shame to our crime.
You have rent asunder the tenderest ties of nature. You have
broken the bonds of conjugal love, which ought ever to be kept
sacred and inviolate. You have filled with grief and discontent
the heart of your amiable wife, whom gratitude, if no other
principle, should have induced you to cherish with tenderness;
and I, wretch that I am, have been your accomplice. But I cease
to reproach you. You have acted but too consistently with the
character which I was sufficiently apprised you sustained. The
blame then may be retorted on myself for disregarding the coun-
sels, warnings, and admonitions of my best friends. You have
prided yourself in the character of a libertine. Glory no longer
in your shame. You have accomplished your designs, your dread-
ful designs, against me. Let this suffice. Add not to the number
of those deluded creatures who will one day rise up in judgment
against you and condemn you."

By this time we had nearly reached the inn and were soon to
part. I seized her hand and exclaimed, "You must not leave me,
Eliza, with that awful anathema on your lips. O, say that you
will forget my past faults." "That," said she, "I shall soon do;
for in the grave there is no remembrance." This, to my mind,
was a harsher sentence than the other and almost threw me into
despair. Never was I so wrought upon before. I knew not what

to say or do. She saw my distress and kindly softened her manner. "If I am severe," said she, "it is because I wish to impress your mind with such a sense of your offenses against your Maker, your friends, and society in general as may effect your repentance and amendment. I wish not to be your accuser but your reformer. On several accounts, I view my own crime in a more aggravated light than yours; but my conscience is awakened to a conviction of my guilt. Yours, I fear, is not. Let me conjure you to return home and endeavor, by your future kindness and fidelity to your wife, to make her all the amends in your power. By a life of virtue and religion, you may yet become a valuable member of society and secure happiness both here and hereafter."

I begged leave to visit her retirement next week, not in continuation of our amour but as a friend solicitous to know her situation and welfare. Unable to speak, she only bowed assent. The stage being now ready, I whispered some tender things in her ear and, kissing her cheek, which was all she would permit, suffered her to depart.

My body remains behind; but my soul, if I have any, went with her.

This was a horrid lecture, Charles. She brought every charge against me which a fruitful and gloomy imagination could suggest. But I hope when she recovers she will resume her former cheerfulness and become as kind and agreeable as ever. My anxiety for her safety is very great. I trust, however, it will soon be removed and peace and pleasure be restored to your humble servant,

<div align="right">Peter Sanford.</div>

LETTER LXXI

To Mrs. Lucy Sumner.

<div align="right">Hartford</div>

The drama is now closed! A tragical one it has proved!

How sincerely, my dear Mrs. Sumner, must the friends of our departed Eliza sympathize with each other and with her afflicted, bereaved parent!

You have doubtless seen the account in the public papers which gave us the melancholy intelligence. But I will give you a detail of circumstances.

A few days after my last letter was written, we heard that Major Sanford's property was attached and that he was a prisoner in his own house. He was the last man to whom we wished to apply for information respecting the forlorn wanderer, yet we had no other resource. And after waiting a fortnight in the most cruel suspense, we wrote a billet entreating him, if possible, to give some intelligence concerning her. He replied that he was unhappily deprived of all means of knowing himself, but he hoped soon to relieve his own and our anxiety about her.

In this situation we continued till a neighbor (purposely, we since concluded) sent us a Boston paper. Mrs. Wharton took it and, unconscious of its contents, observed that the perusal might divert her a few moments. She read for some time, when it suddenly dropped upon the floor. She clasped her hands together and, raising her streaming eyes to heaven, exclaimed, "It is the Lord; let Him do what He will. Be still, O my soul, and know that He is God."

"What, madam," said I, "can be the matter?" She answered not, but with inexpressible anguish depicted in her countenance pointed to the paper. I took it up and soon found the fatal paragraph. I shall not attempt to paint our heartfelt grief and lamentation upon this occasion; for we had no doubt of Eliza's being the person described as a stranger who died at Danvers, last July. Her delivery of a child, her dejected state of mind, the marks upon her linen, indeed every circumstance in the advertisement, convinced us beyond dispute that it could be no other. Mrs. Wharton retired immediately to her chamber, where she continued overwhelmed with sorrow that night and the following day. Such in fact has been her habitual frame ever since; the endeavors of her friends, who have sought to console her, have rendered her somewhat more conversable. My testimony of Eliza's penitence before her departure is a source of comfort to this disconsolate parent. She fondly cherished the idea that, having expiated her offense by sincere repentance and amendment, her deluded child finally made a happy exchange of worlds. But the desperate resolution which she formed and executed, of becoming a fugitive, of deserting her mother's house and protection, and of wandering and dying among strangers, is

a most distressing reflection to her friends; especially is it so to her mother, in whose breast so many painful ideas arise that she finds it extremely difficult to compose herself to that resignation which she evidently strives to exemplify.

Eliza's brother has been to visit her last retreat and to learn the particulars of her melancholy exit. He relates that she was well accommodated and had every attention and assistance which her situation required. The people where she resided appear to have a lively sense of her merit and misfortunes. They testify her modest deportment, her fortitude under the sufferings to which she was called, and the serenity and composure with which she bade a last adieu to the world. Mr. Wharton has brought back several scraps of her writing, containing miscellaneous reflections on her situation, the death of her babe, and the absence of her friends. Some of these were written before, some after, her confinement. These valuable testimonies of the affecting sense and calm expectation she entertained of her approaching dissolution are calculated to soothe and comfort the minds of mourning connections. They greatly alleviate the regret occasioned by her absence at this awful period. Her elopement can be equalled only by the infatuation which caused her ruin.

> But let no one reproach her memory.
> Her life has paid the forfeit of her folly.
> Let that suffice.

I am told that Major Sanford is quite frantic. Sure I am that he has reason to be. If the mischiefs he has brought upon others return upon his own head, dreadful indeed must be his portion. His wife has left him and returned to her parents. His estate, which has been long mortgaged, is taken from him; and poverty and disgrace await him. Heaven seldom leaves injured innocence unavenged. Wretch that he is, he ought forever to be banished from human society! I shall continue with Mrs. Wharton till the lenient hand of time has assuaged her sorrows and then make my promised visit to you. I will bring Eliza's posthumous papers with me when I come to Boston, as I have not time to copy them now.

I foresee, my dear Mrs. Sumner, that this disastrous affair will suspend your enjoyments, as it has mine. But what are our feelings compared with the pangs which rend a parent's heart? This parent I here behold inhumanly stripped of the best solace

of her declining years by the ensnaring machinations of a profligate debauchee. Not only the life—but, what was still dearer, the reputation and virtue—of the unfortunate Eliza have fallen victims at the shrine of *libertinism*. Detested be the epithet. Let it henceforth bear its true signature, and candor itself shall call it *lust* and *brutality*.

Execrable is the man, however arrayed in magnificence, crowned with wealth, or decorated with the external graces and accomplishments of fashionable life, who shall presume to display them at the expense of virtue and innocence. Sacred name attended with real blessings—blessings too useful and important to be trifled away. My resentment at the base arts which must have been employed to complete the seduction of Eliza I cannot suppress. I wish them to be exposed and stamped with universal ignominy. Nor do I doubt but you will join with me in execrating the measures by which *we* have been robbed of so valuable a friend, and *society* of so ornamental a member.

<div style="text-align: right">Julia Granby.</div>

LETTER LXXII

To Mr. Charles Deighton.

<div style="text-align: right">Hartford</div>

Confusion, horror, and despair are the portion of your wretched, unhappy friend. O Deighton, I am undone. Misery irremediable is my future lot. She is gone; yes, she is gone forever. The darling of my soul, the center of all my wishes and enjoyments, is no more. Cruel fate has snatched her from me, and she is irretrievably lost. I rave and then reflect; I reflect and then rave. I have no patience to bear this calamity, nor the power to remedy it. Where shall I fly from the upbraidings of my mind, which accuse me as the murderer of my Eliza? I would fly to death and seek a refuge in the grave, but the forebodings of a retribution to come I cannot away with. O that I had seen her! that I had once more asked her forgiveness! But even that privilege, that consolation, was denied me! The day on which I meant to visit her, most of my property was attached; and, to secure the rest, I was obliged to shut my doors and

become a prisoner in my own house. High living and old debts incurred by extravagance had reduced the fortune of my wife to very little, and I could not satisfy the clamorous demands of my creditors.

I would have given millions, had I possessed them, to have been at liberty to see and to have had the power to preserve Eliza from death. But in vain was my anxiety; it could not relieve, it could not liberate me. When I first heard the dreadful tidings of her exit, I believe I acted like a madman; indeed, I am little else now.

I have compounded with my creditors and resigned the whole of my property. Thus that splendor and equipage, to secure which I have sacrificed a virtuous woman, is taken from me. That poverty, the dread of which prevented my forming an honorable connection with an amiable and accomplished girl—the only one I ever loved—has fallen with redoubled vengeance upon my guilty head; and I must become a vagabond on the earth.

I shall fly my country as soon as possible. I shall go from every object which reminds me of my departed Eliza; but never, never shall I eradicate from my bosom the idea of her excellence nor the painful remembrance of the injuries I have done her. Her shade will perpetually haunt me; the image of her—as she appeared when mounting the carriage which conveyed her forever from my sight, waving her hand in token of a last adieu—will always be present to my imagination; the solemn counsel she gave me before we parted, never more to meet, will not cease to resound in my ears.

While my being is prolonged, I must feel the disgraceful and torturing effects of my guilt in seducing her. How madly have I deprived her of happiness, of reputation, of life! Her friends, could they know the pangs of contrition and the horrors of conscience which attend me, would be amply revenged.

It is said she quitted the world with composure and peace. Well she might. She had not that insupportable weight of iniquity which sinks me to despair. She found consolation in that religion which I have ridiculed as priestcraft and hypocrisy. But, whether it is true or false, would do Heaven I could now enjoy the comforts which its votaries evidently feel.

My wife has left me. As we lived together without love, we parted without regret.

Now, Charles, I am to bid you a long, perhaps a last, farewell.

Where I shall roam in future, I neither know nor care. I shall go where the name of Sanford is unknown and his person and sorrows unnoticed.

In this happy clime I have nothing to induce my stay. I have not money to support me with my profligate companions, nor have I any relish at present for their society. By the virtuous part of the community I am shunned as the pest and bane of social enjoyment. In short, I am debarred from every kind of happiness. If I look back, I recoil with horror from the black catalogue of vices which have stained my past life and reduced me to indigence and contempt. If I look forward, I shudder at the prospects which my foreboding mind presents to view both in this and a coming world. This is a deplorable, yet a just, picture of myself. How totally the reverse of what I once appeared!

Let it warn you, my friend, to shun the dangerous paths which I have trodden that you may never be involved in the hopeless ignominy and wretchedness of

<div align="right">Peter Sanford.</div>

LETTER LXXIII

To Miss Julia Granby.

<div align="right">Boston</div>

A melancholy tale have you unfolded, my dear Julia; and tragic indeed is the concluding scene.

Is she then gone? gone in this most distressing manner? Have I lost my once-loved friend? lost her in a way which I could never have conceived to be possible?

Our days of childhood were spent together in the same pursuits, in the same amusements. Our riper years increased our mutual affection, and maturer judgment most firmly cemented our friendship. Can I then calmly resign her to so severe a fate? Can I bear the idea of her being lost to honor, to fame, and to life? No, she shall still live in the heart of her faithful Lucy, whose experience of her numerous virtues and engaging qualities has imprinted her image too deeply on the memory to be obliterated. However she may have erred, her sincere repentance is sufficient to restore her to charity.

Your letter gave me the first information of this awful event. I had taken a short excursion into the country, where I had not seen the papers or, if I had, paid little or no attention to them. By your directions I found the distressing narrative of her exit. The poignancy of my grief and the unavailing lamentations which the intelligence excited need no delineation. To scenes of this nature you have been habituated in the mansion of sorrow where you reside.

How sincerely I sympathize with the bereaved parent of the dear, deceased Eliza, I can feel; but I have not the power to express. Let it be her consolation that her child is at rest. The resolution which carried this deluded wanderer thus far from her friends, and supported her through her various trials, is astonishing. Happy would it have been had she exerted an equal degree of fortitude in repelling the first attacks upon her virtue. But she is no more, and Heaven forbid that I should accuse or reproach her.

Yet in what language shall I express my abhorrence of the monster whose detestable arts have blasted one of the fairest flowers in creation? I leave him to God and his own conscience. Already is he exposed in his true colors. Vengeance already begins to overtake him. His sordid mind must now suffer the deprivation of those sensual gratifications beyond which he is incapable of enjoyment.

Upon your reflecting and steady mind, my dear Julia, I need not inculcate the lessons which may be drawn from this woe-fraught tale; but for the sake of my sex in general, I wish it engraved upon every heart that virtue alone, independent of the trappings of wealth, the parade of equipage, and the adulation of gallantry, can secure lasting felicity. From the melancholy story of Eliza Wharton let the American fair learn to reject with disdain every insinuation derogatory to their true dignity and honor. Let them despise and forever banish the man who can glory in the seduction of innocence and the ruin of reputation. To associate is to approve; to approve is to be betrayed.

<div style="text-align: right">Lucy Sumner.</div>

LETTER LXXIV

To Mrs. M. Wharton.

Boston

We have paid the last tribute of respect to your beloved daughter. The day after my arrival, Mrs. Sumner proposed that we should visit the sad spot which contains the remains of our once amiable friend. "The grave of Eliza Wharton," said she, "shall not be unbedewed by the tears of friendship."

Yesterday we went accordingly, and we were much pleased with the apparent sincerity of the people in their assurances that everything in their power had been done to render her situation comfortable. The minutest circumstances were faithfully related; and, from the state of her mind in her last hours, I think much comfort may be derived to her afflicted friends.

We spent a mournful hour in the place where she is interred; and then we returned to the inn, and Mrs. Sumner gave orders for a decent stone to be erected over her grave, with the following inscription:

THIS HUMBLE STONE,
IN MEMORY OF

ELIZA WHARTON,

IS INSCRIBED BY HER WEEPING FRIENDS TO WHOM SHE
ENDEARED HERSELF
BY UNCOMMON TENDERNESS AND AFFECTION.
ENDOWED WITH SUPERIOR ACQUIREMENTS, SHE WAS STILL MORE
DISTINGUISHED
BY HUMILITY AND BENEVOLENCE.
LET CANDOR THROW A VEIL OVER HER FRAILTIES, FOR GREAT WAS
HER CHARITY TO OTHERS.
SHE SUSTAINED THE LAST PAINFUL SCENE
FAR FROM EVERY FRIEND
AND EXHIBITED AN EXAMPLE OF CALM RESIGNATION.
HER DEPARTURE WAS ON THE 25TH DAY OF JULY, A. D.--, IN
THE 37TH YEAR OF HER AGE.
AND THE TEARS OF STRANGERS WATERED HER GRAVE.

I hope, madam, that you will derive satisfaction from these exertions of friendship and that, united to the many other sources of consolation with which you are furnished, they may alleviate your grief and, while they leave the pleasing remembrance of her virtues, add the supporting persuasion that your Eliza is happy.

Julia Granby.

THE END